RACE, CRIME, AND THE MEDIA

Robert L. Bing III

University of Texas at Arlington

McGraw Hill

Connect
Learn
Succeed™

Published by McGraw-Hill, an imprint of The McGraw-Hill Companies, Inc., 1221 Avenue of the Americas, New York, NY 10020. Copyright © 2010. All rights reserved. No part of this publication may be reproduced or distributed in any form or by any means, or stored in a database or retrieval system, without the prior written consent of The McGraw-Hill Companies, Inc., including, but not limited to, in any network or other electronic storage or transmission, or broadcast for distance learning.

This book is printed on acid-free paper.

1 2 3 4 5 6 7 8 9 0 DOC/DOC 0 9

ISBN: 978-0-07-340156-0
MHID: 0-07-340156-0

Editor in Chief: *Michael Ryan*
Sponsoring Editor: *Katie Stevens*
Marketing Manager: *Leslie Oberhuber*
Production Editor: *David Blatty*
Manuscript Editor: *Patricia Ohlenroth*
Design Manager: *Ashley Bedell*
Cover Designer: *Mary-Presley Adams*
Production Supervisor: *Laura Fuller*
Composition: *10/12 Palatino by Macmillan Publishing Solutions*
Printing: 45# *New Era Matte, R. R. Donnelley & Sons*

Cover Images: *U.S. Supreme Court:* © *National Geographic/SuperStock; Newsroom:* © *Digital Vision/SuperStock; Reporters:* © *Digital Vision/SuperStock*

Library of Congress Cataloging-in-Publication Data

Race, crime and the media / Robert L. Bing III [editor].
    p. cm.
  Includes bibliographical references.
  ISBN-13: 978-0-07-340156-0 (pbk. : alk. paper)
  ISBN-10: 0-07-340156-0 (pbk. : alk. paper) 1. Mass media and crime—United States. 2. Crime in mass media. 3. Mass media and criminal justice—United States. 4. Mass media and race relations—United States. 5. Criminal justice, Administration of—United States. 6. Mass media—Influence. 7. Journalism—Objectivity—United States. I. Bing, Robert L..
  P96.C74R33 2009
  302.23'4—dc22   2009034763

The Internet addresses listed in the text were accurate at the time of publication. The inclusion of a Web site does not indicate an endorsement by the authors or McGraw-Hill, and McGraw-Hill does not guarantee the accuracy of the information presented at these sites.

This book is dedicated to my daughter, Melissa Bing, and my wife, Cynthia Bing.

Table of Contents

v

Preface

This book, *Race, Crime, and the Media,* is written to describe and discuss the realities of the media and the criminal justice system. The media is critical to an understanding of national and international events. It is also responsible for helping define our understanding of society and is to a large extent responsible for development of stereotypes by its coverage of people and situations. This book represents an effort to draw to the reader's attention the intersect of race, crime, and the media by raising questions about the influence of the media on how we think. Do biases exist in media coverage about crime and race? What are some of the manifestations of this bias? How does the media portray crime committed by racial minorities? How is crime data used by the media to buttress a position on crime? What is the influence of the television network versus 24-hour-cable coverage? How does the media import knowledge or inform the public with respect to the social construction of race, gender, and income.

Race, Crime, and the Media represents an effort to answer many of the questions raised in the previous paragraph and to get individuals to think critically about the realities of the criminal justice system, the media, and race. It is divided into three main sections: (1) The Intersection of History, Race, Crime, and the Media; (2) The Quantification and Contextualization of Crime; and (3) The Social Construction of Crime.

The first section, "The Intersection of History, Race, and Crime and the Media," provides historical context and introduces the reader to some key issues in the area of race and the media, including media coverage of rape and racial profiling.

The second section, "The Quantification and Contextualization of Crime," explores media's use of crime data, the portrayal of blacks as offenders and victims, along with a discussion about the ways crime is politicized.

The third and final section is "The Social Construction of Crime." This section contains coverage on many timely topics; some of these topics include the media's preoccupation with missing white victims to the exclusion of missing black victims, media coverage on cable television, the media's coverage of black athletes, and media coverage about the prosecution of crack cocaine use by people of color.

The book is one of the first to provide a collection of original pieces that address the subject in a way that is balanced and provocative. The chapters in each section will surely open your eyes and create an awareness of issues that must be discussed openly and candidly. In short, these chapters provide the basis for intellectual inquiry into a wide range of topics to help us better understand the intersect of race, crime, and media. It is my hope and belief that you will benefit from the contributions of the many scholars who have written chapters for this book. Read and learn about the influence of the media as well the role it plays in the characterization of crimes committed by racial minorities.

Robert L. Bing III

Acknowledgements

I want to acknowledge the many friends, colleagues, and students who offered support for this book. It could not have been done without your encouragement. Many of you would ask "Bing, how is the book coming along?" Your interest provided the impetus for successful completion of the book. Thanks to Narcel Reedus for helping birth the idea for the book. Thanks to Erica Thomas, Renee Bradshaw, Cynthia Hipolito, and Kelli D. Stevens for their assistance in the research. And a special expression of gratitude to McGraw-Hill, especially Frank, Katie, and Teresa for their encouragement, guidance, and support.

PART I

The Intersection of History, Race, Crime, and the Media

CHAPTER 1

Race, Crime, and the Media in Historical Perspective: An Overview

Robert L. Bing III

A BRIEF HISTORY OF MEDIA

There is a tendency to see the media as something that is a relatively new phenomenon, but the media (less the sophistication that is frequently associated with it today) has been around for a long time. During primitive times, information was passed along via drum beat.[1] The first era of printing emerged in China around the ninth century.[2] The Chinese used small blocks of wood to produce playing cards and small books. The ink came from the soot of burning oil. The process of embedding information on the wood was time consuming, tedious, and laborious. The information was mostly for the elite and frequently related to religion. Over the years, paper was introduced—and large sheets of paper were used to print information. These one-page sheets, called broadsides, might contain information on the life of a deceased person, a schedule of seasonal activities, and/or information about the benefits of eating certain foods. The use of broadsides became popular around the early 1500s.[3]

Although, historians point toward earlier practices, the first official newspaper was printed by Henry Muddiman in 1665. The newspaper was referred to as the *Oxford Gazette* and continued the tradition of passing along ballads and seasonal calendars. The papers were for the elite, as they were the ones who could read. It is interesting to note that these first newspapers served the elite and provided their readers with information about the various planting seasons.

With respect to the growth of the media, historians observe that the first printing press arrived in New England in the 1600s, with the first political cartoon published or printed in 1747. In addition to other things, the newspaper was linked to politics, religion, disasters, and the slave trade.[4] While other ethnic newspapers (during colonial times) were already in existence, the first black newspaper appeared around 1827. It was titled *Freedom's Journal.* The focus of the journal was on black liberation; the newspaper also called into the question the irony of democracy in American society, where black men and women were treated as subhumans, although these same women (subhumans) were raped and subjugated by white men. It is important to know that many of these publications (including *Freedom's Journal*) struggled for sponsorship and there was a lot of turnover; frequently, subscribers did not pay and editors were short on cash.

With this historical perspective offered, this chapter seeks to answer myriad questions, such as: What is the media in contemporary society? How does the media determine what will be covered? What is the synergistic nature of the media? First, the media's influence upon the public is pervasive. The irony behind this pervasiveness is that we tend to take the presentation of information about "late-breaking news" as fact. Many consumers of information may not question the use of data, nor the source of the information presented by the media.[5] It is an established fact that the public is influenced by crime reports, even though the information reported may not be accurate. It is also an established fact that the crime rate may be determined by the media.[6] The media's penchant for covering mostly violent or street crimes is also problematic. This emphasis stems from media focus on maintaining the public's attention. *If it bleeds, it leads* is almost always the corollary. The point here is that media coverage distorts the reality of crime. It can even create the impression that the criminal justice system does not respond very well to crimes of violence, even though it does so for most violent crimes.[7] Further, according to Muraskin, the media covers the less common crimes as if they were common, everyday occurrences.[8] Thus, the media is responsible for reconstructing reality. It is notorious for creating the impression that things are out of hand or that crime is rampant. In one notable example, the media overstated the extent of the crack cocaine epidemic in the mid-1980's and 1990s.[9]

There is apparent bias in the reporting of events for which black men and women may be accountable, and this is not a new phenomenon. In fact, a content analysis by Keever and others reveals that the media has a long history of depicting blacks as physically more threatening; and with respect to politics, the portrayal of blacks may be more demeaning than that of whites.[10] After the racial rioting of the 1960s, President Lyndon B. Johnson established the Kerner Commission in 1967 to investigate the cause of the riots. The Kerner Commission was highly critical of the media and criticized it for its negative portrayal of African Americans. Specifically, the commission found that the media should have done equal coverage on the plight of black Americans. The media failed to inform the viewing white public about the frustrations and the failings of the American dream. As a result of these findings, the Kerner Commission called for a nationwide investigation on the role or impact of media coverage.[11] According to Wilson and Gutierrez, since news reflects what is really important to a society, minority coverage in mainstream news reporting provides insight into the status of minorities.[12] Indeed, an analysis of newspaper coverage on people of color between 1880 and 1990 can provide useful information about the perceived social status of blacks during this time period. Concomitantly, there is a propensity for many journalists to reduce the complexity of situations to more simplistic terms, which may reinforce a stereotype.

SLAVERY AND THE EMERGENCE OF THE BLACK STEREOTYPE

There is a sordid history of slavery in America. With slavery, men and women were subjugated by their slave owners and received subhuman treatment. One of many rationalizations for such barbaric treatment can be directly related to the perception of slaves as primitive people from a dark continent.[13] The negative images of blacks as helpless people from an uncivilized world without industrialization seem to warrant intervention from Europeans. More to the point; the image of the slave as a barbaric savage, lazy and shiftless, engendered the stereotype of the black man from Africa as a Sambo. With the Sambo image emerged two stereotypes: one, that the black man was shiftless and lazy, and the other, that the black man had unrestrained sexual prowess and was potentially violent. In short, the Sambo was to be laughed at— but also feared.

MEDIA COVERAGE AND RACE

There is evidence that broadcast coverage of blacks before WWII was driven by media bias, especially in the South. In other words, the little coverage there was served to maintain stereotypes.[14] One researcher found the pervasive use of stereotypical images of blacks as servants between 1937 and 1957.[15] Other researchers observed that many Northern papers were frequently silent on the issue of oppression in the South.[16] Further, many crimes committed against blacks by whites were back-page stories. This same observation has been made in the case of black-on-black crimes, which were also relegated to the back section of the paper. This writer has found that the media almost ignored coverage of the prospect of a black Jack the Ripper in Atlanta in the early 1900s, when forty-five black females were killed by what many believed was a serial killer. These deaths received little coverage by the *Atlanta Constitution* in the South but more coverage by the *New York Times* in the North.

Shortly after the civil unrest of the 1960s, "managed" media coverage of black Americans was already beginning to change. At the very least, there was greater visibility, as many papers had been notorious for excluding balanced coverage of blacks. In other words, while there was coverage by the media, it was mostly one-sided; few newspapers carried articles about the inequalities and the impediments to the American dream that blacks faced. A major change occurred in 1967 when the *Montgomery Advertiser* dealt with stories about the plight of the underclass and the methods used by law enforcement and the National Guard to control civil rights activists (both black and white).

History has shown that the media has enormous potential to socially construct images of crime or images of people. This potential is powerfully demonstrated in an article by Ted Chiricos,[17] who uses Cohen's phrase "moral panic" to describe how politicians use the media's social construct to advance their own agenda.[18] Chiricos notes that at any particular time a "person or group of persons emerges to be defined as a threat to the societal values and interests."[19] According to Chiricos, the threat may be presented in the media, supported by someone with a presumed expertise, after which there is a response by politicians and a subsequent call to do something that would eradicate the threat.[20] As one of many examples, reports of violence created the impression that crime was out of control in certain communities, resulting in a "moral panic." The net outcome of the moral panic was a call to build more prisons for the presumed violent. Chiricos makes a similar observation with regard to crack cocaine usage. He observes that the crack epidemic was overexaggerated and hypothesizes that the crack cocaine problem was widely overstated for a variety of reasons, ranging from competition between media outlets to political campaigns.[21] More to the point, Chiricos states that beyond advancing a particular political agenda that represses the "have nots" in society, the moral panic serves to "divert attention away from contradictions in American society that have promoted an extraordinary growth of economic inequality and expansion of the underclass."[22] This is one of many ways in which the media can create moral panic. The irony of course is that even use of the term "moral panic" is a contradiction. Why? Because there is little that is moral about the behavior of the media and politicians. Chiricos rightly states "that the same media frenzy that raises decisiveness to the cardinal virtue of public policy lowers the chance that meaningful response to the enduring problem will be undertaken."[23] Concomitantly, the media has an agenda and seeks to motivate change by politicians and legislative bodies.

Black Crime, White Crime, or Crime

The media creates the impression that assaults on the elderly are widespread, when they are not. Similarly, there is a tendency, due to media reporting, for society to feel that whites are more likely to be victimized by urban (or black) youth, but this notion is also not supported by the data. A closer look at the data will reveal that it is urban youth who are at greater risk of victimization, not the elderly. Additionally, since crime is more intraracial, white citizens are not at greater risk from potential black offenders, but from other members of their own race. The same is true for urban youth, who are most likely to be victimized by members of their own race. With this observation in mind, the media has created the term "black on black crime," a phrase that is potentially problematic. Why? The use of the phrase "black on black" or "white on white" creates the impression that crime is indigenous to the neighborhood and some argue that the net effect is to absolve government from any meaningful intervention.[24] Thus, crime and its link to race become socially constructed in the media.

What Is Social Constructionism?

Perceptions of reality, coupled with personal experiences, create what is referred to as *social constructionism*. From this perspective, the media has a lot to do with shaping the construction of crime. Surette, for example, says: "The media influences the social construction of crime . . . by supplying the narrative, symbolic crimes, and basic information . . . needed to create factual and interpretative claims.[25] As Surette and others would argue, the media is the engine by which information is disseminated and subsequently interpreted and reinterpreted by the media and the people and organizations who rely upon it. For example, the Department of Justice is reliant upon the media to disseminate information about crime rates and crime-prevention initiatives. A good example here is the FBI's Crime Clock, a publication of aggregate crime statistics from which the data is easily reinterpreted by viewers of the various media outlets. It is worth noting that sometimes these social constructs are laden with historical stereotypes, such as the black man being prone to savagery. Concomitantly, Surette offers a brilliant example about the use of "frames" and competing lenses by which crime is reconstructed. Surette points toward the video beating of Rodney King in 1991. His point is that the videotaped beating of King provided many media outlets and experts with an opportunity to reconstruct what happened. A parallel situation (not so closely watched) can be found in the second O. J. Simpson criminal trial in Las Vegas, where the jurors and the American people were left to reconstruct what actually happened based upon an audio recording of an armed robbery and kidnapping attempt by O. J. Simpson. In many ways, the 2008 presidential campaign offers another way in which to view the role of the media and social constructionism. Every network and major cable news show (e.g., CNN, MSNBC, and Fox News) had its own brand of news coverage on the campaign, with each network serving as the "engine" and facilitating a social construction of the candidates for their viewers.

According to Surette, there are four stages of social construction. The first is the stage on which many of the perceptions are played out. In other words, the first stage provides context for the social construction. The second stage involves "competing social constructions."[26] Restated, individuals and organizations compete for control of the explanation. In the third stage the media helps filter out nonmainstream viewpoints, frequently yielding to the powerful or the most influential groups. In this way, according to

Surette, the views of the "oppressed" are discounted or filtered out by the media.[27] Finally, the fourth stage is referred to as "winning social construction,"[28] and it represents emergence of a dominant social construction.[29] In this stage, the media has control and legitimates the perspective. In many ways, this fourth stage captures the essence of a position taken by Chiricos in his description of the "moral panic." The media obfuscates reality by carving out a position that results in other perspectives being overlooked. The media shapes our viewpoints and impacts our interpretations. In short, the media poorly describes the realities of crime and the criminal justice system.[30]

CRITICAL THINKING QUESTIONS

1. What is meant by the term *black-on-black crime*?
2. How would you characterize the historical beginnings of the media?
3. What is the role of social construction in the delivery of information by the media?
4. What events shaped the unfolding of media coverage on African Americans in the 1960s and 1970s?

NOTES

1. Hiley H. Ward, *Mainstreams of American Media History* (Boston: Allyn and Bacon, 1997), 1.
2. Ward, *Mainstreams*, 5.
3. Ibid.
4. Ward, *Mainstreams*, 52.
5. Roslyn Muraskin and Shelly Feuer Domash, *Crime and the Media: Headlines vs. Reality* (Upper Saddle River, NJ: Prentice Hall, 2007), 10.
6. Muraskin and Domash, *Crime and the Media*, 11.
7. Samuel Walker, *Sense and Nonsense About Crime and Drugs* (Belmont, CA: Wadsworth, 2005).
8. Muraskin and Domash, *Crime and the Media*, 12.
9. Ted Chiricos, "The Media, Moral Panic and the Politics of Crime Control," in *The Criminal Justice System: Politics and Policies*, ed. George

F. Cole, Marc G. Gertz, and Amy Bunger (Belmont, CA: Wadsworth, 2004), 41–61.
10. Beverly Keever, Carolyn Martindale, and Mary Ann Weston, *U.S. News Coverage of Racial Minorities: A Sourcebook, 1934–1996* (Westport, CT: Greenwood Press, 1997), 14.
11. Keever et al., *U.S. News*, 15.
12. Clint Wilson and Felix Gutierrez, *Race, Multiculturalism and the Media* (Thousand Oaks, CA: Sage, 1995), 34.
13. Ward, *Mainstreams*, 64.
14. Keever et al., *U.S. News*, 80.
15. Keever et al., *U.S. News*, 80.
16. Keever et al., *U.S. News*, 82.
17. See for example Chiricos.
18. Stan Cohen, *Folk Devils and Moral Panics: The Creation of the Mods and Rockers* (Oxford: Blackwell, 1972).

19. See for example Chiricos, 42.

20. See for example Chiricos, 54.

21. See for example Chiricos, 52.

22. See for example Chiricos, 59.

23. See for example Chiricos, 58.

24. Robert Bing, "Black on Black Crime: A Critique of Terminological Preference," in *Black on Black Crime: Facing Facts—Challenging Fictions*, ed. P. Ray Kedia (Bristol, IN: Wyndham Hall Press, 1994), 247.

25. Ray Surette, *Media, Crime, and Criminal Justice* (Belmont, CA: Wadsworth, 2007), 52.

26. Surette, *Media*, 34.

27. Surette, *Media*, 35.

28. Surette, *Media*, 35.

29. Surette, *Media*, 35.

30. Gregg Barak, *Media, Process, and the Social Construction of Crime* (New York: Garland Publishing, 1994), 33.

CHAPTER 2

Rape, Race, and the Media

Frankie Y. Bailey

INTRODUCTION

In June 2003, National Basketball Association (NBA) star Kobe Bryant was accused of rape. His accuser was a nineteen-year-old woman, a member of the staff at the Eagle, Colorado, hotel where Bryant had spent the night. Bryant would eventually reach an out-of-court settlement with his accuser. The massive media coverage of the case placed Bryant and his accuser at the center of the cultural discourse about rape and celebrity. Because Bryant is black and his accuser is white, the case also stirred memories of the history of interracial rape in the United States.[1]

The coverage of rape by the media (both news and entertainment) offers an often distorted view of sexual assault. Historically, myths about rape and about race, class, and gender as factors in sexual assault have been perpetuated in popular culture and the mass media. This chapter examines the intersection of race and rape in the media.

EARLY NARRATIVES

Although the mass media as we know it today did not appear until the nineteenth century, the roots of modern American news and entertainment media can be traced to the colonial era. During this period, religious tracts and gallows sermons and confessions dominated the print culture. The interactions between British colonists and Native Americans ("Indians") gave rise to "captivity narratives." In these works, whites who had been taken captive by Native Americans recounted their experiences. The allegations of sexual abuse/assault on white women and girls by Native American men were presented in language intended to convey horror and outrage. At the same time, the captivity narratives and other accounts of the Indian wars objectified the women and girls who were the alleged victims. Accounts of rape by Native Americans—with no mention of white male assaults on Native American women—presented rape as a weapon used by "savages" against white colonists. Moreover, the focus was on the suffering of the white man who was unable to protect his wife and/or daughters. In contrast to this dominant narrative, in *Six Weeks in Sioux Tepees* (1864) settler and doctor's wife Sarah Wakefield defended Chaska, the Native American man who had sheltered her and her children in his family household, protecting them from harm. Wakefield's captivity narrative appeared as Chaska and other Dakota men were standing trial without counsel with military officers as the jurors.[2] Although "only two of the 393 Dakota tried were convicted of rape," members of Congress alleged that the rape of female captives was "nearly universal."[3] In spite of the reduction in sentence that he had received from President Abraham Lincoln, Chaska was executed in an alleged administrative mistake. He was one of the thirty-eight men hanged in "the largest mass execution in U.S. history."[4] Concerned as much for her own reputation as for that of Chaska, Wakefield published a second edition of her narrative that was also ignored and dismissed.[5]

If the captivity narratives were written from the point of view of European Americans, the slave narratives were written by and from the perspectives of the Africans and their descendants held in bondage. As slave narratives evolved as a unique genre of American literature, former slaves appealed to a Northern abolitionist audience, presenting narratives of captivity and escape to freedom. Male former slaves, such as Frederick Douglass, wrote about the abuse of black women by white slave owners and overseers. But for former bondwomen, such as Harriet Jacobs, it was difficult to speak to their reading audience about the sexual harassment and abuse that they suffered. The stereotypes promulgated by slave owners depicted black women as either asexual "Mammies" or seductive "Jezebels." A white man who had a sexual relationship with a black woman could and often did claim that (a) he had been seduced by the woman, or (b) even if the woman had been coerced, she had not been harmed in the encounter because of the lascivious nature of black women. Female slaves were "property" with no rights concerning their own bodies. Injuries to slave women were viewed as damages suffered to the slave owner's property rather than to the black women as victims.[6] A black woman who claimed the same response to a rape as a white woman challenged one of the myths that allowed slavery to function as an institution. Thus, when former slave Harriet Jacobs wrote her narrative, she needed to speak to her white Northern audience in a language that would evoke empathy rather than disdain or censure. She chose the tropes of the nineteenth-century sentimental novel, positioning herself as the heroine, an innocent victim of male lust, and a mother who sought to protect her children.[7]

Perceptions of African American male slaves were also often based on stereotypes. In counterpoint to "Uncle Tom," the loyal house servant, and "Sambo," the lazy, shiftless field hand, there was "Nat," the violent slave who would kill to obtain his freedom and who struck fear in the hearts of white Southerners.

Neither racial stereotypes nor slavery were restricted to the South. The abolition of slavery in the North did not prevent stereotypes of racial inferiority from affecting white Northern attitudes. In the aftermath of the Civil War, the myth of the "new negro criminal," no longer controlled by bondage and lusting after white women, was prevalent in the South and accepted by many Northerners as factual. In the South, vigilante violence in response to alleged sexual assaults of white women became a form of racial oppression.

THE MEDIA AND LYNCHING

In 1934, Claude Neal, a young African American man in Jackson County, Florida, was accused of the rape and murder of a young white woman, a neighbor. Neal was abducted from jail and held by vigilantes. As newspapers, including those in the North, followed events, the vigilantes announced the time and place of the lynching. A radio station in nearby Dothan, Alabama, "announced the impending event several times."[8] The Associated Press reported the news of the "invitational lynching," with word reaching the National Association for the Advancement of Colored People (NAACP). The NAACP attempted to intervene by contacting the governor of Florida. The governor contacted the county sheriff, offering to send the National Guard; but the sheriff declined the assistance.[9] As the time for the lynching arrived, spectators were in attendance from neighboring states. Neal was tortured (including castration), and then hanged in front of an audience of white men, women, and children. Those present included the relatives of Neal's alleged victim. As on other such occasions, photographs were taken for souvenir postcards. Newspapers in both South and North reported on the lynching as they had the prelude.[10]

Northern and Midwestern newspapers, such as the *New York Times* and the *Chicago Tribune*, respectively, portrayed lynch law in the South as barbarism. However, the white press outside the South did not challenge Southern assertions of the inherent criminality of black males or of black male lust for white women.[11] Conversely, even though it was a risky business for black editors and journalists in the South to challenge the falsehoods that supported lynching, some did. In Virginia, John Mitchell, Jr., editor of the *Richmond Planet,* spoke out against racial oppression and white violence. In Memphis, Ida B. Wells (later Wells-Barnett) became legendary for her reporting.

A turning point in Wells's career occurred when she reported the murders of three black male friends who had fought a gun battle with the white men who had broken into their grocery store. During the battle, they shot one of the intruders. A mob later took the three black men from jail and lynched them. After Wells's article appeared in the *Free Speech and Headlight,* the newspaper in which she was a partner, the newspaper office was destroyed. Her life in danger, Wells was forced to leave Memphis. She moved to Chicago and continued her crusade. In *Southern Horrors: Lynch Law in All Its Phases* (1892), Wells documented the violence occurring in the South. Angering her critics, Wells went to Great Britain to enlist Europeans in the crusade against lynching in the

United States. In her writings and speeches, Wells pointed out the hypocrisy of the white men who claimed to defend the honor of white women while they themselves violated black women. She challenged the idea that rape was the true or primary cause for the lynchings, which were a white weapon in retarding black political, social, and economic progress.[12]

Paramount for African American activists was their participation in the interracial effort to get federal antilynching legislation passed by Congress. Proposed by Representative Leonidas Dyer (R-Missouri), the Dyer Anti-Lynching Bill, which would have made lynching a felony, was defeated by politics and filibuster when it came up in 1922 and 1923. After, reaching a peak in the 1890s, the number of annual lynchings declined in the early twentieth century. However, as the Neal case in 1934 illustrates, such events did not cease. Nor were lynchings solely a Southern phenomenon.[13] Presented as narratives of alleged acts of black sexual violence and outraged white response, stories of lynchings were covered by the wire services and appeared in newspapers across the country.

In his 1915 blockbuster, *The Birth of a Nation*, director D. W. Griffith brought the Old South perspective on the Civil War and postwar Reconstruction to the movie screen. The technical achievements of the film, including such innovations as split screen, delighted the enthusiastic audiences and earned the movie accolades. The film was based on *The Clansman* (1905), by former minister Thomas Dixon. It tells the story of the Civil War and federal occupation of the South from the standpoints of two white families who are friends until the war places them on opposite sides of the bloody conflict. In the aftermath of the war, the Southern family and their neighbors find themselves oppressed by black federal troops, white Northern Republicans, and Yankee "carpetbaggers." Black soldiers patrol the streets of their town. The son of the Southern family is a war hero. Inspired by the sight of white children wearing sheets to frighten black children, he forms a vigilante group, the Ku Klux Klan (KKK). However, he is unable to save his youngest sister from the bestial black soldier, Gus (played by a white actor in "blackface") who stalks her through the woods. "Little Sister" plunges to her death before her brother can arrive to rescue her. She has avoided the "fate worse than death" feared by all virtuous (white) women. Gus is hanged by the Klan, and his body left on the doorstep of the mulatto Lt. Governor, Silas Lynch. Lynch has designs on the beloved of the hero, the daughter of Senator Cameron, the Republican senator. In the climactic final scene, the KKK gallops to the rescue of the besieged Cameron family. North and South are reconciled by the double marriages between sons and daughters of the two families. The threat of black rule ends on election day, when blacks are successfully disenfranchised.

Early film images of bestial blacks—symbolizing "Negro regression"—popularized images of African Americans in the early 1900s in social science literature. For example, criminal anthropologist Cesare Lombroso, the "father of positivist criminology," believed that Africans were less evolved than Europeans. In cartoons of "Darkest Africa," they were cannibals and headhunters. Although well-behaved American negroes were seen as more civilized than their African kin, those who attempted to step "out of their place" were seen as a threat. Southern views on race gained currency in the rest of the country through the works of Southern historians, politicians, and novelists.

However, in the years between the two World Wars, a growing number of Southern newspaper editors and journalists began to make the argument that it was important to bring an end to lynch-law in the South. If the region was to make economic progress, it was necessary that the South overcome its reputation for barbarism and allow the criminal justice process to run its course. Implicit in this argument was the understanding that there was little chance that a black man accused of raping a white woman would be acquitted in a court of law.

WHITE SLAVERY

In urban America, early twentieth-century reformers were expressing concern about "white slavery," the seduction or entrapment of innocent young women into prostitution. The concept of white slavery was linked to beliefs about predatory strangers in the dangerous city. Aside from the white males who might seduce a young white woman, there were also foreigners, such as the Chinese males who were associated in the public imagination with "opium dens." This concern about prostitution—sexual slavery—led to enactment of the White-Slave Traffic Act ("Mann Act") in 1910. The Act was directed at men who took women across state lines for "immoral purposes." The men who were accused of violating the Mann Act included Jack Johnson, the African American heavyweight-boxing champion. The flamboyant Johnson not only defeated white boxers, he flaunted his relationships with white women. His exploits in the ring and out were widely covered by the black press as a celebrity and a hero in the African American community. The white press covered Johnson as it waited for the white boxer (the "Great White Hope") who would be able to defeat him. Lampooned and caricatured in the press, Johnson received death threats from white Southerners who threatened to come to Chicago and lynch him. Facing charges under the Mann Act, Johnson fled the country with his second white wife to avoid prosecution.

THE SCOTTSBORO BOYS

While Jack Johnson had reached the summit of celebrity, the nine black youths involved in what came to be known as the "Scottsboro case" were unknown before they became the focus of the series of trials that attracted international attention. Their story begins in March 1931, when they were aboard a freight train in Alabama. There, a fight broke out between some of the black youths and the white youths, who also were riding the rail in search of work. The white youths lost the fight and were tossed from the slow-moving train. They reported what had happened, and at the next stop in Scottsboro police were waiting. Unknown to the black youths, two young white women were also traveling illegally on the train. Facing arrest, the two women accused the black youths of rape. With that sensational accusation, the black youths—ranging in age from 13–20—became known as the "Scottsboro Boys."

Later, one of the young women, Ruby Bates, recanted her accusation and joined the Communist Party in its crusade for the Scottsboro Boys' freedom. But her friend, Victoria Price, continued to tell and retell her story that she and Bates had been gang-raped. The trials produced two important United States Supreme Court decisions regarding the rights of defendant to adequate legal counsel in *Powell v. Alabama* (1932) and the denial of due process and equal protection when blacks were not allowed to serve on juries in *Norris v. Alabama* (1935). The efforts by the Communist Party to create international support for the Scottsboro Boys and the resulting rallies ensured that a media audience well beyond Alabama was aware of the case.[14]

Three decades later, childhood memories of the case inspired white Southern author Harper Lee as she wrote her coming-of-age novel *To Kill a Mockingbird* (1960), set in Malcombe, Georgia. The film adaptation—starring Gregory Peck as Atticus Finch, the white attorney who takes on the defense of a black laborer accused of raping a white neighbor—immortalized the segregated Southern courtroom. As one of the civil-rights-era novels written by a white Southerner, the novel offered an enduring popular culture image of a white Southern hero standing up for what was right. However, in the novel, Atticus Finch lost his case and his client was kidnapped by vigilantes and murdered.

In real life, the lawyers for Scottsboro Boys managed to save their clients from execution. However, seven of the youths languished in the Alabama prison system until public attention turned to their plight. Then the state of Alabama finally dropped the prosecutions and by 1948 all of the Scottsboro Boys either had been released from prison or had escaped. In 1976, Governor George Wallace, once notorious for his stance against integration, pardoned Clarence Norris, the last living Scottsboro Boy. The legacy of the Scottsboro Boys case continues today in discussions about "racial hoaxes," which depend on stereotypical images of black men.

BIGGER THOMAS AND FICTIONAL RAPE

Chicago was one of those cities where a segregated urban "ghetto" was created by restrictive covenants and other mechanisms. It was in Chicago that African American novelist Richard Wright set his most famous work, *Native Son*.[15] The novel's protagonist is Bigger Thomas, a migrant from the South, who lives with his family in a Chicago tenement. Bigger is hired by Mr. Dalton, a white philanthropist and slumlord, as his family's chauffeur. Mary Dalton, the college-aged daughter, has a boyfriend who is a Communist. Mary and her boyfriend, Jan, befriend Bigger, and insist on having dinner with him at a black hangout. When the inebriated Mary passes out in the car, Bigger tries to get her into her room without waking her parents. Mary's blind mother comes into her daughter's room when Bigger is still there. Panicking, Bigger suffocates Mary while trying to keep her quiet. He attempts to dispose of her body by burning it in the furnace. Then he sends a ransom note to divert attention.

When his crime is discovered, Bigger flees. He kills his black girlfriend, Bessie, before he is taken into custody. But it is Mary's death that leads to his conviction and execution. As he was writing the novel, Wright was reading the newspaper coverage of the sensational, real-life trial of Robert Nixon, a black man who was accused of the rape and murder of a white woman whose apartment he was burglarizing. Wright incorporated the newspaper articles into his novel.[16]

Native Son created its own sensation when it was published. Aside from the positive literary reviews, critics noted Wright's claim that he had presented a fictional version of the young black men that he had known in the South and later in the North. These were the black youths struggling against oppression, driven to violence, and either broken or killed by white society. Bigger Thomas was the white nightmare of black violence personified.[17]

Fifteen years later, it was the contrast between Chicago, in which black males had at least some freedom, and the Deep South, where violations of racial etiquette could lead to death, that was the focus of media discourse. In 1955, the year after the United States Supreme Court declared in *Brown v. Board of Education* that separate public accommodations were not equal, Emmett Till, a Chicago youth, was murdered in Money, Mississippi.

EMMETT TILL AND THE "WOLF WHISTLE"

Till, who was fourteen, had gone to the South with a cousin to visit his great uncle and other relatives. When he and his cousins went into the general store in the small town of Money, Till had an encounter with a white woman, Carolyn Bryant, that would lead to his death. The nature of that encounter remains a matter of debate. However, the woman's husband, Roy Bryant, was told that Till had made a flirtatious comment to Carolyn Bryant and "wolf-whistled" at her. Mamie Till, Emmett's mother, said that her son had a stutter and that what he had said must have been misunderstood. What was in general agreement was that Emmett, born and raised in Chicago, had not realized—until he was taken from his great-uncle's house—how dangerous any violation of the norms regarding black male behavior toward a white female could be.

Although Emmett Till had not been accused of rape or even of physically touching Carolyn Bryant, he was cast in the role of the black rapist. He was punished by Bryant and his half-brother J. W. Milam with an act of vigilante violence that many blacks equated with the lynchings that had occurred earlier in the century. The media coverage of the trial pitted Northern newspapers against Southern newspapers. Editors of Southern newspapers later blamed Mamie Till, the National Association for the Advancement of Colored People (NAACP), and other "outside agitators" for the loss of the initial sympathy that many Southerners had felt for Till. The agitators, they argued, had created a backlash as Southerners defended the region and the two men against attack. Northern interference made the jury willing to believe the defense attorney's assertion of a conspiracy against the accused men.

After they had been acquitted by an all-white, male jury, Bryant and Milam granted a paid interview to a journalist from *Look* magazine. In this interview, they confessed to murdering Emmett Till and tossing his body into the Tallahatchie River. When her son was returned to her in Chicago, Mamie Till had insisted that his battered body be displayed in an open casket. She said she wanted "the world to see" what had been done to her son. The horrific photo of Emmett Till in his coffin appeared in *Jet* magazine, an African American publication. Although his killers were acquitted, the photo in *Jet* galvanized African Americans across the country and became a turning point in the civil rights movement.[18]

RAPE, CIVIL RIGHTS, AND THE WOMEN'S MOVEMENT

The women's movement of the 1960s and 1970s set the stage for the efforts by victims-rights advocates, feminist scholars, and others to challenge myths about rape and the treatment of rape victims by the criminal justice system and in the media. In a seminal work, *Against Our Wills: Men, Women, and Rape*, Susan Brownmiller argued that rape is a weapon used by men in their struggle for dominance. Drawing from the long human history of warfare and conquest, Brownmiller cited examples of women as the "spoils of war," whose rape by the conquerors symbolized their defeat of the losers. Brownmiller argued that rape (or the fear of rape) was a mechanism used by men to keep women subordinate and in need of their "protection."[19]

Feminist challenges to patriarchal assumptions about the nature of sexual relationships between men and women intersected with other social movements. In the 1950s, on the eve of the modern civil rights movement in the South, the rapes of several African American women by white men had become a rallying point for young African Americans. Both regional and national media covered the story of Betty Jean Owens in Tallahassee, Florida. In May 1959 after the Green and Orange Ball at Florida A & M University, the historically black college where they were students, Owens, her escort, and another couple were sitting in their car near a park. Four white men, looking, as they later said, for a "nigger girl" with whom to have an "all night party," approached the car and forced the two young men to get out and leave. The other young woman managed to escape and run into the park. Owens was forced into the four men's car and driven to the edge of town where she was raped seven times.

As noted above, Owens's rape was not an atypical event. By the 1940s and 1950s, other black women were breaking their silence to report attacks by white men. In 1944, for example, the gang rape of Mrs. Recy Taylor in Abbeville, Alabama, became public knowledge and outraged the black community as did the 1949 rape of Gertrude Perkins in Montgomery, Alabama, by two white police officers. Fortunately for Owens, the young, part-time police officer who was on duty when she and her friends went to the station was a college student himself. He set out to look for the men and found them. The four men were put on trial as students at Florida A & M University rallied around Owens, demanding justice.[20]

The African American press cast Owens as a "respectable middle-class co-ed."[21] The mainstream white press also covered the courtroom drama. As McGuire observes, "The Tallahassee case focused national attention on the sexual exploitation of black women at the hands of white men, leading to convictions elsewhere that summer."[22] The four men were found guilty and given life sentences. It was a victory, but some African Americans pointed out the inequity of the sentences given to the white men who had gang-raped Owens and the death sentences given to black men convicted of raping white women.[23]

In 1971, another African American woman, Joan Little, attracted national media attention as both victim and offender. Little was accused of the ice pick murder of a white jail guard, who allegedly had raped her in her cell. She faced a death sentence if convicted. As Little went to trial in a North Carolina courtroom, her case embodied the intersection of post–1960s race, gender, class, and regional politics. Activists (civil rights groups, women's groups, prisoners' rights groups, and opponents of capital punishment) expressed their support of Little, and the Joan Little Defense Fund was started.[24] During the trial, Little attended a press luncheon for female reporters.[25] *Ms.* magazine published an article by Angela Davis, African American intellectual and political activist, who had herself stood trial—and been acquitted—on gun charges related to a courtroom escape by members of the Black Panther Party. In her article about Little, Davis placed the case in the context of the historical legacy of abuse—physical, sexual, and psychological—of black women during slavery and in its aftermath.[26] When Little was acquitted, she quickly disappeared into obscurity.

Twenty years later, although the Anita Hill–Clarence Thomas case did not involve rape, it again focused media and public attention on issues of sex and race. During Thomas's 1991 confirmation hearing for the United States Supreme Court, law professor Anita Hill testified that she had been the victim of sexual harassment by Thomas. Hill alleged that during the period of 1981 to 1983 when Thomas had been her supervisor at the United States Department of Education and then later the Equal Employment Opportunity Commission, he had made sexual overtures to her. Questioned by senators (all white males), Hill recounted episodes that included an occasion on which Thomas had asked who had put a pubic hair in his Coke can. She said on another occasion he had referred to a pornographic film (which gained notoriety during the coverage of the hearing).

Denying Hill's accusations of sexual harassment, Thomas faced the Senate Committee with his white wife sitting behind him. He said that he was being subjected to a "high-tech lynching." The fact that both Hill and Thomas were African Americans who had achieved success and were now on public display created divisions in the African American community. Some African Americans were dismayed that Hill had "aired dirty laundry." Others accused her of conspiring with white feminists to bring down Thomas, who was about to become the second African American (after Thurgood Marshall) to be appointed to the U.S. Supreme Court.

For their part, some black feminists were angered by the fact that white women were the sources sought by the media for statements about the case. As a group, they issued a statement in the *New York Times* and in seven black newspapers. In this statement, they objected to both the stereotyping of black women that was occurring and to Thomas's use of lynching imagery to describe his situation.[27]

Thomas was ultimately confirmed as a Supreme Court justice. Hill continued her career as a law professor and became a nationally sought-after speaker and author. The case remains one of "he said/she said," with supporters on each side convinced that one of the two was lying. One legacy of the case has been increased discourse about the nature of sexual harassment.

Fasson argues that the Hill–Thomas case should be viewed in conjunction with the several "sexual events" (scandals) of the 1990s that attracted massive public attention and media coverage. These events include the abuse of women during the Navy Tailhook gathering, the resignation of Senator Robert Packwood as he faced allegations of sexual abuse and harassment, and the impeachment of President Bill Clinton for perjury concerning his involvement with intern Monica Lewinsky.[28]

RAPE IN THE NEWS

During the 1990s, other celebrities were in the news, accused of rape. In 1991, William Kennedy Smith was accused of the rape of Patricia Bowman, a woman he had met in a bar in Palm Beach, Florida, while in the company of his uncle, Senator Edward Kennedy, and his cousin, Patrick Kennedy. Kennedy Smith claimed the sexual encounter with Bowman on a beach had been consensual. He was acquitted. In January 1992, heavyweight champion Mike Tyson went to trial for the rape of Desiree Washington, a Miss Black American Beauty Pageant contestant, in his hotel room. Tyson was convicted and served three years in prison. If the Kennedy Smith trial had provoked public debate about money, power privilege, and the nature of consent, the Tyson trial led to more discussion about Tyson's controversial career and his image that meshed well with stereotypes of violent black men.

In 1989, a New York City rape case attracted national and international attention. The press called it "wilding," reporting that a group of African American and Hispanic youth had roamed through Central Park assaulting and robbing citizens. The victim of the most vicious attack was alleged to have been a young white woman, an investment banker (the way she was routinely identified) who had been jogging in the park. The group of black and Hispanic youths were accused of brutally attacking, raping, and leaving her for dead. The press carried regular updates of her medical condition, as she first struggled to live and then to recover from the attack. Meanwhile, the young men who had been arrested were the subjects of virulent media coverage. Financier Donald Trump took out a full-page ad in New York City newspapers proclaiming that the death penalty should be brought back.[29] The *Amsterdam News*, a black New York

City newspaper, reported the woman's name in a front-page story, arguing that the intent in doing so was to redress "the racial injustice of naming the black suspects and not the white victim."[30] However, as Benedict observes, both the *Amsterdam News* and the mainstream white press used the sexist language and imagery common to many rape cases. In the mainstream media, the victim was cast in the role of the "virgin" set upon by a pack of wolves.

The teenagers, who had confessed to the crime (although they later said their confessions were coerced), were sentenced to prison. Years later, after the five teenagers had served years in prison and been released, Matias Reyes, already serving time for murder and rape, said that he had attacked the jogger. He said that he had been the lone attacker, and his DNA linked him to the crime scene. The convictions of the five teenagers, now adults, were vacated. In the wake of Reyes's confession, the media looked at the issue of false confessions, particularly in cases involving vulnerable suspects. The following year, in 2003, media attention turned to the victim when she identified herself with the publication of her memoir, *I Am the Central Park Jogger: A Story of Hope and Possibility*. By then married and working with other victims of traumatic events, Trisha Meili said she had no memory of the attack.

The Kobe Bryant rape case mentioned in the introduction is an example of another high-profile "media trial" of the late twentieth century. A "media trial" is a case that receives massive media coverage.[31] Long before such a case is adjudicated in a court of law, citizens have formed opinions about the guilt or innocence of the suspect/alleged offender. They also have evaluated the truthfulness and reliability of statements by the alleged victim and others involved in the case. In this sense, the "trial" occurs in the press.

When Bryant was accused of rape by a white female, many wondered if the allegations were true. The tabloid media sought personal information about Bryant's accuser. The photo of one of her high school classmates was mistakenly identified as the alleged victim and posted on the Internet. Eventually, and contrary to the usual practice in rape cases, the victim's name was released by the media. Advocates for rape victims and others decried this intense media scrutiny and invasion of privacy that might make other women reluctant to report sexual assaults. Supporters and fans of Bryant argued that the woman had no more right to privacy than Bryant, who was being accused of rape. Moreover, they suggested that the alleged victim might be targeting Bryant to extort money from him. Other observers, including some members of the press, suggested that Bryant had run afoul of the law like other male athletes before him. The fact that Bryant was a black athlete and a member of the National Basketball Association (NBA) added a racial subtext to the discussion about athletes "behaving badly."[32]

In an article about media coverage of white criminals, Miller, Like, and Levin discuss the tendency to seek explanations for the behavior of white offenders. Rather than assume that criminal behavior is typical of whites, the mainstream media engage in extensive efforts to find reasons for the lawbreaking of white offenders. Moreover, in American culture, white Western outlaws and gangsters have achieved the status of "folk heroes." In contrast, news media and popular culture depictions of offenders of color often seem to assume that criminality is typical of these groups. There is rarely an effort to provide social context or to examine the lives of individual offenders for factors (e.g., abuse as a child or mental illness) that might have contributed to their criminality.[33]

The 2007 case of the Duke University lacrosse players accused of rape raised questions about the interaction of race, class, and gender in media coverage of rape cases. The white lacrosse players were accused of rape by an African American woman. The woman was an exotic dancer, one of two women hired to entertain at a team party. Supporters of the defendants argued they were themselves the victims of a crusading prosecutor. They argued that the alleged victim had made a false report and was perpetrating a racial hoax. They pointed to the backgrounds of the young men who were "student athletes" and outstanding members of the Duke University community.

Supporters of the alleged victim complained about the media coverage, which emphasized the fact that the woman had been working as an exotic dancer. This served to play into rape myths about "innocent" and "blameworthy" victims and to discredit her testimony. The coverage played down the fact that the alleged victim was a student attending North Carolina Central University, a historically black university. Some supporters tried to place the woman's allegations of rape in the context of the sexual abuse of black women by white males that had been occurring since slavery. They argued that the elite background of the white suspects led them to believe that they could get away with such a crime.

When the charges against the Duke University lacrosse players were dropped, they spoke about the ordeal that they had endured. The prosecutor faced ethics charges for his handling of the case. The young woman continued to maintain that she was raped.[34]

The outcome of the Duke University case brings to mind the still-controversial Tawana Brawley case. In 1987, Brawley, who was then fifteen years old and living in Wappingers Falls, New York, had gone missing for several days and said she had been kidnapped and raped by six white men. Brawley's case attracted support from political activists, including Reverend Al Sharpton. However, lack of physical evidence and discrepancies in her story led to a grand jury report concluding that the crimes Brawley alleged had not occurred. The Brawley case is often characterized as a racial hoax. It remains unclear if this is how the Duke University case will be remembered.

One question we might ask about rape cases and their impact has to do with the images of rape and victims that are prevalent in entertainment media.

RAPE IN FILMS AND ON TV

One of the interesting aspects of post–civil rights era films is the relative lack of images of black male rapists engaged in interracial rape. The films of the "Black exploitation" era of the late 1960s and 1970s featured white male offenders whose crimes include the abuse of black women. One of the superstars of these films, Pam Grier, was often the target of white male physical and sexual abuse. However, in the fashion of action heroes, she responded with lethal violence. These films starring Grier were a forerunner to the "vigilante films" featuring white females who take the law into their own hands to retaliate against their rapists. Such films include *Lipstick* (1976) and the cult-favorite *I Spit on Your Grave* (1978). Although these films often feature despicable white males, black men are rarely depicted as rapists. Even the *Death Wish* series featuring Charles Bronson as a citizen vigilante who, over the course of five films, avenged the rapes and murders of women close to him, depicted the rapists as white or as members of a multicultural gang.[35]

On modern television crime shows, there are also few images of black male rapists. Black men are more likely to appear as police officers, lawyers, or crime scene investigators. These members of the criminal justice system are portrayed as defenders of law and order. For example, on *Law and Order: Special Victims Unit* former rapper Ice-T plays a New York City police detective. He is one of the team of officers who investigate sexual assault, child abuse, and other crimes involving vulnerable victims. As are the other detectives in the unit, he is often shown responding with compassion to these victims. With his colleagues, he works hard to find the perpetrator and see that justice is done. Similarly, other TV crime shows present African American and occasionally Latino or Asian American males in the role of protectors. The question is whether such fictional images serve as a counterbalance to the image of the black male rapist.

Although this chapter has focused on female victims of male rape, it is worth noting that in popular culture male rape in jail and prison settings is often presented as the danger faced by the inexperienced, first-time prisoner. The threat is sometimes played for laughs in television situation comedies. It was treated with grim seriousness in the HBO series *Oz*, set in a fictional and incredibly violent maximum-security prison. In films such as *American Me* (1992), *The Shawshank Redemption* (1994), and *American History X* (1998), prison rape is integral to the plot. However, as Eigenberg and Baro found in their analysis of male rape in prison films, the rapes depicted are generally intraracial.[36] They write: "Victims were most often young, white men of medium build without gang affiliations."[37] They also found that the rapists "were injured and/or killed in the majority of these films, perhaps because so many American films traditionally involve the punishment of evil."[38] These images of male-male rape in correctional settings both reflect and distort a reality of prison life.

In the 1970s and 1980s, the "women behind bars" films became a subgenre featured in video stores. These films depicted the perils of female prisoners—often wrongly convicted or thrown into a foreign prison—who found themselves at the mercy of lustful guards, wardens, or other female prisoners. In R-rated scenes set in showers, cells, huts, or staff offices, the women were often attacked or coerced into sex. These films include *Jackson County Jail* (1976), featuring Yvette Mimieux and Tommy Lee Jones, and low-budget movies filmed in the Philippines, such as *The Big Bird Cage* (1971) and *Women in Cages* (1972), both featuring Pam Grier among the inmates. It is noteworthy that the heroines of these films fought back, often escaping and/or killing their abusers.

MEDIA MISOGYNY

In 2004, *Essence*, a magazine for black women, featured a series of articles in its "Take Back the Music" campaign. The campaign was aimed at increasing awareness of the negative images of women perpetuated in music. Similarly, the women at Spelman, a historically black women's college, canceled the event that would have brought rapper Nelly to the campus to participate in a bone-marrow drive. They were protesting a music video in which the Grammy-winning rapper had swiped a credit card between the buttocks of a bikini-clad woman. The Spelman women described the video and the lyrics of Nelly's music as offensive and misogynistic.[39]

One of the questions posed by social scientists is whether misogynistic images in music serve to reinforce negatives attitudes. Are males who are exposed to music (whether country, heavy metal, or rap) in which women are physically and/or sexually abused more likely to hold attitudes that support such violence? This is not to say that there is a direct cause-and-effect relationship between hearing lyrics supporting sexual abuse of women and engaging in rape. However, it is possible that exposure to such lyrics may be one factor in male support of rape myths, such as the belief that "no" means "maybe".

There is also some concern on the part of researchers about images of physical and sexual violence toward women in magazines, video games, and pornography. The debate about the consumption of such media products by both men and women continues.[40]

LOVE BANDITS

In its three-part series on identity theft, the CBS News *Early Show* featured a segment about online dating scams. The featured scam involved an identity theft in which the photographs of a ruggedly handsome, fortyish, white male model were stolen from other sites on the Internet and posted on almost one hundred dating sites. Posing as the man in the photograph, con artists in Nigeria carried on Internet romances with unsuspecting American subscribers to these dating sites. Telling the women stories of a hardship or an emergency while far from home, the scammers would ask the women to send money. The women, trusting the man in the photo, often complied. Two of the women, who spoke from the shadows to protect their identities, told of the pain and humiliation they had suffered. Susan Koeppen, the show's consumer reporter, traveled to Nigeria to follow the story to its source. Appearing on camera with a black Nigerian man, she reported that he had told her that he made up to $200 a week with this online scam. In Nigeria, he and other such scammers are beyond the reach of American law.[41]

The segment was intriguing not because it depicted a physical sexual assault, but because it raised the spectre of a new kind of black male criminal who can carry out his crime while posing as an attractive white male suitor. Even though their faces were not revealed, the two female victims who spoke appeared to be white women. Their money had been stolen, but they also had suffered what some observers might describe as a "psychological rape" because they had shared their dreams and emotions with men who had deceived them. The CBS News report was offered as a warning to women using Internet dating services to be aware of such scams. However, the fact that the perpetrators shown and discussed were Nigerians might conceivably also have reinforced stereotypes and fears about black male predators.

CONCLUSION

In a paper about media portrayals of sex crimes, Sandler concludes: "Although a great deal of research has been directed toward the media handling of crime in general . . . very little has focused specifically on its handling of sex crime. Simply put, sex crime does not seem to generate as much interest in the research community as other crimes such as murder . . . "[42] Even though social scientists have displayed limited interest in studying how the media covers rape, what we do know is that historically race and rape have received extensive coverage in the news media.

Although sexual assaults are typically interracial, occurring between acquaintances and intimates, race myths often focus on predatory strangers. Historically, relations between men and women have been rooted in the image of the man as both "breadwinner" and "protector." One aspect of the image of the rapist as "other" that cannot be explored here is how this has affected male-female relationships within groups. In political speeches and in the press, white men in the South declared that they were defending the "honor" of white women when they lynched black men. By the early twentieth century, some white women in the South had rejected these acts of vigilante violence in their name. During this same period, African American men struggled with their inability to protect their wives and daughters from white males. As they aspired to attain middle-class "respectability," black men also hoped that this would allow them to isolate their women by taking them out of white households and other settings in which they were particularly vulnerable.[43] To some extent, the ability of a man to protect his "woman" remains linked to perceptions of masculinity. This is a concept that has been perpetuated in popular culture and the mass media. It is thrown into relief in depictions of rape by racial "others."

Taken together, the complex interactions of race, class, gender, and rape in the media merit more research and academic debate. This additional research and discussion will go a long way toward raising awareness of a multitude of problems.

CRITICAL THINKING QUESTIONS

1. Discuss the role of the women's movement in the context of rape and the civil rights.
2. From a historical perspective, please explain or describe media coverage of lynchings.
3. Explain the impact of early films on black Americans.
4. Compare/contrast the author's coverage of "Bigger Thomas" and the "Scottsboro Boys."
5. What is meant by media misogyny?
6. Based upon your reading of this chapter, how would you characterize coverage of rape by the media?
7. What lessons can be learned by the media in its coverage of high-profile cases?

NOTES

1. See Jonathan Markovitz, "Anatomy of a Spectacle: Race, Gender, and Memory in the Kobe Bryant Rape Case," *Sociology of Sport Journal* 23 (2006): 396–418.
2. Janet Dean, "Nameless Outrages: Narrative Authority, Rape Rhetoric, and the Dakota Conflict of 1862," *American Literature* 77 (2005): 96.
3. Dean, "Nameless Outrages," 99.
4. Dean, "Nameless Outrages," 100.
5. Dean, "Nameless Outrages," 93–122.
6. For example, see Wendy Anne Warren, "'The Cause of Her Grief': The Rape of a Slave in Early New England," *The Journal of American History* (2002): 1031–1049.
7. For discussion, see Frankie Y. Bailey, *African American Mystery Writers: A Historical and Thematic Study* (Jefferson, NC: McFarland, 2008).
8. James R. McGovern, *Anatomy of a Lynching: The Killing of Claude Neal* (Baton Rouge and London:

Louisiana State University Press, 1982), 74.
9. McGovern, *Anatomy of a Lynching,* 75.
10. Ibid.
11. For example, see Richard M. Perloff, "The Press and Lynchings of African Americans," *Journal of Black Studies* 30, no. 3 (2000): 315–330; Jean M. Lutes, "Lynching Coverage and the American Reporter-Novelist," *American Literary History* (2007): 456–481.
12. For further discussion, see Frankie Y. Bailey and Alice P. Green, *"Law Never Here": A Social History of African American Responses to Issues of Crime and Justice* (Westport, CT: Praeger Publishing, 1999).
13. See Yohuru R. Williams, "Permission to Hate: Delaware, Lynching, and the Culture of Violence in America," *Journal of Black Studies* 32, no. 1 (2001): 3–29.
14. See James R. Acker, *Scottsboro and Its Legacy: The Cases that Challenged*

American Legal and Social Justice (Westport, CT: Praeger Publishing, 2007); Felecia G. Jones Ross, "Mobilizing the Masses: The *Cleveland Call and Post* and the Scottsboro Incident," *The Journal of Negro History* 84, no. 1 (1999): 48–60.

15. Richard Wright, *Native Son* (1940; repr., New York: Harper Perennial, 1992).

16. Michel Fabre, *The Unfinished Quest of Richard Wright* (New York: William Morrow, 1973), 172.

17. For further discussion, see Bailey, *African American Mystery Writers*, 48–51.

18. See Jacqueline Goldsby, "The High and Low Tech of It: The Meaning of Lynching and the Death of Emmett Till," *The Yale Journal of Criticism* 9, no. 2 (1996): 242–282; Davis W. Houck, "Killing Emmett," *Rhetoric & Public Affairs* 8, no. 2 (2005): 225–262.

19. Susan Brownmiller, *Against Our Wills: Men, Women, and Rape* (New York: Bantam Books, 1976).

20. Danielle L. McGuire, "'It Was Like All of Us Had Been Raped': Sexual Violence, Community Mobilization, and the African American Freedom Struggle," *The Journal of American History* 91, no. 3 (2004): 906–931.

21. McGuire, "'It Was Like All of Us Had Been Raped,'" 922–923.

22. McGuire, "'It Was Like All of Us Had Been Raped,'" 929–930.

23. McGuire, "'It Was Like All of Us Had Been Raped,'" 928–929.

24. James Reston, Jr., *The Innocence of Joan Little: A Southern Mystery* (New York: New York Times Books, 1977).

25. Frankie Y. Bailey and Donna C. Hale, *Blood on Her Hands: The Social Construction of Women, Sexuality, and Murder* (Belmont, CA: Wadsworth, 2004), 161.

26. Bailey, *African American Mystery Writers*, 132.

27. Barbara Ransby, "A Righteous Rage and a Grassroots Mobilization," in *African American Women Speak Out on Anita Hill–Clarence Thomas*, ed. Gail Smitherman (Detroit: Wayne State University, 1995), 45–52.

28. Eric Fasson, "Sexual Events: From Clarence Thomas to Monica Lewinsky," *A Journal of Feminist Cultural Studies* 13, no. 2 (2002): 127–158.

29. Helen Benedict, *Virgin or Vamp: How the Press Covers Sex Crimes* (New York: Oxford University Press, 1992), 287.

30. Benedict, *Virgin or Vamp*, 215.

31. See Ray Surette, *Media, Crime, and Criminal Justice: Images, Realities, and Policies*, 3rd ed. (Belmont, CA: Wadsworth, 2007).

32. For further discussion of this case, see Markovitz, "Anatomy of a Spectacle," 396–418.

33. Jody Miller, Toya Z. Like, and Peter Levin, "The Caucasian Evasion: Victims, Exceptions, and Defenders of the Faith," in *Images of Color, Images of Crime: Readings*, ed. Coramae Richey Mann, Marjorie S. Zatz, and Nancy Rodriquez, (New York: Oxford University Press, 2006), 111–129.

34. For discussion of the various perspectives, see David J. Leonard, "'Innocent Until Proven Guilty': In Defense of Duke Lacrosse and White Power (and Against Menacing Black Student-Athletes, a Black Stripper, Activists, and the Jewish Media)," *Journal of Sport*

and Social Issues 31, no. 1 (2007): 25–44.

35. For further discussion of vigilantism in films, see Frankie Y. Bailey "Getting Justice: Real Life Vigilantism and Vigilantism in Popular Films," special media edition, *The Justice Professional* 8, no. 1 (Summer 1983): 33–51.

36. Helen Eigenberg and Agnes Baro, "If You Drop the Soap in the Shower You Are on Your Own: Images of Male Rape in Selected Prison Movies," *Sexuality & Culture* (2003): 56–89.

37. Eigenberg and Baro, "If You Drop the Soap in the Shower You Are on Your Own," 86.

38. Ibid.

39. Shanara R. Reid-Brinkley, "The Essence of Res(ex)pectability: Black Women's Negotiation of Black Femininity in Rap Music and Music Video," *Meridians* 8, no. 1 (2008): 236–260.

40. For further discussion on theories of media effects, see Surette, *Media, Crime, and Criminal Justice.*

41. CBS, "Online Dating Scammers Using Stolen Images," CBS News website, Adobe Flash Player video file, 4:25, http://www.cbsnews.com/stories/2008/11/18/earlyshow/contributors/susankoeppen/main4613608.shtml?source=search_story (accessed November 18, 2008).

42. Jeffrey C. Sandler, "Media Portrayals of Sex Crime: Is the Public Getting a True Picture?" unpublished paper, no date.

43. Bailey and Green, *"Law Never Here."*

CHAPTER 3

Understanding the Past, Present, and Future of Racial Profiling in the Media

David R. Montague

" . . . most media crime is punished, but policemen are
rarely the heroes."[1]

Racial profiling is a controversial action that deals with society's desire to contain criminals and mete out punishment for those who have broken the law. The epigram above relates one aspect of why this practice is controversial. It relates society's satisfaction in finding that most crime profiled in the media goes punished. However, it also alludes to the fact that police can make mistakes in their pursuit of criminals, and that those mistakes can profoundly impact an innocent person's life. Society expects the police to swiftly ferret out suspects of a crime in the interests of keeping us safe, yet no one spends much time thinking about how the police find their suspects, even when those actions include racial profiling.[2] While the literature overwhelmingly demonstrates that racial profiling is simply not a logical course of action in determining culpability,[3] society seems often to have accepted it or turned a blind eye to its use.[4] The reasons for this willingness to accept an action so inherently wrong are largely historical and have deep roots within American culture and the American psyche. Those roots are largely based on specific indoctrination on matters of race and ethnicity.[5]

Racial profiling has been defined as the following:

> The selective enforcement of the criminal law by police and law enforcement officers, based on a profile regarding a specific criminal activity, heavily influenced by racial/ethnic characteristics.[6]

This definition represents a middle ground on how society and many criminal justice professionals have viewed and addressed racial profiling. To better understand what racial profiling means and the impact that it has, consider the following example:

> Imagine that you are in a medium-sized town and that you are an elderly person living home alone. You awaken to hear a noise in your house and catch an intruder, but the only thing you notice is a hand, a hand you think is "dark" and probably male. In an effort to catch the offender, local police decide to look for a suspect using the descriptors of "young, black, and male," even though you never stated "young" in your description. Officers go to a local college and are provided a list of all the black males attending the college. Armed with this "black list," all the black male students are systematically stopped for questioning. Additionally, any black male on the street is stopped and questioned, sometimes more than once by different officers. As it turns out, a police report indicated that the trail of a possible suspect headed away from the college, bringing into question why a dragnet based on the "black list" is even started. In the end, no suspect is ever caught. You make a statement that your case was never handled properly in that a large number of people were consumed with "race" rather than dealing with what happened to you.[7]

This example shows that racial profiling severely limited what began as good police work and ended in a failed and misguided search.

Figure 3.1 provides a graphic view of a continuum upon which police action can result in reasonable and logical work to identify criminals or a limited search based on racial and/or ethnic biases. Whatever is found within that limited search serves to reinforce notions of criminality. It becomes a self-fulfilling prophecy that seems to justify a continued limited search based primarily upon race and/or ethnicity. This limited search stands in contrast to good police work, driven by objective training.

The media can contribute to awareness of such racial profiling through its reporting. Conversely, a lack of media coverage conveys a disinterest in the significance of the issue. One case in which the mainstream media was visibly absent, while only a few independent minority news organizations and advocacy groups took note, was a 2001 investigation completed by the U.S. General Accounting Office (GAO), now called the General Accountability Office. This case highlighted concerns brought to the attention of U.S. Senator Richard J. Durbin that a disproportionate number of minority airline passengers were stopped and invasively searched by U.S. customs officials in airports. Using the authority of members of Congress via the GAO, an investigative

FIGURE 3.1 Continuum of Effects on Racial Profiling

study determined that minorities were indeed disproportionately stopped and searched, even though nonminorities were found to actually carry more weapons and drugs on them during the course of this investigation. The GAO report explicitly stated that U.S. Customs should use more logical criteria when stopping airline passengers. With the exception of a few minority-related news organizations, this report from the GAO received virtually no mainstream media coverage. This was a "missed opportunity" to demonstrate that the manner in which choices are made can easily make the difference between good police work and a self-fulfilling prophecy.

RACIAL PROFILING IN THE MEDIA: FROM PAST TO PRESENT

Some assert that since circa 1970 the crime-control model, with its emphasis on the criminal justice department's need for efficiency over ensuring fairness, has been the norm within the American criminal justice system.[8] This assertion, referred to by Robinson as "the process of innocent bias," connects how the law impacts the roles of corrections, courts, police, and the media with respect to crime.[9] Historically, the media has reported and created messages about race and ethnicity and crime. For many Americans unfamiliar with the actual experiences of people from different backgrounds, these stereotypical images serve as "reality," their accepted views about others.[10]

Television

The role of the media with respect to television has been historically important. In years past, most Americans did not own televisions and it was common for families and friends to gather at one location to be entertained by the magic of television. Television, regardless of programming, became a sensation and garnered enormous credibility among viewers. It was and in many ways still is an "honor" to get what many call "fifteen minutes of fame." Thus television programming came to yield enormous influence and financial power in America, and it has come to play a historic role in how we understand issues such as racial profiling.

The power of images associated with various television programming helped lay the seeds of how many Americans viewed others, in many ways without actually providing factual programming to counter negative stereotypes.[11] Some of the simplest programming, such as documentaries, which could have countered stereotypes, was not as common. Documentaries could have provided more balance in society by avoiding such stereotypes and by addressing race as a "social construct"[12] rather than as something which was part of the official policy of disenfranchisement known as segregation during the early days of television.

The present represents a new era for television in that the media provides coverage of racial profiling cases that garner the attention of appropriate television personnel. This is a positive reality in that public access to television broadcasts has changed dramatically due to technological advancements and the lower costs of public access. For many, television news stories on racial profiling can be accessed directly at home and on portable televisions, indirectly via the Internet, and even through cell phones. This broad access can profoundly change a story's impact. For example, in one news story a family complained that a crime involving a juvenile used racial profiling.[13] Though a story like this might appear only once on the news, it can be archived on the station's website, where the public can access it repeatedly.

It is imperative that media cautiously and responsibly handle their influence on the public, especially with respect to reality television programming. Some television programming seems like an extension of the news, with videos of possible criminal activity taking place in certain geographic locations. When the media makes decisions about the ways it presents how the police deal with different groups of people, these decisions directly send a message, intentional or not, about the appropriateness of racial profiling.[14] In fact, given the lack of uniform education and understanding nationally on race and ethnicity, since reality television is anything but an accurate representation of reality and simply the reality of what the producers decide to show, this type of programming might reinforce bias against certain racial and ethnic groups.[15] Most dramatically, with respect to television and racial profiling recent research indicates that without doubt the images of crime on reality television do not reflect actual crime statistics along racial and ethnic lines. To quote Monk-Turner and associates, ". . . media images depicted in *COPS* are at odds with UCR [FBI Uniform Crime Reporting] official crime statistics and reinforce stereotypes and myths about the nature of crime in the United States."[16]

Film and Video

The film industry has played the most significant role in how society has addressed race and racial profiling. Like television, movies have played a very important part in the lives of many Americans. The movie theater has been a place to be entertained and a place for temporary sanctuary from things on people's minds. Of course, movies also have represented a means by which many viewers have learned about life outside of their own geographic area. In movie theaters of old, it was common for people, especially children and teens, to spend almost an entire day (on the weekend) at "the movies." During these much anticipated events, children and teens were shown news stories about current events and therefore formed many views about the world from this type of media.

Many scholars have noted the historical negative impact of films and how some have fueled the minds of Americans into thinking racial profiling is not only "logical" but necessary as a form of national security.[17] Movies such as *The Birth of a Nation*, *The Wedding and Wooing of a Coon*, and *The Nigger* were simply manifestations of stereotypes of the time which made people of African descent appear to be savages bent on threatening the fabric of American culture.[18] The importance of this form of media was that it helped develop what the literature refers to as "racial formation." Racial formation refers to the creation of impressions about people as individuals along racial lines.[19] Without doubt, this relationship between the media and the reality of racial profiling explains why this reality is now a legacy.

It has been well documented that those who have controlled the media have often not been culturally sensitive or even concerned about representations of those groups which have generally been outside the power structure. One recent MSNBC news story underscored this point, suggesting that "Hollywood has a fairly despicable history of casting Caucasians as ethnic minorities."[20] The story further explored the sordid history of racial stereotyping of Asian Americans, Latinos/Latinas, and American Indians. In recent history, movies such as *Tropic Thunder* have also used comedy to expose cultural bias. *Tropic Thunder* is a good example of how the movie industry is working at some level presently to help society acknowledge the nonsensical nature of racial profiling. Of course, the motivation for the film/movie industry is in fact profit. At the same time, as the images/views of those in charge of production decisions change to reflect less bias, it stands to reason that the material they create will help combat bias in society.

Print Media

Surette asserts that the print media portrays police as ineffective and incompetent in their methods to address crime.[21] Similarly, Dowler tells us that it is imperative to understand the true relationship between public perception and police effectiveness as influenced by the media, especially print media.[22] What makes print media so important at present is that print media consumption is changing, depending upon the demographic audience. One such demographic factor is the age of the reader. In fact, one source suggests that a decade ago seniors invested approximately 40 percent of their time in reading and watching television compared to a smaller percentage of younger people today.[23] What is important about this finding is that since seniors tend to have more time to focus on what media feeds the public, no matter the form of media exposure, they might be more inclined to develop strong feelings, either positive or negative, with respect to criminality. The significance of this influence cannot be overstated with respect to race and crime within the media, especially racial profiling.

Electronic Media

In recent years there has been a convergence of media types used to provide information to the public, including information on racial profiling. This convergence is important because it means that no matter the distance, time of day, or income level, stories associated with issues such as racial profiling can be disseminated in various ways. This change from the past to the present is profound. Imagine having to rely on telegraph machines years ago to share information about racial profiling in New Mexico and compare that to today's ability to not only send an instant message, but a message that could contain audio and video, and on which others can comment via a connected blog.

FIGURE 3.2 Screen Shot from the *Coconut Grove Grapevine*

The ease of information transfer has also resulted in the media's ability to spread rumor and fear. An example of how a story in a local community news source can spread rumor and fear among the population occurred in Coconut Grove, Florida. A screen shot of this news source is provided in Figure 3.2. Included with the story on the website was text from the accompanying blog in which the readers were able to interactively comment on the story. (See Appendix One for the complete text of the blog.) The story alerted the community to possibly suspicious magazine sales people. The discussion in the blog expanded into racial profiling.

The news story and the accompanying discussion illustrate how media impacts how and what we think about racial profiling. Within the blog (see Appendix One), it is evident that a serious discussion has occurred that not only addresses a situation in the community, but also addresses the merit(s) of how the community should respond to racial and ethnic overtones in public discourse. What becomes so key to this blog is that participants are able to openly discuss the issue of what constitutes "suspicious behavior" in their community; they are able to establish a form of "checks and balances" by bringing up the issue of possible racial profiling on their own to address fundamental fairness and avoid stereotyping. In many ways, the exchange of information within this media type helps to address accuracy of information for residents in that community, thereby reducing the likelihood of bias erupting into a false accusation of a crime.

THE FUTURE OF RACIAL PROFILING IN THE MEDIA: LESSONS LEARNED?

Since the beginning of the twenty-first century the work of the media has provided both progressive and regressive impacts on racial profiling. More importantly the media today has a unique ability to draw attention to how problematic racial profiling is and to more accurately reflect the general societal tenor, which understands racial profiling is not a rational course of action to address crime. Within the last few years, media stories such as the *60 Minutes* program "The Black List" have aired interviews of people involved with such practices. Print and online media have added to news coverage of racial profiling to bring this behavior to the attention of the public; a recent example of such coverage includes the work of a local paper, which addressed the current efforts of the Oneonta community to respond to the famous "Black List" incident.[24]

One might also assert that in the early days the movies and print media helped provide, in many cases, the only knowledge some people had about people with skin color different than their own. In the twenty-first century, the media is reeducating America on how use of the learned bias we all carry at some level is not appropriate within any societal system, especially the criminal justice system. The logical question one might ask is "What is different now versus a few decades ago?" The answer is simple: Society is in a more ameliorative swing at present with respect to biases.

RACIAL PROFILING OF NONMINORITIES AND THE MEDIA: WHY THE SILENCE?

In recent years, another aspect of racial profiling seems evident, but is somehow not discussed explicitly in the literature. There are people in public positions who openly acknowledge their desire and/or their participation in targeting whites as criminals simply based on stereotypes, even though we know that race is a social construct. One example is from online media in which a blogger suggested that if society insisted on profiling based upon race, then it would be appropriate for society to start profiling young white boys as school terrorists.[25] It is presumed that the blogger was being cynical and not endorsing more profiling. However, such profiling occurs. A minority police officer personally told me that when he sees some young white males driving in a car, his first presumption is that there must be some form of methamphetamine in that car and he considers this presumption an appropriate cause to stop them. This statement bothered me as a minority who has been racially profiled many times in life, even when wearing a suit and acting on official business pertaining to national security.

Another profiling-related case became headline news in the fall of 2002, when people were killed by sniper fire in the Washington, D.C. area. This crime stunned the nation's capitol and left many people dead.[26] Initially, media reporters during a press conference encouraged the head of the investigation, Chief Charles A. Moose, to make some statement as to whether the police were searching for a particular suspect based on the fact that some "experts" were saying the suspect was most likely a white male. Chief Moose looked into the cameras and said that it is not good police practice to profile based on race and he wanted to make sure that all possibilities were considered, rather than limiting the search along racial lines. After that press conference, several experts were brought on television to suggest how the police could best use their time, with each pointing toward a profile of a white male with certain other characteristics. Some in law enforcement call this "pattern analysis," but since racial profiling involves making race the primary aspect of what is considered in a search, this case was indeed different. During this sniper investigation, despite the initial public statement that race would not be used as the primary factor to help capture the killer (we now know there were two killers), police stopped the real killers several times as part of an area dragnet, but did not conduct any real search on the unknown suspects, perhaps because they were black rather than white.[27] This is an excellent example of racial profiling gone wrong, yet it was not publicized in most media outlets. In another powerful example, a dragnet singled out over six hundred white males for DNA swabs in the hunt for a serial killer.[28] Again, the reality of needing to address crime is important and is not something to be taken lightly or made "politically incorrect." At the same time, the focus on race rather than actual factors contributing to probable cause is harmful to the true pursuit of justice, a point that was openly stated by the real victim in the Oneonta, New York, case (described earlier). It is disingenuous to ask society to realize racial profiling is happening and is not "good police work" if we do not complain about it or respond to the lack of media coverage on it when it happens to nonminorities.

FUTURE NEEDS IN THIS AREA

It is the opinion of this author, based upon having researched and taught race, ethnicity, and crime courses for almost a decade, as well as having lived as a minority within several criminal justice organizations/agencies, that two directions are needed with respect to the media and racial profiling. Applying Herbert Werlin's *political elasticity theory* herein, it is believed that the most relevant stakeholders might be able to work toward common ground despite differences of opinion.[29] Therefore, it is important that direct and indirect media organizations/agencies play an active role in taking this issue seriously. It is theorized that the more serious the approach, the higher priority of any decision to report allegations of racial profiling.

Finally, as a postscript thought, even after years of experience as a criminal justice professional working for the government as an investigator and now as an academic working to address issues of social justice, I continue to be impacted by projects on which I work. While completing research for this chapter, for example, I was made painfully aware that racial profiling takes a quite different form by the media—in the sense of "who" has access to "what." One recent study in particular caught my attention. The study found that in some newsrooms, stories pertaining directly to minorities are given to minority staff to cover and stories dealing with the general public and issues of more powerful matters in society are given to nonminorities.[30] The implications of the study suggest a "third-wave" (approach) to the issue of race in America, that even assignment to media stories has a racial overtone. The first and second waves respectively would be (1) the initial racist images and overt discrimination against minorities, and then (2) the belief that all things are equal and that the statistical information we have that shows minorities have proportionally more issues than nonminorities is somehow not connected to that first wave.

As one final example of racial profiling, I offer this quote from a blog in which a criminal justice professional is quoted as saying "[I]f I see two guys that look like Aba Daba Doo and Aba Daba Dah, I'm gonna pull 'em over, . . . I wanna find out what you're doing."[31] It is the ability of the media using multiple formats to object or to encourage racial profiling, which makes the role of the media just as influential today as it was many years ago.

Circling back to the continuum of racial profiling in Figure 3.1, it becomes apparent that two major aspects have changed since the early days of media. The first major aspect is how society thinks racial profiling has changed dramatically for the better. At the same time, there are many who do not accept the notion that racial profiling actually exists, even though the literature says otherwise.[32] This is evident in the amount of research acknowledging the unfair bias in the media; these inaccurate and unbiased portrayals have been challenged repeatedly, prompting the need to better understand and embrace cultures rather than to demonize them.[33] The second major aspect is how technology has blurred the lines of content control within the media in the twenty-first century. This second aspect is important because it illustrates how advances in the body of knowledge on racial profiling move into mainstream society with or without the "buy-in" of those who choose to close their eyes to this reality and debate the issue.[34] The technological advances are available to almost anyone, such that even if a news media outlet chooses not to carry a story on racial profiling, then any citizen can download a video, post a blog, or even become an "iReporter" on CNN, providing news uploaded directly and unedited from those people involved in these stories.[35]

CONCLUSION

The media has a tremendous opportunity to address racial profiling at every level. How this power is used in the future will determine the realities of civil liberties for all Americans. Sadly, much progress toward addressing the problems of racial profiling remain. A recent *USA Today* article on the U.S. Border Patrol's practice of allegedly using racial profiling underscores the point.[36] Further, racial profiling knows no socioeconomic boundaries. As an example, Silvio Torres-Saillant, an English professor, says he was stopped three times in one year while purchasing Greyhound bus tickets or waiting in the bus terminal in Syracuse, New York. Torres-Saillant, a U.S. citizen, says this about the reality of how people continue to factor race into criminal justice:

> It's very likely they come to me because of how I look. . . . The idea that there are some people who look more American than others is still very much alive.[37]

APPENDIX ONE: *Coconut Grove Grapevine* Story "Suspicious Magazine Sales People"[38]

SUSPICIOUS MAGAZINE SALES PEOPLE

Magazine sales people have now moved to the Center Grove after residents of both the North and South Grove called police over the past two weeks because of the sales peoples' apparently aggressive behaviors to enter residents' yards and homes . . .

If you see these magazine sales people, please call the non-emergency police number (305-579-6111) and let them know you are calling on behalf of the All-Grove Crime Watch and request a marked unit to come to the area to check out these people who appear to be "casing" homes.

Posted by Grapevine at *8:42 AM* 📧

11 Comments:

👤 *Ben said . . .*

What do you mean by "apparently aggressive behaviors to enter residents' yards and homes?"

Exactly what happened? . . .

Male African American teens go door to door to sell magazines in a white neighborhood and they are accused of "casing the neighborhood". This group has been selling magazines for years door to door in the Grove. They are hard working, harmless college bound students.

The Grapevine should do a little research before promoting racist hate mongering.

Investigate before jumping to conclusions Grapevine.

March 15, 2008 10:33 AM

🅱 Grapevine *said . . .*

I just passed on the police and crime watch report. I didn't write the report.

March 15, 2008 10:36 AM

👤 *Cynthia said . . .*

The ones snooping around the south grove were actually white and maybe Latin. They won't take no for an answer and they try to get into the house, I had to call my husband to get rid of them at the front door.

March 15, 2008 6:53 PM

👤 *Ben said . . .*

Racial profiling is crime most often committed by the police.

Passing on the police and crime watch report does not mean that you've got the whole story. You should know that Mr. Grapevine.

If you are going to request that people "call the non-emergency police number and let them know you are calling on behalf of the All-Grove Crime Watch and request a marked unit to come to the area to check out 'these people' who appear to be 'casing' homes,".....Then you might want to be pretty sure that YOU are not participating in racial profiling.

9 out of 10, Yes that's NINE out of TEN of these calls are a result of racial profiling and THAT is the crime . . .

March 16, 2008 1:11 AM

Grapevine *said . . .*

Shut up Ben. The magazine sellers I saw were not African American so stop making an ass of yourself and put your email address if you want to be taken seriously.

March 16, 2008 8:50 AM

Sarah *said . . .*

If there is a trend in crime it is the duty of the police officers to report it at the crime watch meetings. The Grapevine offers this information as a public service.

There was no mention of race until you brought it up. Get off your high horse and see this issue for what it is. Sales people with overly aggressive behavior . . .

March 16, 2008 12:31 PM

SWLiP *said . . .*

The lesson is to be alert to people who come knocking on your door, or who enter your property, on vague pretenses. They might very well be casing your house.

March 16, 2008 3:44 PM

Anonymous *said . . .*

Racial profiling actually is not a crime and is not illegal. Ethical is another question.

I actually think I saw this same group in the Gables yesterday and I believe they were of Latin background, not that it matters. I am sure people complained there as well and they will be asked to leave. Why? Because door to door stuff this day and age is sketchy . . . I mean think of all the people who have been robbed or assaulted by people posing as FPL workers. If I don't know you, I don't open my door, and if I have the slightest inclination you're up to no good, I will call the cops. PERIOD

March 16, 2008 5:05 PM

Post a Comment

Links to this post:

See links to this post

Create a Link

<< Home

CRITICAL THINKING QUESTIONS

1. Why do you think "history" is important in understanding racial profiling in the media?
2. Given the continuum of views on racial profiling provided within the chapter, explain why there is such a difference of opinion on "racial profiling" among people in today's society. Include in your answer the opinion of those working within the criminal justice system and those within the general public.
3. Explain how television and movies have devalued or added value to a character's race.
4. Explain how the current technology associated with the media (e.g., Internet news, blogs, text messaging, television, radio, hardcopy print, etc.) helps or hinders how society deals with racial profiling.
5. Consider why the racial profiling of nonminorities might not receive the same media coverage as the racial profiling of minorities. What "should" be the appropriate media coverage (and why)?

NOTES

1. L. Lichter and S. Lichter, *Prime Time Crime*. Washington, D.C.: Media Institute, 1983.
2. David A. Harris, "U.S. Experiences with Racial and Ethnic Profiling: History, Current Issues, and the Future," *Critical Criminology* 14 no. 3 (2006): 213–239.
3. Kathryn K. Russell, *The Color of Crime: Racial Hoaxes, White Fear, Black Protectionism, Police Harassment, and Other Macroaggressions* (New York: New York University Press, 1998).
4. Matthew B. Robinson, *Justice Blind?: Ideals and Realities of American Criminal Justice* (Upper Saddle River, NJ: Pearson Education, 2002).
5. Glenn Frankel and Tamara Jones, "In Britain, a Divide over Racial Profiling: Mistaken Killing by Police Sets Off Debate," *Washington Post*, July 27, 2005, http://www.washingtonpost.com/wp-dyn/content/article/2005/07/26/AR2005072601789_pf.html.
6. David N. Falcone, *Prentice Hall's Dictionary of American Criminal Justice, Criminology, & Criminal Law* (Upper Saddle River, NJ: Pearson Education, 2005).
7. CBS, *60 Minutes*, 2002.
8. Matthew B. Robinson, *Justice Blind?: Ideals and Realities of American Criminal Justice* (Upper Saddle River, NJ: Pearson Education, 2002).
9. Ibid.
10. Robert M. Entman and Andrew Rojecki, *The Black Image in the White Mind: Media and Race in America* (Chicago: University of Chicago Press, 2001).
11. Coramae Richey Mann, Marjorie S. Zatz, and Nancy Rodriguez, eds.,

Images of Color, Images of Crime: Readings, 3rd ed. (Los Angeles: Roxbury Publishing, 2006).

12. Eugenia Shanklin, *Anthropology & Race* (Belmont, CA: Wadsworth, 1994).

13. My Fox 13 Utah, "Family Claims Racial Profiling in Arrest of Drive-by Suspect," Television Web cast, Salt Lake City, UT: MyFox13, September 29, 2008, http://www.myfoxutah.com/myfox/pages/Home/Detail?contentId=7542480&version=1&locale=EN-US&layoutCode=VSTY&pageId=1.1.1.

14. Theodore Prosise and Ann Johnson, "Law Enforcement and Crime on *COPS* and *World's Wildest Police Videos:* Anecdotal Form and the Justification of Racial Profiling," *Western Journal of Communication* 68 (2004).

15. Joseph F. Healey, *Race, Ethnicity, Gender, and Class: The Sociology of Group Conflict and Change* (Thousand Oaks, CA: Pine Forge Press, 2005).

16. Elizabeth Monk-Turner, Homer Martinez, Jason Holbrook, and Nathan Harvey, "Are Reality TV Crime Shows Continuing to Perpetuate Crime Myths?" *Internet Journal of Criminology,* 2007, http://www.internetjournalofcriminology.com/.

17. Thomas Cripps, *Slow Fade to Black: The Negro in American Film, 1900–1942* (New York: Oxford University Press, 1977).

18. Jane Rhodes, "The Visibility of Race and Media History," *Critical Studies in Mass Communications* 20 no. 2 (1993).

19. Coramae Richey Mann, Marjorie S. Zatz, and Nancy Rodriguez, eds.,

Images of Color, Images of Crime: Readings, 3rd ed. (Los Angeles: Roxbury Publishing, 2006).

20. Alonso Duralde, "'Thunder' Mocks Hollywood Racial Profiling: What Downey, Jr. Does As a Joke, Satirizes Hollywood's Shameful History," MSNBC.com, August 13, 2008, http://www.msnbc.msn.com/id/26181831/.

21. Ray Surette, *Media, Crime, and Criminal Justice: Images and Realities,* 2nd ed. (Belmont, CA: Wadsworth, 1998).

22. Kenneth Dowler, "Media Consumption and Public Attitudes toward Crime and Justice: The Relationship between Fear of Crime, Punitive Attitudes, and Perceived Police Effectiveness," *Journal of Criminal Justice and Popular Culture* 10 no. 2 (2003): 09–126.

23. Jon F. Nussbaum and Justine Coupland, *Handbook of Communication and Aging Research,* 2nd ed. (Mahwah, NJ: Lawrence Erlbaum, 2004).

24. Denise Richardson, "'Black List' Explores 1992 Oneonta Incident," *The Daily Star: The Newspaper for the Heartland of New York*, February 29, 2008.

25. Cenk Uygur, "Let's Start Racial Profiling—Young White Boys," *The Huffington Post,* August 18, 2006, http://www.huffingtonpost.com/cenk-uygur/lets-start-racial profil_b_27536.html.

26. David A. Harris, "U.S. Experiences with Racial and Ethnic Profiling: History, Current Issues, and the Future," *Critical Criminology* 14 no. 3 (2006): 213–239.

27. J. Michael Kearney, "Before We Lionize Mister Moose," *AuthorsDen.com,* October 22, 2002, http://

www.Authorsden.com/visit/viewArticle.asp?id=7708.

28. *Kohler v. Englade,* 470 F.3d 1104 (5th Cir. 2006).

29.Herbert H. Werlin, *The Mysteries of Development: Studies Using Political Elasticity Theory* (Lanham, MD: University Press of America, 1998).

30. David Pritchard and Sarah Stonbely, "Racial Profiling in the Newsroom," *Journalism & Mass Communication Quarterly* 84 no. 2 (2007): 477–493.

31. A J. Walzer, "Dietl on racial profiling: '[I]f I see two guys that look like Aba Daba Doo and Aba Daba Dah, I'm gonna pull 'em over'." *Media Matters for America,* August 8, 2007, http://mediamatters.org/items/printable/200708080001.

32. Ben Wattenberg, "Is Racial Profiling Real?" *Think Tank with Ben Wattenberg,* PBS, July 19, 2001, http://www.pbs.org/thinktank/show_967.html.

33. John Howard Griffin, *Black Like Me* (Boston: Houghton Mifflin, 1960).

34. Thomas Hickey, *Taking Sides: Clashing Views in Criminal Justice* (Dubuque, IA: McGraw Hill Contemporary Learning Series, 2007).

35. CNN iReporter, December 2008, www.cnn.com.

36. Emily Bazar, "Border Patrol's Methods Criticized: Bus Riders Say Agents Used Racial Profiling,' *USA Today*, October 1, 2008, national edition, P3A.

37. Ibid.

38. Coconut Grove Grapevine: The Daily News of Coconut Grove, "Suspicious Magazine Sales People," online newspaper and blog, March 15, 2008, http://coconut grovegrapevine.blogspot.com/2008/03/suspicious-magazine-sales-people.html.

PART II

The Quantification and Contextualization of Crime

CHAPTER 4

The Media: Crime Rates and Race

Charles Corley

This chapter is a critical portrayal of ways official crime data can be manipulated by the media. The examination begins with an introduction and overview of the two major sources of crime data.

THE UNIFORM CRIME REPORT

In 1929 the International Association of the Chiefs of Police established a method for law enforcement agencies to report crimes across the United States. This voluntary reporting of known offenses by law enforcement became known as the Uniform Crime Report. The Uniform Crime Report (UCR) subsequently became the responsibility of the Federal Bureau of Investigation (FBI), which still serves as a clearinghouse and compiles data for the publication of crime statistics. The UCR Program compiles data from monthly law enforcement reports or individual crime incident records transmitted directly to the FBI or to centralized state agencies that are then reported to the Federal Bureau of Investigation.[1] Thus, the UCR contains information reported to law enforcement agencies. To that end, it should be noted that crimes that are not reported to the police and victimless crimes are not included in the UCR.

Law enforcement agencies active in the UCR Program represented more than 296 million United States inhabitants or roughly 94.1 percent of the total population.[2] To date, there are over 17,000 law enforcement agencies reporting offenses to the FBI. The UCR is divided into Part I and Part II offenses. Of particular interest to media organizations are Part I or Index Offenses. These Part I offenses consist of major felonies and other crimes that have been selected for further analyses because of their seriousness and frequency of occurrence. Part I offenses (Index crimes) include:

- Murder and nonnegligent manslaughter
- Forcible rape
- Robbery
- Aggravated assault
- Burglary
- Larceny-theft
- Motor vehicle theft
- Arson[3]

While the media is more interested in the more serious Part I offenses, it is the less serious Part II offenses that are the most commonly committed types of crimes. Simply put, more persons are arrested for less serious misdemeanor offenses than for the more serious felony offenses. Far more individuals are arrested for committing offenses such as disorderly conduct, driving under the influence, and/or aggravated assault than the more serious crimes such as murder, robbery, and rape. Nonetheless, Part I Offenses are used as a common indicator of the nation's crime and arrest experience, and the media's depiction of crime is heavily weighted toward Part 1 offenses.

Consider that the Uniform Crime Report during 2005 noted 11,424,871 arrests nationwide for all offenses (except traffic violations), with 1,814,761 (16 percent) reflecting Part I or Index Offenses, of which 496,775 were for violent crimes and 1,317,986 were for property crimes. The other 9,610,110 (84 percent) arrests were for Part II offenses.[4] Thus, in accordance with Uniform Crime Report data, the majority of persons arrested in 2005 were for Part II and not Part I offenses. Moreover, it should be noted that less than a third (27 percent) of persons arrested for Part I offenses were for violent offenses.[5]

Uniform Crime Report data enable calculation of more standardized crime statistics. One type of statistic calculated is crime rates. The calculation of crime rates enable maximum comparability. Crime rates specifically allow smaller areas to be compared with larger more populated geographical areas.[6] Dividing the number of particular criminal events by size of the population and then multiplying the product by 1,000 or 100,000 yields a rate. This rate reflects the occurence of such incidents with consideration given to population size.

For instance, it would seem invalid to compare the number of robbery arrests in Michigan (194,101) with the number of robbery arrests in South Carolina (125,699).[7] Michigan is a more densely populated state with more urbanized areas than South Carolina. Yet when rates are calculated with adjustments for the population size in each state, South Carolina yields a higher robbery arrest rate (2,954 per every 100,000 persons) than Michigan (1,918 per every 100,000 persons).[8] Comparing these rates reveal that in the year 2005 Michigan had more arrests for robbery but the robbery rate is actually higher in South Carolina. This would suggest that one would more likely become a victim of robbery in South Carolina than Michigan given the higher rate of arrest.

Uniform Crime Report data from 1986 through 2005 notes that more serious personal offenses (i.e., murder, nonnegligent manslaughter, and forcible rape) have lower rates than other offenses (e.g., burglary, larceny, and motor vehicle theft). For instance, in 1986 the violent crime rate was 620 per every 100,000 persons whereas the property crime rate was 4,882 per every 100,000 persons.[9] Not only does UCR data reveal that violent crimes occur at a lower rate than property offense but neither offense category has risen to their peaks reported in the late 1980s and early 1990s. Consider also that within the same time span, murder decreased from a high (9.8 per every 100,000) in 1991 to a low in 2005 of 6 per every 100,000 persons.[10] Moreover, in this same time period, robbery offenses decreased 22.1 percent. These facts are not always evident when the media presents information about crime rates, nor is there a meaningful dialogue about the differences between Part 1 and Part 2 offenses.

Crime has proven itself more an urban than rural phenomenon. That is to say, more crime occurs in urban than suburban and rural areas. This is somewhat expected given the larger size populations found in urban areas. However, when crime rates are calculated, smaller, less-populated areas can be legitimately compared to more densely populated urban areas. Hence, it was not surprising in 2005 to find metropolitan counties with 100,000 or more persons produced higher violent crime rates (403 per every 100,000 persons), than nonmetropolitan counties numbering between 10,000 and 24,999 (181.5 per every 100,000 persons).[11] Yet, nonmetropolitan counties with populations of less than 10,000 produced violent crime rates of 236 per every 100,000 persons.[12] This underscores the point that while the numbers of violent crimes are higher in metropolitan areas within the United States, it is not restricted to these areas alone and media portrayals should go beyond the minority-inhabited inner cities in their crime coverage. It does a public disservice not to portray the realities of crime. Earlier it was mentioned the state of South Carolina—with less than half the population of Michigan—had a higher robbery rate. Well, the same is true about crime in general. That is, while there may be more arrests in urban areas, the outlying nonmetropolitan areas may actually have higher crime rates. Thus, media focus on crime riddled inner-city minority communities does not reveal the true nature of crime in America.

THE NATIONAL CRIME VICTIMIZATION SURVEY

A somewhat similar picture of crime across the United States emerges upon examining National Crime Victimization Survey (NCVS) data. However, first we must understand the purpose of this survey. Since 1973, the Bureau of Justice Statistics (BJS) has conducted biannual surveys of approximately 43,000 households of persons ages 12 and older to ascertain victimization information regarding rape, sexual assault, personal robbery, aggravated and simple assault, household burglary, theft, and motor vehicle theft (Department of Justice, 2005).[13] Unlike UCR data, which is a summary and a hierarchically based response to reported or known offenses, the NCVS (given that it is a survey) contains information on both reported and unreported offenses. Specifically, the NCVS tends to be more incident based than the Uniform Crime Report and will provide insights into the victim's experiences with the criminal justice system. It is with these data that minorities as victims of crime most often emerge.

Although the Uniform Crime Report and National Crime Victimization Survey measure similar types of offenses, these programs were designed for different purposes. The UCR began as an effort to address law enforcement operations, management, and budget issues, whereas the NCVS was designed to provide information on both reported and unreported offenses, victims and offenders.[14] Both programs measure similar offenses and results are also similar but with some noted differences. Consider that for the year 2005 the NCVS reported 23,440,720 victimizations; whereas for the same year the UCR reported 11,424,871 arrests.[15] Hence, the National Crime Victimization Survey tends to always show a higher volume of victimization than arrests as reported by the Uniform Crime Reports.

Additionally, when crime trends are examined, similar patterns emerge between the UCR and NCVS. The National Crime Victimization Survey shows victimization rates are higher for property than violent crimes. This same pattern is found when property and violent crimes are compared using UCR data. Yet, these findings are rarely displayed through media depictions of crime. One would think that violent crimes occur more often than property offense given depictions on television. The old adage which suggests that "if it bleeds, it leads" seems appropriate given media depictions which seemingly promulgate a higher occurrence of violent than property crimes.

It was noted earlier that crime was more an urban than rural phenomenon, particularly in reference to the numbers of arrests. This finding has race-based implications as well. The previous findings combined with the fact that blacks are primarily an urban-based group with socioeconomic disadvantages suggest a tautological reasoning for the higher victimization rates of blacks. That is to say, the poor often victimize the poor.

Currently, the inhabitants of the inner city are persons of color and the whole phenomenon of "black-on-black" crime is really a situation of "poor-on-poor crime." It just so happens that the persons inhabitating the inner city at this particular time in history are both minority and poor. Earlier ethnic immigrant groups (Irish, Italians, Jews, and Poles) who inherited the inner city with its crime-prone environment eventually migrated to suburban America. However, it has proven more difficult for racial minorities to achieve these patterns of assimilation and hence we see generations of poverty among these inhabitants of the inner city. Historically, the inner-city enviornment continues to produce crime and higher arrest rates among its inhabitants. To that end, this explains both the intraracial and intraclass nature of crime in America.

Rennison notes that blacks are six times more likely than whites to die by homicide, a crime that is overwhelmingly intraracial in nature.[16] Similarly, Sampson and colleagues found that blacks are segregated by neighborhood and thus differentially exposed to key risk and protective factors, an essential ingredient to understanding the black-white disparity in violence.[17] Noticeably, the intraracial and intraclass nature of crime in America is not made apparent through media sources and the greater fear of crime among African Americans is seldom noted. Notwithstanding, these findings surrounding violence are not new. And more to the point, the Department of Justice's analysis of national crime statistics reveal that while blacks have victimization rates that far exceed their white counterparts, blacks are rarely portrayed in the media as victims.

Similar to the UCR, the National Crime Victimization Survey notes that violent victimizations peaked during the early to mid-1990s and have since shown a steady decline. The survey data also reveals that males, blacks, and lower-income single persons are the more likely victims of crime. These findings are further supported by Sampson and colleagues, who observe that over 60 percent of the violence gap between blacks and whites is explained by immigration status, marriage, length of residence, verbal/reading ability, impulsivity, and neighborhood context.[18] Yet Goering concludes that policies such as housing vouchers to aid the poor in securing residence in middle-class neighborhoods may achieve the most effective results in bringing down the long-standing racial disparities in violence.[19] The truth, however, is that much of the violence experienced in inner-city America could be alleviated with measures that improve the quality of life and stabilize neighborhoods that are not presented in mainstream media.

Moreover, official crime reporting agencies (e.g., Bureau of Justice Statistics) should report racial findings within data as such without attempting to explain away racial implications. For instance, in a report conducted by the U.S. Census Bureau on behalf of the Bureau of Justice Statistics (BJS), 18 million persons reported contact with the police in 2005 for a traffic stop.[20] While it was reported that most persons felt they were stopped by the police for legitimate reasons, it was further reported that about five percent of all vehicles were searched. However, in 2005 police searched 9.5 percent of stopped African Americans and 8.8 percent of stopped Hispanics, compared to 3.6 percent of white motorists.[21] While this finding tended to coincide with other findings from around the nation, the report further noted that "while the survey found that African American and Hispanic drivers were more likely than whites to be searched, such racial disparities do not necessarily demonstrate that police treat people differently based on race or other demographic characteristics."[22] The authors note that other factors may have contributed to the disproportionate searching of vehicles driven by African Americans; however, these factors were not included as part of their study. Hence, an opportunity to engage meaningful dialogue where race appears to influence vehicle searches is lost and so is the opportunity to explore the impact of race-based decisions on both perpetrator and victim.

It seems the aforementioned social facts pursuant to crime in the United States are rarely depicted in media portrayals of crime and victims of crime. It appears that irrespective of what crime data shows to be the reality of crime, media abounds with distorted images of crime. On television we see folk monsters who are psychopathic killers or serial murderers, yet offenders who even remotely fit these caricatures are extremely rare. The reality of crime is far more humdrum. The nature of crime, of victimization, and of policing is thus systematically distorted in the mass media.[23]

MEDIA IMPACT ON PUBLIC PERCEPTIONS OF CRIME

Research assessing the influence of media on fear of crime began in the 1970s by George Gerbner. Gerbner reported that heavy television viewers possessed what he termed a "mean world view."[24] Additional research has characterized similar viewers as fearful, alienated, and suspicious of others.[25] These types of viewers believe that crime is steadily on the increase. Yet data reviewed from both the Uniform Crime Reports as well as the National Crime Victimization Survey show that criminal victimizations have declined since the mid-1990s. One possible explanation for this inconsistency between public opinion and the actual crime rate is that the preponderance of police and crime television programs is simply creating what Felson calls the "dramatic fallacy."[26] This refers to the perception that the crime rate is much greater than it actually is. Moreover, this fallacy provides a distorted image of victims and alleged perpetrators. For instance, it seldom denotes blacks as more the victims of property and personal crimes. Furthermore, the public also believes that violent crimes predominate when, as noted, property crimes such as burglary, robbery, and drug-related crimes are far more common.[27]

Then again, media coverage fueled by the motives to bolster ratings through sensationalism can promote public fear. Signorielli suggests:

> "Fearful people are more dependent, more easily manipulated and controlled, more susceptible to deceptively simple, strong, tough measures and hard-line postures—both political and religious. They may accept and even welcome repression if it promises to relieve their insecurities and other anxieties . . . When reel-world violence is compared to real-world crime as measured by official statistics, it appears that the media images exaggerate the probability and severity of danger. This is said to 'cultivate' a misleading view of the world based on unnecessary anxiety about levels of risk from violent crime.[28]

Moreover, when race is mixed in with media perceptions of crime, blacks become a repository for fear of crime in the United States.[29] In other words, blacks become associated with crime as perpetrators and not as victims. This racially influenced construction of crime negates accurate reporting. Hence, America can then launch a "War on Drugs" which rapper Tupac Shakur referred to as a "war on me" given the misperception that illicit drug users are primarily black. This biased type of media coverage contributes to the establishment of inequitable drug laws, from which conviction of possession of five grams of crack cocaine can be punished by a prison term of five years, while it takes conviction of possession of at least 500 grams powdered cocaine to obtain a comparable sentence.

Research by Entman reports that in television news stories, black (compared to white) suspects are less likely to be identified by name, are not as well dressed, and are more likely to be shown physically restrained.[30] This depiction contributes to the promotion of the fear of not only the alleged black criminal but also blacks in general. Fear of blacks has a range of social implications. It makes it almost impossible for a black man to hail a cab due to the cab driver's fear. It also makes people reluctant to hold open an elevator door for a black person arriving just as the doors are starting to close.

While blacks are overrepresented as offenders, they are typically under-represented as victims in the news.[31] This runs contrary to National Crime Victimization Survey data, which shows that members of minority groups have significantly higher rates of victimization than members of the majority group. Yet, it is the fear of crime experienced by majority group members that appears reinforced by media coverage of crime. Persons are made fearful of the male, dark figure lurking in the background when in reality it is that dark, male figure that is the more likely the victim. This comes about in part because of the social construction of crime. Official data and statistics focus solely on street crimes. The Uniform Crime Report as well as the National Victimization Survey does not by creation focus upon white-collar crimes involving deceit, and/or concealment and violation of trusts that are usually committed by higher-status majority individuals. Hence, most Americans may not realize that it is white-collar crimes that cost society the most monetary resources. The imagery of crime as Quinney suggests is related to an acceptance of the prevailing social order where physical types of offenses are perceived as more of a threat to the existing social order.[32] Fewer persons of color occupy positions of trust and are able to commit white-collar crimes. Moreover, our construction of crime generates acceptable images of marginalized minorities as a more legitimate threat to the existing social order than the more costly white-collar crimes committed primarily by whites.

Russell further suggests this association of crime with black males as perpetrators has become so entrenched in public perceptions of crime that blacks have become "entrapped by media imagery."[33] This entrapment leads to pre-emptive responses when whites encounter black males. That is to say, this projection of the black male criminal has persons fearful of black males. Such self-induced fear contributes to a lack of positive interaction and perpetuates stereotypes. Hence, individuals become mentally stuck in the images that portray black men as criminals and cannot free themselves to communicate freely. Moreover, such individuals may experience forms of cognitive dissonance and anxiety when they encounter black men who are doctors, lawyers, teachers or other professionals who contradict the popularized black male criminal stereotype.

This nonfactual depiction of minorities in general and black males in particular fits within the context of what sociologist Hubert Blalock terms the "The Minority Threat Hypothesis."[34] This hypothesis is rooted in conflict theory whereby members of the proletariat group (workers) continually challenge the bourgeoisie (ruling class) for wealth, status, and power. This perceived threat then becomes more intense when racially and otherwise culturally heterogeneous groups comprise members of the proletariat and are perceived by others in the group as a threat to the existing social order.[35] To that end, the dominant group encourages use of mechanisms that instill greater sources of control over the increasingly marginalized group. Consider the experiences of many of the ethnic groups migrating from certain parts of Europe. While welcomed as cheaper sources of labor by the industrialists, workers perceived the Irish, Italian, Polish and Jews as a threat to the existing social order, in part because these marginalized workers would accept lower wages and cross picket lines during labor strikes.

Thus, more repressive measures were instituted as the perception of threat increased. The "paddy wagon" became known as such due to the numbers of Irish targeted and arrested prior to and during the Civil War. To this end, the criminal justice system has been perceived as a tool of the ruling class that serves to protect their interests resulting in increased arrests and incarceration of subordinate and marginalized groups.[36]

Perceptions of marginalized groups as a threat to America's social order continues with depictions of violent crimes that contribute to overall sensationalism of crime that in turn sells newspapers and increases television ratings. This sensationalism of crime occurs regardless of the factual information regarding crime. Though crime rates are down for much of this present decade, media still tends to report on crime through usage of crime clocks that show how often someone is assaulted or murdered in increments of seconds or minutes.

Moreover, the media may often report an increase in a city's overall crime rate without specifically denoting that increase was directly related to an increase in larceny or theft and not personal offenses. In fact, the Urban Institute attributed an increase in crime rates for 2005 and 2006 to thefts of iPods and MP3 players that do not have manufacturer-installed security codes.[37] Nonetheless, these less than accurate depictions of crime can alarm readers and viewers and instill a sense of fear.

CONCLUSION

The media plays a significant role as a mechanism of social control in that it can convey, instill, and normalize public reactions to various social groups. Jacobs suggests that news work is not shaped by the desire to include the greatest number of voices or the most compelling argument, but by the journalist's desire to tell the better story.[38] Further, the media presentations of crime, whether fictional or real, are based on a general acceptance of the prevailing social and economic order.[39] The better stories are based upon representations of reality that viewers can believe. Historically, marginalized groups, whether ethnic or racial, have been perceived as a threat to the general social order. Stories that depict black males as perpetrators of crime more than victims of crime perpetuate stereotypes Americans have come to believe. These images, whether real or fictional, have profound consequences and may leave many Americans in a state of bewilderment and anxiety as the United States has elected its first African American male president. The cognitive dissonance some Americans experienced before the election of Barack H. Obama is a direct result of the negative portrayals of black men in media, where blacks and other minorities are demonized as criminals and relegated to lower social positions that are not necessarily based on truth.

CRITICAL THINKING QUESTIONS

1. What are some shortcomings in the media's coverage of minorities as offenders?
2. How does the media contribute to fear of African Americans? Do you agree?
3. How does the Bureau of Justice Statistics contribute to misrepresentation of African Americans in media coverage?
4. How is it that media focus on inner-city crime does not reveal an accurate portrayal of crime in the United States?
5. Media as it relates to crime influences the social construction of reality. How does this reality differ from trends revealed in the Uniform Crime Reports and National Victimization Survey?
6. The term *black-on-black crime* refers to the intraracial nature of crime. With this in mind, explain how "black-on-black crime" is comparable to "poor-on-poor" crime.

NOTES

1. Federal Bureau of Investigation, "Crime in the United States," *Uniform Crime Reports* (Washington, D.C.: U.S. Government Printing Office, 2005).
2. Ibid.
3. Ibid.
4. Ibid.
5. Ibid.
6. Ibid.
7. Ibid.
8. Ibid.
9. Ibid.
10. Ibid.
11. Ibid.
12. Ibid.
13. Bureau of Justice Statistics, National Crime Victimization Survey (Washington, D.C.: U.S. Government Printing Office, 2005).
14. Ibid.
15. Ibid.
16. C. Rennison, *Violent Victimization and Race, 1993–98.* Washington, D.C.: Bureau of Justice Statistics; Publication NCJ 176354: 2001.
17. Robert Sampson, J. Morenoff, and S. Raudenbush, "Social Anatomy of Racial and Ethnic Disparities in Violence," *American Journal Public Health* 95 (2005): 224–232.
18. Ibid.
19. J. Goering and J. Feins, *Choosing a Better Life? Evaluating the Moving to Opportunity Social Experiment* (Washington, D.C.: Urban Institute Press, 2003).
20. Matthew R. Durose, Erica L. Smith, and Patrick A. Langan, *Contacts between Police and the Public* (NCJ-215243) BJS, Department of Justice, 2005.
21. Ibid.
22. Ibid.
23. J. Young, "The Failure of Criminology: The Need for Radical Realism," in *Confronting Crime,*

edited by R. Matthews and J. Young (London: Sage 1986).

24. George Gerbner and Larry Gross, "Living with Television: The Violence Profile," *Journal of Communication* 26 no. 2 (1976): 173–199.

25. George Gerbner, Larry Gross, Michael Morgan, and Nancy Signorelli, "Living with Television: The Dynamics of the Cultivation Process," in *Perspectives on Media Effects,* edited by J. Bryant and D. Zimmerman (Hillsdale, NJ: Lawrence Erlbaum, 1986).

26. Marcus Felson, *Crime and Everyday Life,* 3rd ed. (Thousand Oaks, CA: Sage, 2002).

27. Ibid.

28. N. Signorielli, "Television's Mean and Dangerous World: A Continuation of the Cultural Indicators Perspective," in *Cultivation Analysis: New Directions in Media Effects Research,* edited by N. Signorielli and M. Morgan (Newbury Park: Sage, 1990), 85–106.

29. Dennis Rome, *Black Demons: The Media's Depiction of the African American Male Criminal Stereotype* (Westport, CT: Praeger, 2004), 2.

30. R. M. Entman, "African Americans According to TV News," *Media Studies Journal* 8 (1994): 29–38.

31. A. Weiss, and S. Chermak, "The News Value of African American Victims: An Examination of the Media's Presentation of Homicide," *Journal of Crime and Justice* 21 (1998): 71–88.

32. Richard Quinney, *The Social Reality of Crime* (New York: Little Brown, 1970), 22.

33. Katheryn Russell, *The Color of Crime: Racial Hoaxes, White Fear, Black Protectionism, Police Harassment and Other Macro-aggressions* (New York: University Press, 1998), 70.

34. Hubert M. Blalock, *Toward a Theory of Minority Group Relations* (New York: Wiley, 1967).

35. Allen E. Liska, *Social Threat and Social Control* (Albany, NY: State University of New York Press, 1992).

36. Richard Quinney, *Class, State, and Crime,* 2nd ed. (New York: Longman, 1980).

37. Arnold Zafra, "Ipods and Media Players Increase Crime Rates," *Digital Magazine* (2008); http://www.digitalmagazine .com.au/2008/03/06/ipods-and-media-players-increase-crime-rate/.

38. Ronald Jacobs, *Race, Media and the Crisis of Civil Society: From Watts to Rodney King* (Cambridge, UK: Cambridge University Press, 2000), 26.

39. Jacobs, *Race,* 92.

CHAPTER 5

Politicization of Crime by the Media

Renee M. Bradshaw
Robert L. Bing III

Following the terrorist attacks on September 11, 2001, media outlets throughout the United States began 24-hour news coverage of the attacks, the attackers, and potential future targets. Even following the return to regular television programming, news programs continued to cover the attacks extensively. During the ensuing weeks, many Muslim Americans endured harassment and violence as a result of publicity about Al Qaeda, the terrorist group linked to the attacks. Some citizens indiscriminately persecuted anyone who appeared to be of Middle Eastern descent, relying solely on propaganda and stereotypes to guide them.[1]

On October 4, 2001, Mark Anthony Stroman entered a Shell convenience store in Mesquite, Texas, armed with a .44-caliber handgun. Behind the counter was the owner, Vasudev Patel, an Indian immigrant and married father of two. Stroman demanded money and when Patel reached for a weapon behind the counter, Stroman shot him. Patel later died in the hospital.[2]

When questioned, Stroman stated that he had shot Patel and two other immigrants in retaliation for the 9/11 terrorist attacks. He believed that terrorists were all over the U.S. and stated he had targeted anyone he thought looked to be of Middle Eastern descent. Stroman's reaction to a perceived threat, fueled by stereotypes, resulted in the murders of two men and the permanent injury of another.[3]

With this is mind, the media plays a vital role in the public's perception of the world around them. Television, newspapers, and the Internet consistently appear in Gallup polls as sources of information for the public. Although people claim to be skeptical about how much they trust the media,[4] the exposure still has an affect on their schema.[5] These subtle influences are reflected in their policy concerns and voting behavior.[6] It is essential, then, that criminologists understand the politicized nature of the media.

THE ROLE OF THE MEDIA

We are in the middle of an era that thrives on information.[7] Society wants data at their fingertips—whether through the television, the Internet, or the radio. Today, individuals are accustomed to watching 24-hour news stations or visiting online news sources to gain information.[8] The problem of such behavior stems from how the public interprets the information they obtain.

Although public opinion polls reveal decreased trust in the media, they also illustrate that the primary source of information for the public is television.[9] A recent Gallup poll shows that 47 percent of people believe that media stories are generally accurate.[10] If they see a great deal of crime on the news, then it sometimes translates into the belief that there is a great deal of crime in their communities. What they fail to consider is the primary purpose of the media. Media enterprises are businesses, with the goal of earning money. This is done by entertaining the public. Sensational stories tend to be the most entertaining, but they do not represent the overall crime atmosphere in the country.[11]

This chapter examines how the media relates to crime and the criminal justice system. The authors discuss the media's role in creating and dramatizing crime; in triggering moral panics; and in influencing politics and agenda setting.

THE RELATIONSHIP BETWEEN CRIME AND THE MEDIA

The media is affected by politics; it is driven by the political climate and affects that climate in turn. The media also has power over and is controlled by the public.[12] In the end, the media politicizes crime, by keeping criminal actions at the forefront of everyone's minds.[13] This can then influence their concerns and voting behavior, which can influence the types of laws and codes that are created.[14]

The Media's Creation of Crime

Because the media has such an influence on how people perceive the world, it is in a unique position to emphasize or de-emphasize stories. For example, on a slow-news day, a reporter could present a dramatic five-minute segment about alleged abuse at a day care center, causing uproar and panic from the parents of other children enrolled there. The next day, a big-news day, the news station discovers that the allegations against the day care center were false. Because of the amount of news to be covered that day, the news anchor makes a brief statement, if any at all, that the previous story proved to be false. However, the damage to the hypothetical day care center has already been done. Parents and neighbors are convinced about the truth of the allegations. In this example, the media has both emphasized and de-emphasized stories. With an emphasis on "alleged" actions, the media is able to create crime, whether or not any true criminality exists.[15]

Additionally, the media's emphasis of some stories can create crime trends. When looking for themes in reporting the news, a reporter may discover two or three alleged incidents against children and then decide to focus on this theme rather than on the unrelated crimes themselves. Conversely, other reporters may look into the cases and discover and report on three or four other crimes against children, creating the impression among viewers of an emerging crime trend against children. In actuality, three or four unrelated incidents were grouped together for ease of reporting and no trend exists. Therefore, the media has an ability to create both crime and crime trends.[16]

This seeming omnipotence of the press is even more apparent with the advent of 24-hour news stations and the Internet. There is never a shortage of crime, so there is an ever-revolving set of stories to be covered. By covering crime 24/7, the media creates the impression that crime is so rampant that it *needs* to be covered continuously. This establishes a sort of self-fulfilling prophecy: The media searches for crime to cover, creating the impression of a crime problem; the public and police then focus attention on a particular type of crime, meaning arrests and other police data will reflect the new focus. In the end, the media reported a particular crime problem, and that crime became a problem due to increased public and police focus.[17]

The Media's Dramatization of Crime

In addition to creating crime and crime trends, the media also dramatizes crime and crime data. By dramatizing these issues, the media is able to make news and stories more entertaining than they would be otherwise. The public is drawn to sensational news and the media produces and reports it. Rape and murder, for example, are not the most prevalent forms of crime, but they are the crimes most often reported by the media.[18]

According to Friedman and Percival, crimes can be divided into tiers much like a wedding cake (Figure 5.1). This wedding cake model contains, at the top, the very few sensational, or "celebrated," cases. This is the smallest tier and includes such things as school shootings and celebrity cases. The second tier

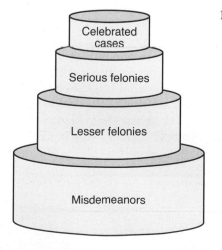

FIGURE 5.1 The Wedding Cake Model

FIGURE 5.2 The Media's Coverage of Crime

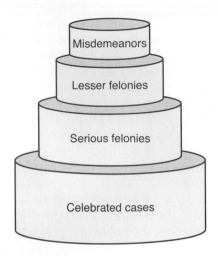

contains major felonies such as rape and murder, as well as crimes committed by repeat offenders. The third tier includes lesser felonies, such as property crimes, and first offenses. The bottom—and largest—tier contains the misdemeanors, such as criminal mischief and public-order crimes.[19]

The media, however, reports news inversely to this model (Figure 5.2). Sensational cases, which make up the smallest amount of crime, are the cases the media covers most heavily. The second tier, which is the second smallest in volume of crimes, is the second most covered by the media. Finally, the third and bottom tiers, which account for the majority of crimes committed, are covered the least by the media.[20]

In another way, the media dramatizes crime by improperly using crime statistics published in the FBI's Uniform Crime Reports (UCR). The UCR contains a large amount of information but has various validity issues in its data collection method.* Typically, the media treat the information or data as facts. And media outlets tend to use in their reporting only a small part of the UCR, often the Crime Clock (Figure 5.3).[21]

Racial Disparity   Another issue in media's dramatization of crime is racial disparity. The media has a tendency to emphasize or over-report stories in which the perpetrator is young, black, and male. This emphasis can subsequently cause viewers to assume that most crimes are committed by young black men.[22]

When Barlow looked at the content of fifty years of *Time* and *Newsweek* cover stories, she discovered a high number of articles connecting black men to crime. She claimed that this association, which she called "symbolic racism," was much less

---

* Because it relies on numerous law enforcement agencies with varying definitions and procedures for each type of crime, the UCR lacks consistent variables. Also, the UCR reporting standard requires agencies to report only the most severe crime when multiple crimes are committed in a single incident. For example, if a man breaks into a home, rapes and murders a woman, then kidnaps her child and steals her television, the incident would be reported to the UCR as a murder. The other crimes committed during the incident are not reported on the UCR.

Every 22.2 seconds	One Violent Crime
Every 30.9 minutes	One Murder
Every 5.7 minutes	One Forcible Rape
Every 1.2 minutes	One Robbery
Every 36.6 seconds	One Aggravated Assault

Every 3.2 seconds	One Property Crime
Every 14.4 seconds	One Burglary
Every 4.8 seconds	One Larceny-theft
Every 26.4 seconds	One Motor Vehicle Theft

http://www.fbi.gov/ucr/cius2006/about/crime_clock.html

FIGURE 5.3 Crime Clock for 2006

explicit in later stories. Barlow states that the damage has already been done; young black men and crime have been irrevocably linked in the minds of the public.[23]

In 2002, Chiricos and Eschholz analyzed local broadcast news content in Orlando, Florida. They found that, although the media did not drastically distort the number of minority offenders, they did frequently present them in more menacing contexts. Minorities were shown as suspects more often than their white counterparts. The authors speculate that this could be a factor in why some people feel so threatened by someone of another race.[24]

Pollack and Kubrin later compared news broadcasts to newspaper and news magazine coverage. They learned that for basic facts both mediums reported the same information. However, this changed when looking at their coverage of subjective factors in the stories. Broadcast media tended to play on emotions and create fear or anxiety in viewers in regards to crime. This was a tendency not present in print media.[25] This stereotyping by the media has several ramifications, two of which are discussed below.

The first is the "demonization" of young black men. Some people might begin to believe that young black men are dangerous and should be avoided. These people could eventually come to fear young black men, when there is no logical cause for such fear.[26] This irrational fear is illustrated in Randall Kennedy's book, *Race, Crime, and the Law.* Kennedy mentions how Jesse Jackson once described hearing footsteps behind him on the street and was later relieved when he realized that it was a white man. Even Jackson, whose name is frequently linked with equal rights activism, had fallen prey to media stereotyping.[27]

The second ramification is what Russell refers to as the racial hoax. Once society demonizes young black men, it becomes easy to blame them for crimes they did not commit. There are two types of racial hoaxes. One is when a crime actually occurs, and the other is when there is no crime.[28]

The Racial Hoax   The first type of racial hoax occurs when a fictitious offender is blamed for a real crime solely because of race. An example of this type would be the case of Susan Smith. On October 25, 1994, Susan Smith allowed her car to roll into a lake with her sleeping children in the backseat. She then notified police that a middle-aged black man had driven off with her children in the car. She even went so far as to assist with a composite drawing of the alleged offender. Nine days later, she admitted to killing her children and fabricating the story of the carjacker. Smith fabricated a black criminal, playing on local prejudices, in an effort to deter authorities from discovering her crime.[29]

The second kind of racial hoax happens when a fictional perpetrator—predicated upon race—is accused of a crime when no crime has actually occurred. For example, in 1990 Miriam Kashani told campus newspaper reporters at George Washington University that a white woman had been raped by two black men. The next day, Kashani held a press conference and revealed that the whole story was concocted to increase rape awareness on campus. In this case, Kashani created two black offenders when no true crime had occurred.[30]

The greatest trouble with the racial hoax is that it increases interracial tension and mistrust. After Susan Smith accused a "fabricated" black man of abducting her children, people everywhere began looking for this alleged offender. This resulted in the unnecessary scrutiny of many black men nationwide. These racial hoaxes add to the public's belief that young black men are inherently criminal.[31] As Welch stated, "The mere existence of racial hoaxes . . . offers support for the notion that blacks have been stereotyped in criminally coded ways."[32]

The Media and Moral Panic   Because of the media's creation and dramatization of crime and violence, the press is able to influence the thoughts and fears of its audience. In this way, the media can create (as they can with crime or crime trends) feelings of panic and anxiety with viewers. When the media identifies a specific crime wave, whether it exists or not, the result can be known as a moral panic.[33]

A moral panic is typically characterized by the use of stereotypes against those who are different[34] and the consequences can be long lasting and damaging to all involved.[35] Various examples of moral panics are available in scholarly literature, some of which are discussed below.

Many researchers have characterized fear of gangs in specific cities as moral panics.[36] In these circumstances, increased media attention to gang crimes leads to increased fear of gangs. Unfortunately, the public's perception of the stereotypical gang member is far from accurate. This image comes from and is reinforced by the media. The media's representation of a gang member is usually young, male, and a minority.[37] The public's fear of gangs often leads to fear of anyone meeting this distorted image of gang members—another manifestation of the demonization of young black men. This elevated fear among the public leads to increased political action against gangs and gang crimes.

Colomb and Damphousse contend that the public's fear of hate crimes during the late 1990s was another example of moral panic. People were disproportionately afraid of hate crimes and a great deal of media attention was focused on the subject during that time period. The subject also engendered feelings of extreme passion and hostility, which the researchers tied to spikes in media coverage about hate crimes. These fears brought about policy proposals regarding hate crimes. And when media attention shifted, public interest in the issue waned somewhat.[38]

Fear of school violence, and especially school shootings, is another example of moral panic, according to Killingbeck. Statistically speaking, most schools are relatively safe environments. Yet after the media paid attention to the recent occasions of school shootings, many in the public began to believe that school violence was indeed rampant and out of control. This belief is reflected in the scrutiny paid to children in schools and the government money dedicated toward preventing school violence. As the media loses focus on school violence, people's thoughts swing to other concerns.[39]

More recently, research has turned to terrorism as another occurrence of moral panic.[40] After 9/11, the American public was in a state of panic. People expected more attacks to come at any minute, and their anxiety led them to support actions from the government that many may have been previously opposed.

This moral panic regarding terrorism also results in racial tensions, as illustrated in the case of Patel outlined earlier. The fear of terrorism can cause people to be suspicious of other races, leading to discrimination or violence. This is what Mythen and Walklate refer to as the "nonwhite terroristic other."[41]

THE RELATIONSHIP BETWEEN THE CRIMINAL JUSTICE SYSTEM AND THE MEDIA

In addition to its relationship to crime, the media is also related to the criminal justice system. There are various dynamics to this relationship. These dynamics include the way the media represents crime and the legal system, the power of the media over the criminal justice system, and how the news media affects real-life policy.

The Media's Representation of the Criminal Justice System

Several content analyses have been conducted on criminal justice programs on television, with similar results, such as an overrepresentation of high-speed chases, murders, and other violent crimes. These activities are presented far in excess of their relative occurrences in real life. On the other hand, many common duties of law enforcement officers are left out. Patrolling and filling out paperwork seldom make it onto television. Property crimes, white-collar crimes, drug offenses, and family violence are also underrepresented by the media.[42]

Alternatively, television tends to overestimate the number of employees within the criminal justice system. Although TV police officers respond immediately to each crime and seem to have inexhaustible resources, real law enforcement agencies are often understaffed and underfunded. This reality could result in long waits for assistance and subsequent dissatisfaction with the criminal justice system.[43]

The legal system is also frequently misrepresented in the media[44] and due process is frequently minimized.[45] Television also has a distorted number of successful convictions, with criminals almost always apprehended and convicted within the program. This is one of the biggest discrepancies from reality, as crime clearance rates are nowhere near 100 percent.[46]

The Media's Power over the Criminal Justice System

The media has the ability to indirectly exercise considerable power over the criminal justice system. This is most obvious in its ability to influence a district attorney's decision to prosecute. In 1986, Pritchard analyzed the relationship between the amount of newspaper attention to a given incident and the prosecutor's decision to plea bargain. He found that the less media attention devoted to a case, the more likely the prosecutor was willing to offer a plea bargain. This observation suggests that the media has the potential to influence the prosecutor's decisions.[47]

The Media's Role in Agenda-Setting and Policy

As a result of the media's influence over public perception, it also has an influence on agenda setting and public policy. When the media covers a crime extensively, the public's reaction can result in policy proposals and funding reallocations. If people are concerned with crime, then politicians are concerned with crime, and the public agenda will reflect that concern.[48]

Another example of the media's role in agenda setting was explored by Adcock, who researched how media coverage affects the United States' humanitarian efforts. She claimed that the public's emotional reactions to the crisis in Somalia in 1992 led the government to enter the situation without fully considering the consequences.[49]

CONCLUSION

When considering the politicization of crime by the media, two policy implications become apparent. First, steps should be taken to dispel many of the myths associated with crime and the criminal justice system. The media must adopt policies that would lessen the misinformation they convey, while the criminal justice system should take steps to educate both the media and the public about crime. Next, the government and other state employees (like the district attorney) should acknowledge the error of enacting policies and making decisions based upon the uninformed opinions of the public. Restated, media and criminal justice officials should work jointly to explore ways to better educate the public, as only through continued exposure and attention can we begin to alter the negative effects of the media's influence.

CRITICAL THINKING QUESTIONS

1. How does the media politicize crime? Do you agree?
2. Discuss the dramatization of crime by the media. What examples can you point toward?
3. What is the essence of the moral panic?
4. How do the authors characterize the media's representation of the criminal justice system?
5. What is meant by the creation of crime?

NOTES

1. Robert Pierre, "Victims of hate now feeling forgotten; family of man killed after 9/11 finding little charity but much hardship," *The Washington Post*, September 14, 2002.
2. Holly Becka, "Police: Suspect changed his story—hate crime motive weighed after he said after he said owner slain in holdup," *The Dallas Morning News*, November 3, 2001.
3. Cherie Bell, "Widow struggles after 9/11—backlash victim's case not unusual, aid official says," *The Dallas Morning News*, October 13, 2002.
4. Gallup, Inc., "Media Use and Evaluation," http://www.gallup.com/poll/1663/Media-Use-Evaluation.aspx (accessed June 12, 2008).
5. George Gerbner, "The Stories We Tell," *Peace Review* 11, no. 1 (1999): 9–15; Daniel Romer, Kathleen Jamieson, and Sean Aday, "Television News and the Cultivation of Fear of Crime," *Journal of Communication* 53, no. 1 (March 2003): 88–104.
6. Oscar Gandy et al., "Race and Risk: Factors Affecting the Framing of Stories about Inequality, Discrimination, and Just Plain Bad Luck," *The Public Opinion Quarterly* 61, no. 1 (1997): 158–182.
7. David Alberts and Daniel Papps, eds. *The Information Age: An Anthology on its Impact and Consequences* (Washington, DC: National Defense University Press, 1998).
8. David Altheide, "The News Media, the Problem Frame, and the Production of Fear," *The Sociological Quarterly* 38, no. 4 (1997): 647–668.
9. Gallup, "Media Use and Evaluation;" Lydia Saad, "Local TV Is No. 1 Source of News for Americans," (January 5, 2007), http://www.gallup.com/poll/26053/Local-No-Source-News-Americans.aspx (accessed June 12, 2008).

10. Gallup, "Media Use and Evaluation."
11. Altheide, "The News Media," 647–668.
12. Ibid.
13. Romer, "Television News," 88–104.
14. Gandy, "Race and Risk," 158–182.
15. Altheide, "The News Media," 647–668.
16. Ibid.; Killingbeck, "The Role of Television News in the Construction of School Violence as 'Moral Panic'," *Journal of Criminal Justice and Popular Culture* 8, no. 3 (2002): 186–202; Jessica Pollack and Charis Kubrin, "Crime in the News: How Crimes, Offenders and Victims Are Portrayed in the Media," *Journal of Criminal Justice and Popular Culture* 14, no. 1 (2007): 59–83.
17. Altheide, "The News Media," 647–668.
18. Romer, "Television News," 88–104.
19. Lawrence Friedman and Robert Percival, *The Roots of Justice: Crime and Punishment in Alameda County, California, 1870–1910* (Chapel Hill: University of North Carolina Press, 1981).
20. Pollack and Kubrin, "Crime in the News," 59–83.
21. Altheide, "The News Media," 647–668.
22. Melissa Barlow, "Race and the Problem of Crime in *Time* and *Newsweek* Cover Stories, 1946–1995," *Social Justice* 25, no. 2 (1998): 149–183; Pollack and Kubrin, "Crime in the News," 59–83.
23. Barlow, "Race and the Problem of Crime," 149–183.
24. Ted Chiricos and Sarah Eschholz, "The Racial and Ethnic Typification of Crime and the Criminal Typification of Race and Ethnicity in Local Television News," *Journal of Research in Crime and Delinquency* 39, no. 4 (2002): 400–420.
25. Pollack and Kubrin, "Crime in the News," 59–83.
26. Barlow, "Race and the Problem of Crime," 149–183.
27. Randall Kennedy, *Race, Crime, and the Law* (New York: Vintage Books, 1997).
28. Katheryn Russell, "The Racial Hoax as Crime: The Law as Affirmation," in *African American Classics in Criminology and Criminal Justice*, eds. Shaun Gabbidon, Helen Greene, and Vernetta Young (Thousand Oaks, CA: Sage, 2002), 349–376.
29. Susan Chira, "Murdered Children: In Most Cases, a Parent Did It," *New York Times*, November 5, 1994; Russell, "The Racial Hoax as Crime," 349–376; Kelly Welch, "Black Criminal Stereotypes and Racial Profiling," *Journal of Contemporary Criminal Justice* 23, no. 3 (2007): 276–288.
30. Felicity Barringer, "False Rape Report Upsetting Campus," *New York Times*, December 12, 1990; Russell, "The Racial Hoax as Crime," 349–376; Welch, "Black Criminal Stereotypes," 276–288.
31. Russell, "The Racial Hoax as Crime," 349–376; Welch, "Black Criminal Stereotypes," 276–288.
32. Welch, "Black Criminal Stereotypes," 284–285.
33. Michael Welch, Eric Price, and Nana Yankey, "Moral Panic over Youth Violence: Wilding and the Manufacture of Menace in the Media," *Youth Society* 34, no. 3 (2002): 3–30.
34. Jodi Lane, "Fear of Gang Crime: A Qualitative Examination of the Four Perspectives," *Journal of Research in Crime and Delinquency* 39, no. 4 (2002): 437–471.

35. Welch et al., "Moral Panic over Youth Violence," 3–30.

36. Joel Best, *Random Violence: How We Talk about New Crimes and New Victims* (Berkeley: University of California Press, 1999); Lane, "Fear of Gang Crime," 437–471; Mercer Sullivan and Barbara Miller, "Adolescent Violence, State Processes, and the Local Context of Moral Panic," in *States and Illegal Practices*, ed. Josiah Heyman (New York: Berg, 1999), 261–283.

37. Finn-Aage Esbensen and Karin Tusinki, "Youth Gangs in the Print Media," *Journal of Criminal Justice and Popular Culture* 14, no. 1 (2007): 21–38.

38. Wendy Colomb and Kelly Damphousse, "Examination of Newspaper Coverage of Hate Crimes: A Moral Panic Perspective," *American Journal of Criminal Justice* 28, no. 2 (2004): 147–163.

39. Donna Killingbeck, "The Role of Television News," 186–202.

40. Gabe Mythen and Sandra Walklate, "Communicating the Terrorist Risk: Harnessing a Culture of Fear?" *Crime Media Culture* 2, no. 2 (2006): 123–142.

41. Mythen and Walklate, "Communicating the Terrorist Risk," 123–142.

42. Joseph Dominick, "Crime and Law Enforcement on Prime-Time Television," *Public Opinion Quarterly* 37, no. 2 (1973): 241–250; James Garofalo, "Crime and the Mass Media: A Selective Review of Research," *Journal of Research in Crime and Delinquency* 18 (1981): 319–350; Jason Low and Kevin Durkin, "Children's Conceptualization of Law Enforcement on Television and in Real Life," *Legal and Criminological Psychology* 6 (2001): 197–214.

43. George Gerbner and Larry Gross, "Living with Television: The Violence Profile," *Journal of Communication* 26, no. 2 (1976): 172–199.

44. Kenneth Dowler, "Introduction to the Special Issue: Media Criminology in the Television World," *Journal of Criminal Justice and Popular Culture* 14, no. 3 (2007): 237–242.

45. Jason Low and Kevin Durkin, "Children's Understanding of Events and Criminal Justice Processes in Police Programs," *Journal of Applied Developmental Psychology* 18 (1997): 179–205.

46. Dominick, "Crime and Law Enforcement," 241–250; Valerie Hans and Juliet Dee, "Media Coverage of Law," *American Behavioral Scientist* 35 (1991): 136–149.

47. David Pritchard, "Homicide and Bargained Justice: The Agenda-Setting Effect of Crime News on Prosecutors," *The Public Opinion Quarterly* 50, no. 2 (1986): 143–159.

48. Franklin Zimring and David Johnson, "Public Opinion and the Governance of Punishment in Democratic Political Systems," *The Annals of the American Academy of Political and Social Science* 605 (2006): 265–280.

49. Jennifer Adcock, "The Effects of Television on Public Opinion and Intervention: The Lessons of Somalia," (master's thesis, Dalhousie University, 1997).

CHAPTER 6

Victims-Offenders: What Is the Role of Race in the Media's Portrayal of Crime?

Charisse T. M. Coston

The topic of race and crime is often cloaked in soothing rhetoric, full of euphemisms and anti-inflammatory words. Yet beyond this rhetoric lie serious social issues. At the core of many social issues, including school busing, poverty, and welfare, are problems related to persistent racial tension in America. Likewise, at the core of the crime problem is also race. According to Pollack and Kubrin, there is no escaping the intersection of race and crime.[1]

The question is not why so many black offenders compared to whites in the U.S. population are engaging in crime, or why others are arrested and convicted by prejudiced criminal justice officials, but rather why, given centuries of oppression, so few have resorted to violence. This question is particularly interesting when we talk about the large numbers of poor blacks in the United States. The treatment of blacks as invisible throughout history has made many blacks angry and as a matter of protest has led them to engage in violence. This violence has created victims as well as offenders. By responding with violence, blacks become responsible for their own victimization.[2]

The media has a duty to fairly and accurately report the news. We have often seen that the news and its portrayal of blacks is often slanted, presenting the worst picture of the black culture and its relation to the crime problem. Thus, when the media covers violence in the black community, society often gets a distorted image that taints the view of black culture for some and frustrates others.

As an example of media distortion, consider the portrayal of football legend O. J. Simpson, who was accused of murdering two white people: one female and one male. The news story began over a decade ago with the slow-speed chase of O. J. Simpson in his Bronco by the police on a Los Angeles freeway, a chase witnessed by many on various news channels. One of myriad of controversies surrounding the O. J. Simpson case developed when both *Time* and *Newsweek* magazines depicted darkened pictures of Simpson on their covers. Minority groups cried "foul" immediately for the darkening of Simpson's face and accused both magazines of racism. The magazines' reply was that the image manipulation was done intentionally to show that Simpson had fallen from grace. However, the two magazine covers were immediately replaced and only those who had a subscription to the magazine "supposedly" saw the darkened picture of Simpson on the cover.

Based upon a survey of the literature on media and crime, it is difficult for any minority group to be depicted positively in the media. There are flaws in the portrayals of Mexicans, Arabs, Africans, Indians, and other ethnic groups.[3] However, this chapter focuses on the fantasy, reality, and the portrayal of blacks as victims and offenders of crime in the media. Although there have been some attempts by Hollywood to represent various types of black families, it is often that Hollywood movies create the basis for misinformation that is then used by news media to make social judgments about blacks in their reports.[4] We still have a long way to go to accurately portray black offenders and victims in the media, whether it is in a movie, a TV sitcom, local news, or national news.[5] As stated, the media has a responsibility for neutral reporting, not selective journalism. Without balanced media reporting, we get a polarization of the citizenry, as slanted views by white-dominated media outlets fuel misinformation and racial tension.

PORTRAYALS BY MEDIA OUTLETS

There are a few distortions in the media depiction of crimes and natural tragedies that feed the public misinformation about race in America. One distortion is the relative lack of information about successful blacks whose contributions are great but who lack celebrity. For example, Dr. Mark Dean is a black man who has been a senior vice president at IBM, and who has three of the nine patents for the IBM/PC. Most people probably have not heard of him because it is not sexy and mainstream to show a successful black man from Stanford University in the news. But most people do know Snoop Dogg, P. Diddy, and O. J. Simpson. Some believe that the media uses the names, images, and activities of the more notorious black men to reinforce negative imagery of all black men.[6]

Another distortion is the slanted coverage of whites versus blacks. During Hurricane Katrina there were both whites and blacks who were looting stores as a way of surviving until they could receive aid. In the midst of the storm, efforts at survival by whites were seen as necessary; yet similar measures taken by blacks were seen as negative.[7] News reports referred to New Orleans blacks who were taking items from stores as a means of survival, as hoodlums and thieves. These media outlets showed blacks searching in vain for food and clean water. Conversely, there were several black men who stepped up to pay for recovery efforts in New Orleans, but their stories and good will received little press coverage.

Yet another distortion creates fear of blacks as a whole and black men in particular. In the National Football League (NFL) between 2005 and early 2007, there were about forty-one football players who had been arrested. In one article, the pictures of all forty-one arrested players were shown. Thirty-nine of the players were black. One can imagine the image that this picture invoked in the media readership and the resulting fear of black men it created.[8]

Studies on the news and crime suggest that blacks are depicted as aggressive criminals in reality-based crime and new shows. Entman, for example, found that blacks more so than whites, were shown in handcuffs and mug shots.[9] Oliver found that more blacks were represented than whites in crime stories in the newspaper.[10] Dixon also described whites as having fewer troublesome and criminal portrayals than blacks in news stories and reality-based crime shows.[11] While the creation of more racial diversity in the media workplace has shed light on black stereotypes, misperceptions still exist. In a 2008 groundbreaking study by Radio One and the highly respected Yankelovich research firm that has been hailed as the most thorough and accurate study ever conducted on black America (www .newsone.com), it was reported that most black people agreed that mainstream media reinforces black stereotypes and portrays blacks in a negative light.

REALITY: BLACKS AS CRIME VICTIMS AND CRIMINAL OFFENDERS

Contrary to what we have seen in the media, juveniles are less likely than adults to be victims or offenders. Stories involving black juveniles as victims and offenders of violent crime are disproportionately represented in broadcast and print media outlets.[12] Official crime statistics suggest that most crime is nonviolent. However, media reports of crimes suggest that there are more violent crimes.[13] Researchers studying victims and offenders frequently refer to the overreporting of violent crimes. In reality, there is a smaller percentage of black victims and offenders in the criminal justice system than media reports would lead us to believe. A larger proportion of blacks and minorities than whites are shown as victims and offenders, especially when the offense is violent.[14] Black murder victims are given shorter reports in the news than white murder victims.[15] Researchers have found that some people are more crime prone than others. Their results show that black males are at a higher risk for criminal victimization than any other persons.[16] Yet we rarely see black males depicted as crime victims in crime news reports. The nature of crime itself is intraracial, with victims and offenders from the same race. The media and official statistics report accurately that there are more black males than black or white females who have been arrested for crimes.

Overall, the media depicts blacks as committing more violent crime than official statistics show. This is yet another distortion of reality that instills fear in the citizenry, making people feel less safe and secure in their property and with their personal belongings around blacks, particularly black males. On the other hand, the media typically underrepresents black victims in its reporting of crime news, as if these victims are unworthy of recognition. This fact underscores the racial bias in the media today. Only with the correction of such distortions will the topic of race and crime reflect reality in the media.

CRITICAL THINKING QUESTIONS

1. What was the justification given behind the darker images of O. J. Simpson on the covers of *Newsweek* and *Time* magazines? What are your reactions to this justification?
2. Discuss the disconnect between media reports of crimes, relative to the official crime statistics. Do you agree?
3. What does the author suggest about media coverage in the aftermath of Hurricane Katrina? Is this a fair criticism? Why?

NOTES

1. J. M. Pollack and C. E. Kubrin, "Crime in the News: How Crimes, Offenders, and Victims Are Portrayed by the Media," *Journal of Criminal Justice and Popular Culture* 14 (2007): 1–33.
2. R. Surrette, *Media Crime and the Media Criminal Justice: Images, Realities, and Politics* (Belmont, CA: Wadsworth, 2007).
3. R. Muraskin and S. F. Domash, *Crime and the Media: Headlines vs. Reality* (Upper Saddle River: NJ: Pearson-Prentice Hall, 2007).
4. H. Adoni and S. Mane, "Media and the Social Construction of Reality," *Communication Research* 11 no. 3 (1984): 323–340.
5. Pollack and Kubrin, "Crime in the news."
6. T. Gest, *Crime and Politics* (London: Oxford University Press, 2001).
7. R. Surrette, *Media Crime and the Media Criminal Justice.*
8. Muraskin and Domash, *Crime and the Media.*
9. R. Entman, "Blacks in the News: Television, Modern Racism, and Cultural Change," *Journalism Quarterly* 69 (1992): 341–361.
10. M. B. Oliver, "Portrayals of Crime, Race and Aggression in 'Reality-Based' Police Shows: A Content Analysis," *Journal of Broadcasting and Electronic Media* 38 no. 2 (1994): 179–192.
11. T. Dixon, "A Social Cognitive Approach to Media Stereotypes," *African-American Research Perspectives* 6 (2000): 60–68.

12. Pollack and Kubrin, *Crime in the News.*

13. S. Chermak, "Predicting Crime Story Salience: The Effects of Crime, Victim, and Defendant Characteristics," *Journal of Criminal Justice* 26 (1998): 61–70.

14. Pollack and Kubrin, *Crime in the News.*

15. Entman, "Blacks in the News."

16. Dixon, "A Social Cognitive Approach to Media Stereotypes."

CHAPTER 7

Images of African Americans in the Media

Erica Thomas
Robert L. Bing III*

Ubiquitous and powerfully influential are accurate descriptions of the mass media. There is no question that the media plays a major role in shaping peoples' beliefs, values, knowledge, and understanding of their social environment. The power the mass media has in affecting perceptions is advantageous to some and disadvantageous to others. The advantaged group consists of privileged individuals who are rich and powerful, as they control the mass media. The disadvantaged group consists of less-privileged individuals, who are in the majority but represent the minority from the standpoint of power and control. Consequently, a reality is created of these individuals (those in the minority) that is negative, misleading, and stereotypical.

Historically, members of minority groups have had limited participation in the mass media. The images and sounds offered by the media have been stereotypical and often harmful. Today, there is a trend toward improving the quality, frequency, and accuracy of mass media portrayals of minorities. However, this chapter will explore how media depictions of African Americans have remained unchanged. It will discuss the historical evolution of minorities in print and broadcast advertising and examine the portrayals of minorities in the most powerful medium: television. The influence on the perception of minorities in both fictional entertainment and reality television will be discussed, as well as possibly a new form of racism known as modern racism, which is the source of harmful stereotypical portrayals of minorities.

* We are very grateful for the assistance of Cynthia Hipolito, who was instrumental in the collecting of research articles for this chapter.

This chapter will focus on the portrayal of minorities as criminals and crime victims. It will discuss the impact of these stereotypical portrayals on viewer perception and explore possible explanations based on various theories and perspectives. Exploration of this topic will begin with how African American women are generally portrayed in the mass media, beginning with the controversy that surrounded radio personality Don Imus in 2007. His degrading comments about the Rutgers women's basketball team were a prime example of how sexism and racism are often present in media characterizations of minority women. An *Advertising Age* editorial writer noted that "Imus may not have broken the law, but a crime was committed." [1] He committed a crime that is still committed today against the image of black women in the media.

If there was anything positive that stemmed from the Don Imus controversy, it was that the media redirected or increased the public's attention to how women, especially black women, are portrayed in various mediums. It added contributing members to a public dialogue that was long overdue. Unfortunately, as this chapter will highlight, more attention should be paid specifically to how minority women are depicted as criminals and victims in the media.

HISTORICAL EVOLUTION OF MINORITIES IN THE MEDIA

Many studies have acknowledged a relationship between the mass media and how it influences the beliefs and knowledge of the dominant group about minorities. [2] This relationship is significant, considering the low visibility of some minority groups in the mass media along with their frequent negative and stereotypical portrayal. In the past, for instance, African Americans were limited in their roles on television. [3] Unfortunately, negative portrayals of black women have influenced how the dominant group views them in "real world" situations. According to the cultivation hypothesis, television in particular can communicate information about the social environment that influences an individual's perceptions about the social world. [4] This hypothesis, however, is concerned with long-term exposure to television programming, rather than single exposure. In essence, an individual who is exposed to certain consistent portrayals or images on television may assume that those depictions are a true reflection of reality. Thus, it is important to examine how accurate these representations are of minority groups, such as African Americans on television and in other media.

Research indicates that the presence of African Americans in the mass media has increased over the years. [5] And while their presence has improved dramatically, some studies indicate that their portrayal remains negative and stereotypical. [6] In television, the increase in appearances of African Americans has been primarily limited to sitcoms or disparaging characterizations. [7] Before the civil rights movement, African Americans were virtually invisible and the roles that were available depicted them as lazy and unintelligent, images intended to entertain a white audience. [8] Most of the characters held low-status positions and lived in the ghetto or slums. [9] The invisibility of minority characters and alleged discriminatory hiring practices at television networks resulted in a presidentially commissioned investigation of television's impact on perceptions of minorities. The investigation found that portrayals of African Americans and other ethnic minorities influenced the way whites and nonwhites perceived minorities.[10]

In the 1970s, the number of African Americans on television remained significantly disproportionate to the total population of African Americans in the country. Many were still portrayed as deviant and criminal, but that began to disappear by the 1980s. An upward trend began in 1984, with more African Americans represented on television.[11] African Americans, especially in sitcoms, began to reach equal status to whites. Greater equivalence in this genre has been mostly attributed to the success and popularity of *The Cosby Show*. This signaled the beginning of African Americans depicted with professional careers and normal to upscale lifestyles.[12] A more recent study has shown that African Americans have definitely carved a niche in prime time television in situational comedies, with 21 percent represented in sitcoms.[13]

HISTORICAL EVOLUTION OF MINORITIES IN ADVERTISING

Similar to the interest in how African Americans are portrayed in entertainment television, researchers have been studying how African Americans are portrayed in consumer media for over fifty years, particularly in print advertising.[14] Some individuals believe that advertising perpetuates stereotypes and bolsters pre-existing social inequalities, while others believe it can affect social change by replacing stereotypical portrayals with realistic ones.[15]

Stevenson examined the quantitative and qualitative portrayal of African Americans in business advertising to find if the portrayals reflect or shape society.[16] The six-decade study revealed that prior to the 1970s African Americans were rarely used in advertising. A surge in portrayals occurred in the 1970s and again in the new millennium following a period of stagnation in the 1980s and 1990s. The most significant increase was in the types of portrayals. Between 1957 and 1977 there was a sharp increase of African Americans portrayed in managerial and professional roles and a significant decline in their portrayal as blue collar and clerical workers. Perhaps advertisers were following the social changes that occurred prior to 1977. However, by 2005 African Americans portrayed as managers and professionals exceeded the actual numerical presence of African Americans in those business occupations.[17] The presence of minorities in prime-time television advertising has not followed the same pace as print advertising. Mastro and Stern[18] found 12 percent African Americans, 2 percent Asians, and 1 percent Latinos were represented in a week's worth of television commercials. Interestingly, findings of representation on television based on ethnicity, race, and age compared to the general U.S. population show that African Americans are the only group who appear in excess on television, compared to their representation within the U.S. population.

Greenberg and Worrell examined *TV Guide's* fall preview issue from 1993 to 2004, seeking to find the proportions of minorities represented on television.[19]

African Americans comprised 25 percent of the characters shown on television across the more than thirty seasons analyzed. Two events may have contributed to the increase in African American representation: the introduction of the UPN and WB networks in 1995 and the NAACP threatening lawsuits and boycotts of broadcast networks in 1999 after a discovery of low African American representation. This discovery found there were increases in African Americans shown on television, but that the overall increase masksed the year-to-year fluctuations.

Today, the number of African Americans on television is proportionate to the African American population in the United States, but the quality of their depictions continues to be examined.[20] For example, Mastro and Robinson reviewed over two thousand prime time television commercials and how African Americans were portrayed in those commercials.[21] They found that African Americans are generally depicted in advertisements for financial services or food. Their depictions were comparable to whites and not considered harmful to self-perceptions.

Yet some advertisements can be harmful to self-perceptions. The images and ideas in television ads not only persuade individuals to purchase products and services, they also influence beliefs and values.[22] According to market researchers, advertisers understand the power of symbols and signs, and position their products to invoke realities for consumers.[23] The social learning theory contends that individuals learn beliefs and behaviors from observing others.[24] Similarly, cultivation theory suggests that constant exposure to certain beliefs and ideas about an object leads to a perpetuation of those beliefs and ideas about that object.[25]

Stereotyping minorities in advertisements has been shown to occur across different mediums for several years. For example, Lieata and Biswas found in a 1993 study that African American models were associated with low-value products more often than whites.[26] Taylor and Stern in 1997 found that certain minority groups in prime-time television advertising were associated with different products, such as Asians being associated with technology-oriented products.[27]

A 1998 survey of children aged ten to seventeen found that children, especially those of color, believed race representation was important in commercials. Most of the children believed minorities were portrayed more negatively than whites and 71 percent believed that when bosses are portrayed in the workplace on television they are often white. The study highlighted the importance of accurate racial representation in television advertisements and how advertising can affect the socialization process of children. Bang and Reece examined the portrayals of African American, white, and Asian children in television commercials.[28] Unlike previous studies, their research found that minorities were portrayed in more television commercials that targeted children. And African Americans were the most overrepresented of minority groups. Previous studies have shown that whites dominate in representation on television while minorities are virtually invisible.[29]

In a study of television advertisements, a look at the top ten comedies in 1999 found that racial diversity was limited.[30] People of color primarily held peripheral roles and were limited to certain products. Whites were associated with expensive, domestic, and household products. "People of color, on the other hand, were closely tied to low-cost, low-nutrition products such as fast food and soft drinks, candy, and gum." [31] African Americans are often stereotypically linked to fried chicken and athletic apparel commercials as well. Henderson and Baldasty concluded that the association of people of color to low-cost products symbolizes their perceived lack of worth as consumers and members of society.[32]

Covert and Dixon found hopeful results for women of color in the media. The researchers performed a content analysis of popular women's magazines from 1999 to 2004 to examine the effect of counterstereotypical portrayals on readers. Their hypothesis that white women would be overrepresented and Latina and African American women would be underrepresented in women's magazines was supported. This trend, however, was lessened in 2004 when there was a reversal of findings, and African American women were overrepresented as professionals and white women were underrepresented. Interestingly, this reversal had more positive occupational expectations among white readers than those of color.[33]

Covert and Dixon concluded that while African American women have better representation in magazines, their journey to equal exposure as white women continues.[34] Furthermore, the perceptual change of women of color was explained by sub-grouping theory. The sub-grouping theory suggests that different positive portrayals work to weaken the support for negative stereotypes. The diverse representation of African American women prevented readers from arguing that certain African American women were the exception to the rule. It also encouraged readers to acknowledge the variation within a racial group and the inconsistencies with stereotypes. People of color, however, who had the opposite reaction may have compared their experiences to those of the successful women of color featured in the magazines and assumed those women were atypical. The researchers suggested further study of this phenomenon.

FREQUENCY AND QUALITY OF PORTRAYALS OF MINORITIES IN FICTIONAL ENTERTAINMENT TELEVISION PROGRAMS: SOME CHANGES IN IMAGERY?

Mastro and Robinson studied the frequency and quality of television portrayals by ethnic minorities in the United States from fictional programming featured on ABC, CBS, Fox, and NBC.[35] They found that while other ethnic minorities were near exclusion in major roles, African Americans appeared to have found their niche in sitcoms and crime shows. Over half of the African Americans represented on television were in major roles. However, compared to white and Latino characters, African Americans were the most negatively portrayed. Consistent with past findings, Mastro and Robinson found that minorities in general are overrepresented in depictions as officers and underrepresented in their depictions as criminals.[36] Replications have also revealed similar findings: Another study found that African Americans comprised 10 percent of the criminal portrayals on prime-time television.[37] That is five times lower than real-world figures.

FREQUENCY AND QUALITY OF PORTRAYALS OF MINORITIES IN NEWS TELEVISION PROGRAMS

These stereotypical portrayals are not limited to fictional television programming. Perhaps it is the reinforcement of stereotypes depicted on reality programming, such as local and national news programming, that is more harmful to the perception of African Americans. Crime stories in the news may influence how people perceive order and justice in society.[38] And if news programming depicts people of color as mostly perpetrators of crime, then some viewers may conclude that people of color are evildoers who need to be controlled.[39] Concomitantly, Entman's study of local television news programming in Chicago found that the local news contributes to "modern racism."[40] In crime reports of both violent and nonviolent offenses and every case where there was a difference in how African Americans and whites were portrayed, the stories appeared more likely to stimulate negative emotions toward African Americans. Similar to the Mastro and Robinson study, Entman found that African Americans were much more likely to be shown in the grip of a restraining officer than whites, reinforcing the idea that African Americans are more threatening than whites.

Gilliam and Iyengar argue that minorities, African Americans in particular, are more likely to be shown as suspects of crimes in the local news due to the almost exclusive coverage of violent crimes.[41] The researchers studied over three thousand crime stories that aired in the Los Angeles market. They found that most crime stories were violent and there was a reference made to the racial ethnicity of the suspects. When nonviolent crime stories are aired, the suspect is most typically white. They argue that crime stories are told as narrative scripts. A script is defined as a consistent sequence of events expected from the observer of the script. Since scripts have predictable roles and scenarios, people are able to fill in versions of scripts they are familiar with. The researchers believe viewers of local television news "fill in the blanks" of the crime script.

The crime script is typically violent and episodic with a focus on discrete events rather than collective outcomes[42] and also requires a prime suspect. What viewers typically learn about prime suspects is limited to visual attributes, especially the race or ethnicity of the individual. The research also uncovered the impact that the racial element in the crime script has on the perceptions of white viewers. White viewers who viewed five seconds of an African American perpetrator in crime news stories had small increases in the belief that their criminality could be attributed to individual failings. They tended to support punitive crime policies and believed African Americans were not in sync with mainstream culture. The opposite effect was found in African Americans who viewed the crime news stories. Although race was discovered to be a visual cue in eliciting negative perceptions of African Americans by whites, the effects of race are quite modest when compared to years of socialization and numerous other visual cues not controlled in the study.[43]

It could be that structural limitations may help explain the overrepresentation of African Americans as "blue-collar" or "street" criminals. It is easier, for example, to identify perpetrators of blue-collar crimes than white-collar crimes.[44] Second, the television news format usually encourages an emphasis on what is visual and dramatic.[45] Unfortunately, the emphasis on reporting so-called blue-collar crime is more likely to draw attention to African American perpetrators, given that a sizeable number of African Americans often do not have the resources, nor the opportunities to commit white-collar crimes. We believe that the focus on blue-collar crime is the result of the purposeful exaggeration of blue-collar crimes committed by African Americans, relative to the white-collar crimes committed by whites.

THE IMPACT OF STEREOTYPICAL PORTRAYALS OF AFRICAN AMERICANS

The unfortunate consequence of negative portrayals of African Americans is that it could lead to the aforementioned cultivation effect where individuals may believe what is seen on television is reality.[46] It could also lead to a social cognitive paradigm where news images could affect viewer perceptions by reinforcing a cognitive association with a particular racial/ethnic group and a particular role. The stored cognitive information may be primed with each stereotypical portrayal. The point here is that if African Americans are commonly depicted as criminals rather than as victims, this could affect decision makers who base their judgments about race-related policies upon their racial perceptions.[47] As noted in Gilliam and Iyengar's study, for example, whites who perceived African Americans as perpetrators based on news stories tended to support punitive crime policies and believed African Americans were not in sync with mainstream culture.

Indeed, news programs that negatively portray African Americans may influence viewers' beliefs. Gorham, for example, found that people who frequently consumed a large amount of television news, television in general, and read the newspaper were more likely to exhibit linguistic intergroup bias (LIB)—the use of different levels of abstract language to describe someone who belongs to an "in group" or "out group."[48] Here is the point, individuals with LIB were not necessarily conscious of their thought processes, nor was there an explicit measure of prejudice present in any of them. Essentially, race-related news stories primed dominant stereotypes about blacks, which influenced the interpretation of behavior and language process of the respondents.

The priming of stereotypes can cause viewers to misidentify suspects. In one study, respondents attributed the causes of crime with the characteristics of African American suspects as opposed to white suspects. This finding came after the respondents were asked to watch a fifteen-minute local news segment that included a crime story and mug short of the suspect.[49] Oliver also found that individuals were more likely to misidentify African Americans as suspects, even after seeing a white suspect arrested for murder.[50]

Dixon and Azocar examined the relationship between long-term news viewing and the stereotyping of African Americans.[51] There was evidence that showed that African Americans were overrepresented as lawbreakers in the news. The researchers concluded that the racialized crime news eventually leads viewers to perceive that crime is a serious problem that requires severe punishment for offenders. Similarly, there is evidence that television uses a script that associates African Americans with criminality. This was supported by the finding that heavy news viewers exposed to stories with unidentified suspects were more likely than heavy news viewers exposed to noncrime stories to have biased racial perceptions. Thus, more exposure to news stories leads to more exposure to the black crime script and the activation of the black criminal stereotype.

PORTRAYAL OF AFRICAN AMERICAN WOMEN IN THE MEDIA

The evidence shows that African Americans are portrayed negatively throughout the media. And priming stereotypes can cause an automatic association of negative, dangerous behavior with members of the African American community. Arguably, the negative associations may be applied automatically for more African American men than women. Certainly, there is a difference in the portrayals of African American men versus women. Generally, studies have found that women are not usually shown as violent predators who are forcibly detained by the police.[52]

Chesney-Lind and Eliason examined the recent increase of women as violent-crime perpetrators and the relationship to race.[53] They argue that the second wave of feminism contributed to the increase in women's crime, which prompted the media to showcase stories and images. By the 1990s, the news media began coverage of "bad girls," particularly those of color in gangs. Specifically, *Newsweek* often used ethnically coded names in addition to publishing images of African American girls wearing gang attire.[54] This motif in the media continued and by the end of the 1990s depictions of the "bad girl" morphed into depictions of the "violent girl." For instance, in movies and books there are media constructions of the sneaky, "mean" white girl, but they are usually positioned against the violently aggressive, masculinized Latina and African American girls.

Perhaps media portrayal of the violently aggressive female of color is justified. Chesney-Lind and Eliason contend that changes in policing and policies, such as zero-tolerance initiatives in schools, contributed to the surge in girls of color judicially processed and detained. For example, between 1992 and 2000 the number of detained African American girls increased by 90 percent and there was a 209 percent increase in the detention of Hispanic girls in San Francisco alone.[55] Chesney-Lind and Eliason believe that the increase in female criminality has created a backlash. Women who do not conform to gender roles prescribed by white males in society are most likely to experience the backlash in the criminal justice system. This is most significantly experienced by poor women of color. They argue that the media and the criminal justice system have complementary roles in controlling women. The media demonizes and masculinizes women who do not conform to stereotypical gender roles. And the argument goes that the criminal justice system is able to justify the processing of cases.[56]

THE PORTRAYAL OF AFRICAN AMERICAN WOMEN AS CRIMINALS AND VICTIMS

Generally, studies about the victimization of women indicate that women are blamed for their victimization in news coverage and a good girl/bad girl or virgin/whore dichotomy has been created.[57] News coverage of African American women victimized by violence is rare, unless the victimization is unusual or sensational.[58] African American feminist theorists contend that the sexual harassment, sexual assault, and violent victimization of African American women is not portrayed or viewed sympathetically due to the stereotypical view of African American women as promiscuous. Furthermore, within the African American community, males have been socialized to dominate as men by oppressing women.[59] When women of color accuse men of color of sexual assault, they are often not believed by their communities and are labeled traitors to their race.[60] Thus, their victimization is silenced while they rally around the men that abuse them.[61]

Meyers studied the news coverage of the victimization of African American women at the annual college spring break ritual known as Freaknik in Atlanta, Georgia, in the 1990s.[62] This study was designed to explore the intersection of race, class, and gender and its influence on the representation of African American women. Major findings revealed that the news coverage of violence against African American women blamed the women for their victimization and lessened the seriousness of the violence. Most commonly, these women were portrayed as oversexed jezebels whose lewd behavior provoked men to assault them. Men were largely either not believed to have attacked or raped the women or were unnamed in the assault and portrayed to have been enticed by the women's scantily clad dancing bodies. The news criminalized African American men for property crimes, but decriminalized them for abuse of African American women.

Similar to contributions of Meyers, Donovan studied the relationship between sexist and racist stereotypes of African American women and the rape blame attribution.[63] Donovan explored the racist stereotypes of the jezebel and the matriarch. African American women who are stereotyped as jezebels may be perceived as contributors to their victimization. The matriarch stereotype is the tough, strong, independent black woman who emasculates an African American man and takes over his role as head of the household. We should add that previous studies have found that the rape of whites is perceived as more serious than the rape of African Americans.[64]

To test the persistence of these stereotypes, Donovan surveyed over four hundred undergraduate students in New England. White male participants tended to view the African American victim as more promiscuous than the white victim when the perpetrator was white. When the perpetrator was African American, promiscuity of the victim was viewed similarly. This may be due to the jezebel stereotype of African American women. Also, more than half of the white female and male participants incorrectly chose white women as most likely to be victims of African American rapists. This further supported the myth of the African American rapist. In sum, racist and sexist stereotypes still exist in modern society. And if the victimization of African American women is not blamed on them, then it may be ignored by the media. Consider the following: The media has begun to question lack of coverage of minority women as victims. A May 2005 *Chicago Tribune* commentary, for example, entitled "Missing White Female Alert: Why Won't the Media Cover Missing Minority Women?" was written by Douglas MacKinnon, press secretary to former U.S. Senator Bob Dole. He wrote that the coverage of missing, attractive white women demeans the news media profession and slaps the faces of minority mothers and parents who search for their missing children with little help. He blamed the ugliness of the television ratings game for the underreporting of missing minority women, emphasizing that coverage of missing, attractive white women draws more viewers. Ironically, the same day as McKinnon's commentary was published, an editorial was written in the *Atlanta Journal-Constitution* also noting the tragic reality that missing minority women are unable to provoke interest or sympathy in the media.[65]

CONCLUSION

Taken together, while the experiences of blacks in the media have changed over time, stereotypes persist. And the media still manages to influence our values and perspectives toward other individuals, with African American images that remain negative. Last, despite the realities illustrated within this chapter, we believe that things will change when the focus of the media shifts from coverage of blue-collar crimes to corporate crimes, and when the media decides that it can have an audience without reconstructing racial biases and playing into the fears of Americans.

CRITICAL THINKING QUESTIONS

1. The subgrouping theory suggests that different positive portrayals work to weaken the support for negative stereotypes. Explain your thoughts about this perspective.
2. Discuss the role of stereotyping in the media. Why might it be important for the representation of minorities in the media to be proportionate to their representation in the country?
3. Is the media playing a "ratings game" when it comes to their coverage of "majority" women as missing persons and rape victims? If so, what does that suggest about American society and its values? What message does it send to women and girls of color?
4. Which is more influential in shaping beliefs and perpetuating stereotypes: fictional entertainment or reality-based programming, such as news broadcasts? Explain.

5. How does the demonizing and "masculinizing"of women by the media serve as a form of control?
6. Dixon and Azocar concluded that the racialized crime news eventually leads viewers to perceive that crime is a serious problem that requires severe punishment for offenders. What is the significance of the finding?

NOTES

1. Women of Color, *Media Report to Women* 33 (2005): 1–2.
2. D. E. Mastro and Bradley S. Greenberg, "The Portrayal of Racial Minorities on Prime Time Television," *Journal of Broadcasting & Electronic Media* 44 (2000): 690–703.
3. Ibid.
4. Ibid.
5. Ibid.
6. Ibid.
7. Ibid.
8. Ibid.
9. Ibid.
10. Ibid.
11. Bradley S. Greenberg, and Tracy R. Worrell, "New Faces on Television: A 12-Season Replication," *The Howard Journal of Communications* 18 (2007): 277–290.
12. D. E. Mastro and Amanda L. Robinson, "Cops and Crooks Images of Minorities on Primetime Television," *Journal of Criminal Justice* 28 (2000): 385–396.
13. Greenberg and Worrell, "New Faces on Television."
14. Thomas H. Stevenson, "A Six-Decade Study of the Portrayal of African Americans in Business Print Media: Trailing, Mirroring, or Shaping Social Change," *Journal of Current Issues and Research in Advertising* 29 (2007): 1–14.
15. Ibid.
16. Ibid.
17. Ibid.
18. D. E. Mastro and S. R. Stern. "Representation of Race in Television Commercials: A Content Analysis of Prime Time Advertising," *Journal of Broadcasting and Electronic Media* 47 (2003): 638–647.
19. Greenberg and Worrell, "New Faces on Television."
20. Mastro and Robinson, "Cops and Crooks Images."
21. Ibid.
22. H. Bang and Bonnie B. Reece, "Minorities in Children's Television Commercials: New, Improved, and Stereotyped," *Journal of Consumer Affairs* 37 (2003): 42–67.
23. S. Coltrane and Melinda Messineo, "The Perpetuation of Subtle Prejudice: Race and Gender Imagery in 1990s Television Advertising," *Sex Roles* 42 (2000): 363–389.
24. Bang and Reece, "Minorities in Children's Television Commercials."
25. Ibid.
26. Ibid.
27. Charles Taylor and Barbara Stern. "Asian Americans: Television Advertising and the 'Model Minority' Stereotype." *Journal of Advertising* 26 (Summer, 1997): 47–61.
28. Ibid.
29. Ibid.
30. J. J. Henderson and Gerald J. Baldasty, "Race, Advertising, and Prime-Time Television." *Howard Journal of Communication,* 14 (2003): 97–112.

31. Ibid.

32. Ibid.

33. J. J. Covert and Travis L. Dixon, "A Changing View: Representation and Effects of the Portrayal of Women of Color in Mainstream Women's Magazines," *Communication Research* 35 (2008): 232–256.

34. Ibid.

35. Mastro and Robinson, "Cops and Crooks Images."

36. Ibid.

37. Mastro and Robinson, "Cops and Crooks Images."

38. T. L. Dixon and Daniel Linz, "Overrepresentation and Underrepresentation of African Americans and Latinos as Lawbreakers on Television News," *Journal of Communication* 50 (2000a): 131–154.

39. Ibid.

40. Robert M. Entman, "Blacks in the News: Television, Modern Racism and Cultural Change," *Journalism Quarterly* 69 (1992): 341–361.

41. F. D. Gilliam Jr. and Shanto Iyengar, "Prime Suspects: The Influence of Local Television News on the Viewing Public," *American Journal of Political Science* 44 (2000): 560–373.

42. Ibid.

43. Ibid.

44. Ibid.

45. Ibid.

46. Mastro and Robinson, "Cops and Crooks Images."

47. Travis L. Dixon, "Crime News and Racialized Beliefs: Understanding the Relationship between Local News Viewing and Perceptions of African Americans and Crime," *Journal of Communication* 58 (2008): 106–125.

48. Bradley W. Gorham, "News Media's Relationship with Stereotyping: The Linguistic Intergroup Bias in Response to Crime News," *Journal of Communication* 56 (2006): 289–308.

49. Gorham, "News Media's Relationship with Stereotyping."

50. M. B. Oliver and Dana Fonash, "Race and Crime in the News: Whites' Identification and Misidentification of Violent and Nonviolent Criminal Suspects," *Media Psychology* 4 (2002): 137–156.

51. T. L. Dixon and Cristina L. Azocar, "Priming Crime and Activating Blackness: Understanding the Psychological Impact of the Overrepresentation of Blacks as Lawbreakers on Television News," *Journal of Communication* 57 (2007): 229–253.

52. Marian Meyers, "African America Women and Violence: Gender, Race, and Class in the News," *Critical Studies in Media Communication* 21 (2004a): 95–118.

53. M. Chesney-Lind and Michele Eliason, "From Invisible to Incorrigible: The Demonization of Marginalized Women and Girls," *Crime Media Culture* 2 (2006): 29–47.

54. Ibid.

55. Ibid.

56. Ibid.

57. Meyers, "African America Women and Violence."

58. Ibid.

59. Ibid.

60. Ibid.

61. Ibid.

62. Ibid.

63. Roxanne A. Donovan, "To Blame or Not to Blame: Influences of Target Race and Observer Sex on Rape Blame Attribution," *Journal of Interpersonal Violence* 22 (2007): 722–736.

64. Ibid.

65. Women of Color, *Media Report to Women* 33 (2005): 1–2.

PART III

The Social Construction of Crime

The Missing White Women Syndrome: Why Missing Women of Color Are Easy for the Media to Ignore

Stephanie A. Jirard, J.D.*

She was so pretty. Sparkling eyes, thick hair, and a coquettish smile that only girls who are fast becoming women can wear well. Her photograph caught and held attention. From Modesto, California, Chandra Levy was a 24-year-old intern at her local congressman's office in Washington, D.C. Chandra disappeared while jogging on May 1, 2001, and until fragments of her body were discovered one year later in Washington's Rock Creek Park, the nation witnessed the growing media obsession with females who were white, and missing or dead, especially those who may have been victims of sexual foul play. After she disappeared, the nation learned that the married congressman, Gary Condit, had taken his intern as his young lover. During the summer of 2001, Chandra's disappearance generated 739 stories in print, which was more news coverage than the contentious G-8 summit of world leaders in Italy and the stem-cell debate that raged in Congress.[1] The national media's selective coverage of pretty, young white kidnapping, sexual assault, and murder victims to the exclusion of girls and women of color who have met the same fate has been coined the "missing white women syndrome."[2] The media saturation that defines the

* I am grateful for the assistance of my good friend and valued colleague, Professor Donna C. Hale of Shippensburg University, in the preparation of this chapter.

syndrome that began with Levy's disappearance continues today. In July 2008 the *Washington Post* ran a twelve-part series on Chandra's unsolved murder, a series the breadth of which the paper has not devoted to an unsolved murder of a woman of color.

This chapter examines the media whirl that catapults missing white females into the national spotlight and turns them into household names overnight— among them, Laci (Peterson), Natalee (Holloway), and Elizabeth (Smart)— while missing females of color—such as Stepha (Henry), Tamika (Huston) and LaToyia (Figueroa)—go largely unnoticed. The keystones that support the syndrome are the rise of *infotainment* (a term meaning the marriage of news and entertainment), the media-generated fear of crime represented by tabloid television shows such as Fox Television's *COPS* and *America's Most Wanted*, and the perpetually elevated status of the white victim in the criminal justice system. The cultural narrative of the missing white woman goes beyond media hype; the syndrome spurs lawmakers to honor the white sexual assault or murder victim by enacting a number of laws in their names that punish offenders severely. On July 27, 2006, President George W. Bush signed into law the *Adam Walsh Protection and Safety Act* that imposed a mandatory minimum sentence of thirty years for child rape and established a national sex offender registry. Congress states on the law's face the purpose for its enactment is "in response to the vicious attacks by violent predators against the victims listed below" and names seventeen sexual assault and kidnapping victims (thirteen were murdered), including eleven girls under the age of sixteen, four women and two boys: Every single named victim is white.[3] It is no surprise, then, that if America's federal government cannot list at least one man, woman, or child of color on behalf of enacting strong laws against sexual predators and killers that the media, as a reflection of society's values, ignores those missing women and girls.

WHITE NEWS

> Whiteness is not only an identity, but the power to name and shape identities. Whiteness not only has control of valuable resources, but has the ability to limit access to those resources to those who reflect its own image. Whiteness not only constitutes a distinct perspective on events, but has the authority to generate definitive cultural narratives.[4]

When a white woman or girl goes missing, embedded within the media frenzy is the dual social construct that white life in America is important and colored life in America is valueless. Since America imported her first slaves, race has been about power and the power to control the media lies with the dominant culture. A few corporations define what news gets covered by owning and controlling mass media outlets. Time Warner owns Cable News Network (CNN), and the cable entertainment station Home Box Office (HBO). It publishes 120 magazines, including *Time*, the black-female magazine *Essence*, and the celebrity magazines *People* and *Entertainment Weekly*. It also co-owns with MSNBC the real-life courtroom drama station and website *Court TV,* and with America Online (AOL) the black-themed Internet site BlackVoices. Rupert Murdoch's News Corporation owns MySpace, Fox News, Fox Television, the *New York Post,* and the Twentieth Century Fox movie company. The Disney Corporation owns American Broadcasting Network (ABC) News, the tabloid shows *PrimeTime Live, Nightline, 20/20, Good Morning America,* and the *Lifetime* Channel.[5] When news coverage comes to missing, kidnapped, or dead victims, no one is more important than a white woman or girl.

America has long been segregated. People of color have been denied equal opportunity for so long that many live at or below the poverty line. According to the U.S. Bureau of the Census Report on Poverty in 2004, 24.7 percent of blacks (including those not African American) and 21.9 percent of Hispanics were poor, while only 8.6 percent of whites fit the category.[6] People of color are overrepresented on the poverty table because easy access to professional life—medicine, law, business—has been available for only the past thirty years. Journalism remains the bastion of white influence; from 2001–2005, seven hundred minority journalists joined newsrooms and newspapers across America, but only thirty-four were African American, the rest were Hispanic, Asian or another minority.[7] Where white images dominate news, media, and entertainment, whites are seen as individuals and are less vulnerable to stereotypes, unlike darker people, who tend to get lumped together in one negative stereotype.[8] Many poor people of color live in the dense inner city, culturally isolated from mainstream America, which means as Fahizah Alim reports, that when women or girls of color go missing, "the assumption is that there must be some pathology involved."[9] If the cultural narrative of the media is that white newsrooms cover the news that is important to them, the nature of crime news as entertainment is a value shared by everyone.

Crime stories as news have a life of their own, especially salacious stories about sex and murder. News reports about the latest development in high-profile criminal cases keep the public interested in the news source. America's appetite for sensational news has at its core "its appeal to the emotions."[10] The early nineteenth-century crime beat focused on graphic news peppered with damnation rhetoric about the criminal's soul. When millions of new immigrants "whose only literature was the family story paper or the cheap novel" arrived in America's cities, newspapers moved toward news storytelling with illustrations to entice new readers.[11] With the rise of storytelling journalism is a parallel emergence of American celebrity. From 1890–1930 and beyond, newspaper reports about high society were designed to humanize the prominent, which "not only encouraged the public to identify with the successful and well-to-do, obscuring the fault lines of class," but made the famous accessible.[12] The mixture of sensational crime as prominent news and imagined access to the rich created the first national media frenzy over a missing and then dead white child, the kidnapping of Charles A. Lindbergh Jr.

The aviator Charles Lindbergh was the hero of his day. Flying solo from New York to France in his plane, the *Spirit of St. Louis,* in 1927 he became a national icon of courage, power, and megacelebrity. When in 1932 his first-born son was kidnapped for ransom from his crib, the story transfixed America. Few things for parents are more frightening than the kidnapping of a child and such news stories invoke the uncertainty and tragedy of everyday life; if it could happen to Lucky Lindy, it could happen to anyone. Millions of extra newspapers were published to cover the latest development in the search for baby Lindbergh, for the first time radio saturated the airwaves for twenty-four hours to satisfy the demand for kidnapping-related news, and the few televisions in existence kept vigil night and day with a continuous beam of the baby's photograph.[13] By 1936 when Bruno Hauptmann was executed for murdering junior Lindbergh, America had suffered a rash of ransom kidnappings. Most victims were upper-class businessmen, their sons, and daughters. This had two consequences still relevant today: one was media exploitation of murdered children, as with the baby Lindbergh story "with its reams of publicity and its association with fame, the crime of kidnapping would be infused with the glamour of association,"[14] and the second was that the moneyed status of the victims influenced passing laws aimed at protecting rich whites to the fullest extent possible.[15] But today's legal protection in the name of missing white women accrued from the cultural shifts in news reporting and use of women in advertising from the 1960s to the 1990s.

Once television was established as a household device, the three major networks that presented nightly news were ABC, the Central Broadcasting Network (CBS), and the National Broadcasting Network (NBC). In the 1960s, newscasts expanded from fifteen to thirty minutes and filled the extra time with movie clips and other visual stimuli.[16] Longer newscasts allowed viewers to grow fond of specific news anchors, such as Walter Cronkite on CBS, which increased the competitive market for advertising rates. The way women were represented visually in mainstream media changed, too. Women were portrayed as alluring, desirable, and sexy, a freedom unleashed by the social upheaval of the civil rights and burgeoning women's rights movements. Advertisers began to sell sex and sex "never fails as an attention-getter, and advertisers like to bet on a sure thing. By showing flesh, advertisers work on the deepest, most coercive human emotions of all."[17] The growing erotica in advertising combined with the increased visual presentations in the nightly news intertwined news and entertainment. As advertised, the sexually free woman, the pure woman, was a white woman. Women of color depicted in advertisements then, and today, are portrayed as exotic, predatory, and are used to sell socially undesirable products such as alcohol, cigarettes, and plus-size pantyhose.[18] Even in magazines devoted to a black female audience, the white beauty standard applies:

> In ethnic magazines women are exhorted to change their appearance by straightening or texturing their apparently unruly hair, lightening or covering up their skin, and generally conforming to the flawless appearance of models. It is positive that magazine ads feature more Afrocentric-looking models but there are vestiges of perhaps a realistic reminder that white females continue to epitomize what society deems to be beautiful.[19]

Beauty worthy of media attention is "all the more unattainable for women of color"[20] and reinforces the woman of color's low status in society. As the value of the black woman increases with how light she can get her skin or how straight she can get her curly hair, stories of missing women of color attract attention precisely because such stories are ignored. Take for example the disparate media coverage of pregnant women gone missing, white Laci Peterson, black–Hispanic LaToyia Figueroa, and Hispanic Evelyn Hernandez. By far, the close to five hundred news stories, the made-for-television movie, the $500,000 dollars in reward money raised for information about her whereabouts, the books, and the subject of many covers of tabloid glossy magazines, the media's supernova focus on Laci Peterson's disappearance and murder dwarfed the coverage of the same stories for Figueroa and Hernandez. Most stories of missing white women have, according to Sheila Brown, author of *Crime and Law in Media Culture,* all the subplots of a good fiction crime novel—the youth, the innocence, and the unanswered questions—all of which make for a perfect media story. Pretty, energetic, outgoing, and expecting her first son whom she planned to name Conner, Laci was a twenty-seven-year-old college graduate, future stay-at-home mom allegedly happily married to a financially secure fertilizer salesman. Laci's disappearance also had independent newsworthy subplots: She went missing on Christmas Eve while her husband was "fishing" in the San Francisco Bay; her husband Scott immediately acted suspiciously; and the public quickly learned that Scott was having an affair with a massage therapist. Undeniably, a big factor in the extensive media coverage of Laci's disappearance was her universal appeal to the American public. When Kelly St. John wrote an article about Laci and interviewed people in her shared hometown with Chandra Levy of Modesto, California, people remarked that Laci appeared from her missing person photographs "like a warm, beautiful daughter. You see nothing but a big smile."[21] A man said, "She was a happy-go-lucky lady. In a way I feel like I wish I would have known her." In an article John Johnson and Christine Hanley wrote about Laci, women interviewed found religious significance in her disappearance on Christmas and discovery of her body near Easter; one woman said, "She definitely had to be an angel."[22]

In contrast, missing women of color rarely have subplots worthy of attractive fiction. No community members referred to Figueroa and Hernandez as angels or spoke about identifying with them as family members by virtue of seeing their faces. Both women had messy lives. At the time they went missing, they were mothers of children to whom they gave birth as teenagers and were pregnant by men to whom they were not married. They had no real education and worked odd jobs. Hernandez was a legal immigrant from El Salvador who went missing in May 2002 with her five-year-old son Alex. When her torso washed up on shore in San Francisco Bay in July 2002, the same Bay where Laci's torso would wash ashore in April 2003, there was no national spotlight. In contrast to the hundreds of local new stories about Peterson, the *San Francisco Chronicle* had written just five stories about Hernandez over the eleven months from the time she went missing in May 2002 to April 2003, when she became known as the "other body in the bay." Alex has never been found.

Figueroa was discovered missing when she failed to pick up her seven-year-old daughter from a Philadelphia daycare, but it took a few days for someone to report her missing. As the days stretched to weeks with no media coverage of her disappearance, the community complained about the lack of Petersonlike coverage. How can communities of color generate interest when there is none? Rather than admit the inherent bias in news reporting exclusively on white female victims who go missing, news executives deflect charges of unmitigated racism by focusing on the universal appeal of the type of story represented by the disappearances. Television morning show *Good Morning America* executive Shelley Ross incredulously explained, as reported by Peter Johnson, that the excessive media interest in missing females was the result of a renewed post 9/11 community spirit as "all Americans have become citizen deputies. We care about our neighbors more."[23] Executives also absolve their responsibility in deciding which stories to cover and which ones appeal to viewers by pointing to a white victim's family's public relations' savvy in generating and holding the media spotlight on their missing girls and women. As reported in *The Sacramento Bee*, Paula Skuratowicz, executive director of the Polly Klaas Foundation said in 1995, "The [minority] community needs to learn how to generate that kind of interest."[24] And such public interest pays off, as fourteen-year-old Elizabeth Smart, kidnapped from her upper-middle-class bedroom in Salt Lake City on June 5, 2002, was found in March 2003 after her captor, Brian Mitchell, was spotted walking down the street with two women, one of whom turned out to be Smart. Two alert people who recognized Mitchell from the intense media coverage of Smart's disappearance notified police.

Do black communities in particular contribute to their own alienation from mass media? If the urban poor communicate with mainstream culture through music, videos and movies, do minority communities telegraph a misogynistic view of women and girls through rap? Rap lyrics are notorious for referring to women as whores, female dogs who are "scheming, vain, whining mercenaries whose goal is to deprive black men of their self-esteem, money and possessions."[25] The message then from people of color about their own women is that they are only good for sex, can take care of themselves, and need to be treated violently, as rapper Snoop Dogg sings "a b***h is just a b***h." Scholars resist blaming communities of color for their own marginalization and look instead to the reasons for their anemic response to missing females in the crushing weight of high crime, high unemployment, and high poverty rates.[26]

The minority-focused media outlets are little better at highlighting the stories of their own missing women. Specifically, the blog "Black and Missing But Not Forgotten"[27] was started as a direct result of the lack of mainstream media coverage. Powerful minority media is owned and controlled by white media. The first black-owned cable network, Black Entertainment Television (BET), is now owned by Viacom and Time Warner owns *Essence* magazine. *Essence* did in 2005 write one story about the gross disparity in the detail and sheer number of media stories between white and minority missing women at the urging of Tamika Huston, the aunt of a twenty-four-year-old woman who disappeared in Spartanburg, South Carolina. The article features Huston and six other missing women of color who as a whole lived far from the middle-class lifestyle mainstream media represents.[28] The missing women ranged in ages from nineteen to forty. At the time they went missing, none were married, only two were not pregnant or had no children, and at least two of the women had at least five children. One of the missing girls featured, Kineasha Pam Linkhorne, would not know where to find her family even if she did make it back; the family had moved away and left no forwarding address. African American women who have middle-class backgrounds are no more marketable to the media; stories about their disappearances never reach national dissemination. In May 2007 Stepha Henry, a twenty-two-year-old John Jay College of Criminal Justice honors graduate with law school plans, went missing from a date while visiting family in Florida. Like Hernandez and Figueroa before her, Henry received national attention for the lack of coverage her disappearance generated. As with the white standard of beauty, the woman or girl of color is valued only as she relates to the dominant culture. Henry's body was never found, but Kendrick Williams has been arrested for her murder. Tamika Huston's body was found one year after she disappeared, and her boyfriend was convicted of first-degree murder.

WHITE FEAR

"Your continual focus on and reporting of, missing, young, attractive white women not only demeans your profession but is a televised slap in the face to minority mothers and parents the nation over who search for their own missing children with little or no assistance or notice from anyone."
—Douglas MacKinnon, former Press Secretary to Senator Robert Dole[29]

According to U.S. Department of Justice statistics, the majority of juveniles under the age of eighteen who go missing are runaways or snatched by a noncustodial parent. The smallest numbers of children who go missing are abducted by strangers, but that number has the most likelihood of being sexually molested and murdered.[30] But fear as a media marketing tool is big business because fear "is what makes victimization meaningful and plausible to audiences" and news is not above "showing programming that attracts ratings by exploiting people's vulnerabilities."[31]

As broadcast deregulation shook the industry in the 1980s and allowed for the proliferation of many new stations, the conditions were perfect for the advent of tabloid television and its sleaze appeal to attract new audiences. Tabloids are often associated with wild stories. In the late 1970s and 1980s, the tabloids, those magazines filled with stories of Elvis Presley sightings long after his death in 1977, pregnant aliens, and man-eating hogs, gained a wide audience. Tabloids became a breathing link with crime victims who, like celebrities, became household names by the constant media coverage of their tragedy. "The hunger for dirt and the thirst for scandal that fueled the tabs' immense popularity in the 1970s and 1980s had spread like a virus through every level of "serious" journalism."[32] When millionaire-turned-media-mogul Ted Turner launched the first twenty-four-hour all-news cable station in 1980, CNN, and by the time Rupert Murdoch launched Fox Broadcasting in the late 1980s to, as one commentator noted, "make Fox into America's tabloid network," the public was ready for the continuous mix of news, sex and crime.[33]

As the number of television stations increased so, too, did the demand for shows, specifically shows that could be packaged, sold, and re-run over and over in syndication. At a time in the late 1980s and early 1990s when the crime rate in America was in decline, the increased prominence of tabloid television made reality-based shows easy and cheap to produce. John Walsh was catapulted to national prominence when his six-year-old son, Adam, was abducted from a Florida mall and found murdered weeks later. Frustrated by the unavailability of a cohesive law enforcement effort to track and find missing children, Walsh started the National Center for Exploited or Missing Children and became the host of the Fox Network's *America's Most Wanted*. Missing kids were a great tie-in for tabloid television and served to keep the public glued with stories of good guys getting hurt by bad guys who might get caught as a result of the show. In the media, images of missing children became touchstones for fear in American culture, which was exacerbated by the constant media presence of cable news.[34]

The nature of cable subscriptions with access to the three primary cable news channels, Fox News, MSNBC, and CNN, saturated the market quickly. On regular television, news is covered, packaged, and edited for the nightly broadcast—an expensive and time-consuming method of delivery. To save money, cable news moved away from the packaged format to "live" interviews with newsworthy people.[35] While the talking-head format was more off-the-cuff, news anchors were forced to fill the 24-hour news cycle and by 2005, the format for constant cable news was set. Station managers decide which one or two stories to cover throughout the day and then run those stories over and over. Constant reference to "breaking news" or "updates" are many times nothing more than a repeat of earlier information. As *The Annual Report on American Journalism* reported in its 2005 State of the News Media Review, "60 percent of all stories aired on cable through the day are simple repetition of the same information. Just one in three stories in the course of a cable day is new, or something not aired earlier."[36] Evidence of the repetitive-with-nothing-new-to-report format was in the cable news coverage of beautiful, blond, and blue-eyed Alabama teenager Natalee Holloway. Natalee Holloway disappeared on May 30, 2005, while on a high-school trip in Aruba. All news stations flocked to Aruba and her telegenic family and friends made every effort to secure the media and legal resources to find Natalee. In the 2005–2006 news cycle on cable news alone, Fox News had presented 434 stories, CNN had reported 75 stories, and MSNBC (owned jointly by NBC and Microsoft), had aired 103 stories on Natalee,[37] and her story graced at least nine *People* magazine covers. No girl or woman of color could compete in her disappearance and death.

In the process of the press scares with tales of the maniacal sex fiend who kills children in the home the day after Christmas, such as Colorado's first-grader beauty queen Jon Benét Ramsey, or abducts them on the street in broad daylight, such as five-year-old Samantha Runnion who was playing with her friends in her California front yard, American television viewers become also indulgent voyeurs by watching reality television, a different type of information and entertainment. A study of the gratification about why people watch reality television found that "the mode of engagement with reality television was rather passive, and designed to fill time when no other activities are available."[38] The interest and needs satisfied by reality television are voyeurism, judgment of others, social comparison, and especially in crime-based reality shows, heightened emotions including disgust, anger, and sadness.[39]

The media plays a vital role in shaping public opinion on how women are viewed as victims of murder, rape, assault, and other crimes of personal violence in society. By mixing the fear of kidnapping with advertising to sell goods, for example, the ubiquitous photographs of missing children on the side of milk cartons or in advertising inserts, increase society's anxiety of its missing children but do not provide the "means to defeat the enemy who seem(s) everywhere."[40] People who watch more news about crime believe they live in a more dangerous world than those who do not watch a steady diet of crime news. The need to protect women and children from the unseen enemy heavy in all missing white women stories is the metaphor for social control in the form of draconian sentencing schemes for those who wish to prey upon such victims.

THE WHITE VICTIMS

> "You could abort every black baby in this country,
> and your crime rate would go down."
> —William Bennett, former Secretary of Education[41]

Secretary Bennett claimed his words were taken out of context because he did say it would be morally reprehensible to abort black babies. Citing the work of University of Chicago economists Steven Leavitt and Stephen Dubner in their wildly popular book, *Freakonomics*, all Bennett was trying to say, he insisted, was that abortion reduces the crime rate: It was his cultural interpretation of crime rates that blacks commit more crimes than whites. Despite media representations on the nightly news or crime shows where blacks are underrepresented as crime victims, black people are far more likely to be victims of violent crimes than whites. When black people are crime victims, they have less value than a white victim in the eyes of the media.[42] It is well documented that the government is three times more likely to seek the death penalty for a white, and not a black, murder victim, regardless of the killer's color.[43] A 1996 study of Kentucky's death row revealed everyone was there for murdering a white person, even though since 1976 over 1,000 blacks had been murdered.[44] The federal government released a report on the death penalty and race and found:

> In 82 percent of the studies, race of the victim was found to influence the likelihood of being charged with capital murder or receiving a death sentence, i.e., those who murdered whites were found to be more likely to be sentenced to death than those who murdered blacks. This finding was remarkably consistent across data sets, states, data collection methods, and analytical techniques.[45]

If the murder victim is a white female, death may be sought as punishment because "white females may be perceived as the group most in need of protection from violence and least likely to be responsible for their victimization."[46] The decision to commit state money to a death-penalty prosecution, from expensive jury selection and sequestration throughout the trial, to paying for expert witnesses for both the defense and prosecution, to the expensive appeals process that will last maybe for decades to relitigate the case if the appellate court finds a mistake and sends the case back for a new trial (sometimes more than once), are all resources dedicated to avenging the white victim. The same racial corollary holds true for state resources used to vindicate white rape victims. When black women were slaves, they could not legally be raped.[47] Today the devaluing of the black sexual assault victim continues as "black women are less likely to have their cases prosecuted and perpetrators of sexual assaults on black women will more likely escape punishment."[48] The justice system's devaluing victims of color logically extends to the laws enacted in the name of, and on behalf of, the missing white women and girls.

The 1990s witnessed the enactment of a host of state and federal laws to protect victims as embodied by the kidnapping, rape, and murder of three young white girls, Polly Klaas, Megan Kanka, and Amber Hagerman. Polly Klaas, the white twelve-year-old abducted in 1993 from her bed in California, reportedly spurred the state to enact its "three strikes" law "to ensure longer prison sentences and greater punishment" for repeat offenders.[49] Megan Kanka, the white seven-year-old from New Jersey murdered in 1994 by a neighborhood sex offender, has an eponymous series of federal and state laws collectively known as "Megan's Laws" that require police registration of sex offenders and notification of the communities in which they live.[50] An Amber Alert, electronic notification on television and highway signs when a child is reported missing, was named for Texan Amber Hagerman, a nine-year-old kidnapping victim raped and murdered in 1996.[51]

Missing college women are well represented in the number of laws in their name. The *Kristin Smart Campus Safety Act* (1988) requires sharing of information about missing students between campuses and local law enforcement. The beautiful white college girls who went missing in the 1990s and have never been found had their law enacted, the *Jennifer Kesse–Tiffany Sessions Missing Persons Act* (2008), which expands the class of people who can report people missing and collects family DNA if the person is not found in ninety days.[52] Clicking on the U.S. Department of Justice's homepage leads to the "Dru Sjodin National Sex Offender Public Website," named after the blond, blue-eyed, twenty-two-year-old North Dakota college student who in 2003 was raped and murdered by a repeat sex offender.

Even when women of color are clearly the victim demographic, as in women who are pregnant and killed or murdered within one year after giving birth, the laws are enacted in the name of white victims. The *American Journal of Public Health* reported that from 1991 to 1999 "homicide ratios were about seven times higher among black women than for white women" even when every characteristic such as age, income, and access to medical care was examined.[53] The laws enacted to punish those who kill pregnant women and their babies are the federal *Laci and Conner's (Peterson) Law* (2004) and *Lori's Law* (2005), a Utah law that raised the minimum sentence for murder from five to fifteen years and that was named for pregnant Lori Hacking killed in 2004 by her husband.[54]

There is no sign that the missing white women syndrome will abate anytime soon. As of late July 2007, the federal government continued to direct its attention and resources to validating the elevated status of the white female crime victim, even if she was not American, and did not disappear on American soil. The U. S. Attorney General Alberto Gonzales, the chief law enforcement officer of the country, held on July 22, 2007, a private meeting with British citizen Gerry McCann. In May 2007, the McCanns had left their three-year-old-daughter, Madeleine, in a Portugal hotel room with infant twins to eat in a nearby restaurant. There was a global search for the child, who remains missing. The handheld video is grainy, but as Gerry McCann shakes Gonzales's hand for photographs, Gonzales manages a meek smile and makes a verbal commitment of America's awesome power to help find the beautiful white toddler. In America on that day like so many other days, Gonzales and the rest of the federal government paid no homage to any missing girl or woman of color.

CONCLUSION

While analysis shows media coverage is overblown if the missing woman is white, in reality, the stories are repetitive given the new technology of 24-hour cable news programs and the emotional appeal of tabloid television shows. The excessive media coverage of missing white women treats their tragedies as entertainment, but the strength and power of the white victim in the criminal justice system mobilizes the public and legislators to enact laws in the missing women's names, thereby making the syndrome a legitimate expression of the heightened societal value of the white woman in American culture. From the time of the early newspapers that moved from a factual to a heavily-illustrated storytelling approach, people have been attracted to sensational crime stories. The Lindbergh baby kidnapping infused kidnapping crimes with a sense of glamorous drama that surrounded the rich and famous. When the 1960s ushered in a new era of sexual liberation, advertisers portrayed women as sexy and when news broadcasts expanded to include more advertising, the sexy white woman and news reporting appealed to the public, but the public appeal was limited to white women.

By the 1980s and 1990s when the television industry was deregulated, there were many new stations that had to attract a limited number of viewers. Programming decisions offered reality television programming with a crime focus, such as *COPS* and *America's Most Wanted,* and the 24-hour-news format on cable television, which creates the opportunity to replay through the news cycle, over and over, the relatively rare occurrences of stranger kidnapping, rape, and murder, although there is often no new news to report. Corporate media interests controlled by a few companies that can report on a story of a missing white woman in the news, or in a made-for-television movie, or put the story on the cover of a glossy tabloid that the company owns, lead to the saturation of the news market with stories of missing white females. Missing females of color are not attractive to mainstream media because their life stories rarely contain the middle-class story lines to which the viewing public can personally relate. The media appears justified in ignoring stories on missing women and girls of color because they are devalued—not only in how they are portrayed in the media through rap music or advertising, or how they are marginalized by being poor– –but even within the criminal justice system. Even when women of color are overrepresented as crime victims, such as in cases of pregnancy-related homicides or in sexual assault cases, perpetrators are prosecuted less and offenders receive less severe sentences. The marriage of the sexy white woman and the voyeuristic appeal of crime-focused, reality-based television, combined with the devaluation of the female crime victim of color, indicates the missing white woman syndrome is not going to end anytime soon.

CRITICAL THINKING QUESTIONS

1. Does the history of slavery have any impact on media portrayals of people of color as crime victims? Why or why not?
2. Name three concrete steps communities of color can do to increase awareness and visibility of their missing members.
3. Is media coverage merely a reflection of public interest or is it a spotlight on American culture which media highlights for society, especially when reporting about crime?

NOTES

1. "Missing Intern Mystery," *Media Monitor* 15, no. 4 (July/August 2001): 1–6.
2. The term "missing white women syndrome" has been credited to journalist Gwen Ifill and University of Maryland Professor Sheri Parks who openly criticized the excessive news coverage of prominent white kidnapping victims. Also disturbing, but not covered in this chapter, is the lack of media coverage of missing persons who are male, Hispanic, Asian, or African American, such as the young men

and boys who were the victims of black serial killer Wayne Williams.
3. The list of victims for whom 42 U.S.C.S. §16901 et seq. (2006) was enacted includes: Jacob Wetterling, Megan Kanka, Pam Lychner, Jetseta Gage, Dru Sjodin, Jessica Lunsford, Sarah Lunde, Amie Zyla, Christy Fornoff, Alexandra Zapp, Polly Klaas, Jimmy Ryce, Carlie Brucia, Amanda Brown, Elizabeth Smart, Molly Bish and Samantha Runnion.
4. Barbara J. Flagg, "Whiteness: Some Critical   Perspective: Forward:

Whiteness as Metaprivilege," *Washington University Journal of Law & Policy* 18 (2005): 1–8.

5. The information was compiled from the following sources: Time Warner businesses http://www.timewarner.com/corp/businesses/index.html; News Corporation corporate governance http://www.newscorp.com/corp_gov/index.html; Walt Disney corporate governance http://corporate.disney.go.com/corporate/overview.html.

6. Bureau of Census, *Income, Poverty*, 46.

7. American Society of Newspaper Editors, "News Staff Shrinking While Miniority Presence Grows," April 12, 2005, http://www.asne.org/index.cfm?ID=5648.

8. Leonard M. Baynes, "White Out: The Absence and Stereotyping of People of Color by the Broadcast Networks in Prime Time Entertainment Programming," *Arizona Law Review* 45 (Summer 2003): 303.

9. Fahizah Alim, *The Sacramento Bee*, June 28, 2005.

10. Joy Wiltenburg, "True Crime: The Origins of Modern Sensationalism," *American Historical Review* 109, no. 5 (December 2004): 1379.

11. Neal Gabler, *Life the Movie: How Entertainment Conquered Reality* (New York: Knopf, 1998), 65.

12. Charles L. Ponce de Leon, *Self Exposure: Human Interest Journalism and the Emergence of Celebrity in America 1890–1940* (Chapel Hill: University of North Carolina Press, 2002), 139.

13. Paula S. Fass, *Kidnapped: Child Abduction in America* (New York: Oxford University Press, 1997), 98.

14. Ibid.

15. Ernest Kahlar Alix, *Ransom Kidnapping in America/1874–1974: The Creation of a Capital Crime* (Carbondale and Edwardville: Southern Illinois University Press, 1978), 176.

16. Kevin Glynn, *Tabloid Culture: Trash Taste, Popular Power, and the Transformation of American Television* (Durham, NC: Duke University Press, 2000), 20.

17. Jack Solomon, *The Signs of Our Times: The Secret Meanings of Everyday Life* (New York: HarperCollins, 1990), 66.

18. Janis Sanchez-Hucles, Patrick S. Hudgins, and Kimberly Gamble, "Reflection and Distortion: Women of Color in Magazine Advertisements," in *Featuring Females: Feminist Analyses of Media*, ed. Ellen Cole and Jessica Henderson Daniel (Washington, D.C.: American Psychological Association, 2005) 194.

19. Ibid., 195.

20. Deborah L. Schooler, Monique Ward, Ann Merriwether, and Allison Caruthers, "Who's That Girl: Television's Role in the Body Image Development of Young White and Black Women," *Psychology of Women Quarterly* 28 (2004): 39.

21. Kelly St. John, "Eerily Similar Case Languishes in Obscurity," *San Francisco Chronicle*, April 21, 2003, http://www.sfgate.com/cgi-bin/article.cgi?file=/c/a/2003/04/21/MN275651.DTL.

22. John Johnson and Christine Hanley, "Appetite for Laci's Story Endures," *Los Angeles Times* May 07, 2003, http://article.latimes.com/2003/may/07/local/melaci7.

23. Peter Johnson, "Missing Women: Why the Hype?" *USA Today,* April 4, 2004, http://www.usatoday.com/life/columnist/mediamix/2004-04-04-mediamix_x.htm.

24. Paula Skuratowicz, *The Sacramento Bee,* June 28, 2005.

25. Douglas S. Massey and Nancy A. Denton, *American Apartheid: Segegation and the Making of the Underclass* (Cambridge, Massachusetts: Harvard University Press, 1993), 176.

26. Wendy Kliewer, Katie Adams Parrish, Kelli W. Taylor, Kate Jackson, Jean M. Walker, and Victoria A. Shivy, "Socialization of Coping with Community Violence: Influences of Caregiver Coaching, Modeling, and Family Context," *Child Development* 77 (May/June 2006): 607.

27. "Black and Missing and Not Forgotten," http://blackandmissing.blogspot.com/.

28. "Have You Seen Her?" http://www.essence.com/essence/.

29. Douglas MacKinnon, "Missing Female Alert," *Chicago Tribune,* May 8, 2005, www.chicagotribune.com.

30. David Finkelhor, Heather Hammer, and Andrea J. Sedlak, "Nonfamily Abducted Children: National Estimates and Characteristics," Office of Justice Programs, 2002: 7.

31. David L. Altheide, *Creating Fear: News and the Construction of Crisis* (New York: Aldine de Gruyter, 2002), 41.

32. Bill Sloan, *I Watched a Wild Hog Eat My baby: A Colorful History of Tabloids and Their Cultural Impact* (Amherst, NY: Prometheus Books, 2001), 209.

33. Kevin Glynn, *Tabloid Culture: Trash Taste, Popular Power, and the Transformation of American Green* (Durham, NC: Duke University Press, 2000), 27.

34. Paula S. Fass, *Children of a New World: Society, Culture, and Globalization* (New York: New York University Press, 2007), 154.

35. Andrew Tyndall, "State of the News Media 2004," Annual Report on American Journalism: Cable TV, 24, http://www/stateofthemedia.org/2004/.

36. http://www.stateofthenewsmedia.org/2005/cabletv_contentanlysis.asp.

37. Jeffrey J. Pokorak, "Rape as a Badge of Slavery: The Legal History of, and Remedies for, Prosecutorial Race-of-victim Charging Disparities," *Nevada Law Journal* 7 (Fall 2006): 4, n.7.

38. Zizi Papacharissi, and Andrew L. Mendelson, "An Exploratory Study of Reality Appeal: Uses and Gratifications of Reality TV Shows," *Journal of Broadcasting & Electronic Media* (June 2007): 365.

39. Robin L. Nabi, Carmen R. Stitt, Jeff Halford, and Keli L. Finnerty, "Emotional and Cognitive Predictors of the Enjoyment of Reality-Based and Fictional Television Programming: An Elaboration of the Uses and Gratifications Perspective," *Media Psychology* 8 (2006): 440.

40. Fass, *Kidnapped,* 237.

41. Bill Bennett's Morning in America broadcast on Salem Radio Network, 28 September 2005.

42. Travis L. Dixon, Cristina L. Azocar, and Michael Casas. "The Portrayal of Race and Crime on Television Network News," *Journal*

of Broadcasting & Electronic Media, December (2003): 504.

43. Richard Deiter, "The Death Penalty in Black and White: Who Lives, Who Dies, Who Decides," Death Penalty Information Center 2008, http://www.deathpenaltyinfo.org/.

44. Ibid.

45. *Death Penalty Sentencing: Research Indicates Pattern of Racial Disparities*, U.S. General Accounting Office, Washington, D.C.: U.S. Printing Office, 1990.

46. Marian R. Williams, Stephen Demuth, and Jefferson E. Holcomb, "Understanding the Influence of Victim Gender in Death Penalty Cases: The Importance of Victim Race, Sex-Related Victimization, and Jury Decision Making," *Criminology* 45 (2007): 872.

47. Pokorak, *Rape as a Badge of Slavery*, 8.

48. Ibid.

49. Cal. Penal Code Ann §667(b); *Ewing v. California*, 538 U.S. 11 (2001).

50. Violent Crime Control & Law Enforcement Act of 1994, 42 U.S.C. §13701.

51. Public Law 108–21, 117 Stat. 650 (2003).

52. Cal. Education Code §72330; Florida Stat. §937.021 (2008).

53. Jeani Chang, Cynthia J. Berg, Linda E. Saltzman, and Joy Herndon, "Homicide: A Leading Cause of Injury Deaths among Pregnant and Postpartum Women in the United States, 1991–1999," *American Journal of Public Health* 95, no. 3 (March 2005): 473.

54. Unborn Victims of Violence Act of 2004, 18 U.S.C. §1841; Utah H.B. 102, Sessions Law Ch. 348.

CHAPTER 9

Banned in the U.S.A.: The Convergence of Hip-Hop, Crime, and the Media

Jason Naumann
Robert L. Bing III

From its emergence in the underground of the 1970s Bronx, a borough of New York City, to its rise as one of the premiere musical art forms in the world, hip-hop, and its much-maligned offshoot "Gangsta Rap," has been the focus of more media attention and debate than any of its predecessors. No art form has provoked so much support or opposition; and no art form garners such strong opinions or media appeal. From their inception, hip-hop and rap have been criticized for both the glorification and the cause of criminal activity. And while there have always been critics of the music in both white and black communities, members of the African American community in particular have become outspoken critics of the negative impact rap music has upon their neighborhoods, children, and social outlook. Their accusation is that "the genre's glorification of thug culture—often for the entertainment of white youths—drags down the black community."[1] Is this criticism fair? Does rap or any other musical genre have the power to influence an entire culture? The difficulty in achieving a quantifiable answer to this question is that so much of the information studied is anecdotal. In an effort to sift through the rhetoric, this chapter analyzes the characterization of hip-hop by minority and majority populations. This examination then attempts to draw meaningful conclusions about the way the media has influenced the hip-hop movement.

Seemingly, the toughest battle hip-hop has faced is not record sales, lack of material, or public exposure, but the constant negative characterizations that have defined its public image since birth. The earliest days of hip-hop were replete with negative perceptions and stereotypes, even though it now may "seem innocent in light of the violence that now seems inseparable from [it]."[2] On the tail of the civil rights push of the 1960s and prior to the "crack cocaine" epidemic of the 1980s, hip-hop moved quickly from the "apartment building community rooms, playgrounds, and street corners"[3] of New York City to the national, and even worldwide, spotlight (by 1979) with release of "Rapper's Delight." During these early years, hip-hop was closely linked to a group of freethinking street artists focused on graffiti writing. Even then, when presented with the newly forming hip-hop subculture, "New Yorkers in general and city government officials saw the graffiti crews as vandals."[4] In this instance, the *Washington Post* was quick to play upon the forming rift by referring to hip-hop as "the newest craze among 17-to-21-year-olds" and "a bit of New York City party culture."[5] With public perceptions quickly forming, hip-hop was about to enter into its most tumultuous era. In more recent years, hip-hop has become a hot issue for the entertainment industry, academia, and the government. The characterizations offered by these groups, including the media, have resulted in the creation of negative images.

Some of the biggest critics of hip-hop have been entertainers and other celebrities. This observation is especially true for the 1980s and early 1990s, with the emergence of "gangsta rap," when notables such as Bill Cosby and Oprah Winfrey have lambasted the genre with claims that the artists are "terrible role models for impressionable inner-city youths" and that "hip-hop presents a caricature of black America that damages how young black people view themselves and how they're viewed by others."[6] Stanley Crouch, an author and jazz critic, has said "ordinary African Americans [have been] bearing the consequences of a genre in which 'thugs and freelance prostitutes' have been celebrated for a number of years."[7] Crouch even went so far as to place blame for thousands of African Americans "murdered or beaten up or terrorized" on the shoulders of the rap community, and that although most hip-hop fans are white suburban teenagers, their "class privileges [. . .] largely shield them and their communities from the [negative] outcome."[8] Chris English, a budding producer and website developer, was more direct in his criticism. He stated, "There's a big correlation between rap and the breakdown of the black community in general. Regardless of what people say, it is affecting kids . . . I see kids who would rather be on the corner drinking 40's [40-ounce glasses of malt liquor] and smoking [marijuana] blunts [because of rap]."[9] In all, many have relegated blame for the ills of the African American community on the emergence of rap music.

Over the past thirty years, many individuals (including professors and authors) have made their opinions on hip-hop known. Not surprisingly, a majority encourages the study of the rap culture as a result of cultural and social phenomena. Even among the more educated and freethinking, there is outspoken criticism. Heru Ofori-Atta, author of *The Unapologetic African: Inside the Mind of a Frontline Poet*, remaining true to his self-imposed label, unapologetically offers a glimpse of his critical view of hip-hop when he says, "I care about the minds of black children more than I care about my freedom of speech. I care about setting high standards for my people more than I care about capitulating to the low cultural standards set by white culture."[10] Restated, Ofori-Atta would rather give up his First Amendment right than surrender to white America's imposed low cultural expectations presented in hip-hop.

No criticism of rap was so sharp, and no media coverage was so sensational, as that given during the 1990s, when the government tried to intervene on behalf of "respectable" citizens. The major factor behind this anti-rap movement was the birth of violent, anti-establishment "gangsta rap." The rap group Niggaz With Attitude (N.W.A) is considered the originator of the gangsta rap phenomenon, and their second album sold three million copies. This new movement within the hip-hop community was characterized by ultraviolent lyrics against whites, authority figures, and the government. There were also charges that women were depicted as baseless sexual objects. The FBI was the first to get involved, when an assistant director accused a record company of "encouraging violence against and disrespect for law-enforcement officers."[11] It wasn't long before gangsta rap was embroiled in a fight for survival. The Parents Music Resource Center, an organization cofounded by Tipper Gore, wife of former Vice President Al Gore, had already been opposing sexual lyrics in rock music; in 1990 Mr. and Mrs. Gore turned their attention to gangsta rap. Concurrently, the rap group 2 Live Crew, produced by member Luther Campbell, was engaged in litigation about the suitability of his group's lyrics, as obscene and criminal. And even though the U.S. Supreme Court issued a favorable ruling, the underlying hostility toward the government can be heard in their song "Banned in the U.S.A." In this song, they rhyme about "corrupted politicians playing games/bringing us down to boost their fame," but warns officials to "wisen up, cuz on election day/we'll see who's banned in the U.S.A."[12]

Without an understanding of the real social and economic problems facing the African American community, C. Delores Tucker, a Democratic politician and founder of the National Political Congress of Black Women, told the Senate Judiciary Committee in 1994 that it was "an unavoidable conclusion that gangsta rap is negatively influencing our youth . . . [and it] explains why so many of our children are out of control and why we have more blacks in prison than we have in college."[13] To attempt to place the blame for a majority of African Americans' societal problems on rap was not uncommon during this time period, and the government spearheaded the movement to rein in the outspoken, and often politically incorrect, artists of the genre.

It is easy to suggest that rap (specifically gangsta rap) has been negatively characterized by entertainers, intellectuals, and those running or influencing government—and more to the point, that the media has capitalized upon these characterizations. Newspapers and broadcast news depicting the sensational violence within the hip-hop community, and movie production companies releasing strings of racially charged films, and record companies profiting over 1 billion dollars from rap music (by the end of the 1990s) were all instrumental in helping people, especially the detractors, crystallize their view of rap.

Not surprisingly, one may always expect the media to portray the more violent and sinister side of hip-hip. One example of this proclivity is illustrated by the mid-1990s murders of Tupac Shakur and Notorious B.I.G. There remain, however, those who seek to understand the truth and not the hype of hip-hop. Those who seek to do so attempt to show that rap is not degrading the community but is simply a reflection of African American culture. For better or worse, rap represents the cultural heart of the community. Through such underlying themes as a revolt against oppression and the depiction of the plight of the inner-city community, rap becomes a study of the strength and unity within the African American community.

"African Americans have engaged in an ongoing struggle for liberation— from slavery, discrimination, and the various manifestations of racial oppression" in which they "have often used violence as a tactic or strategy."[14] In response to numerous African Americans beaten or murdered in the postslavery era, there was often a taking up of arms against the white oppressors. These ancestors of today's African American created a legacy of attempting to make things right by use of violence when little else seemed to help. There are those who argue that even today, as a result of the fundamental deprivations felt by a large percentage in the African American community, the use of violence can be cathartic and even instrumental as a means toward self-actualization. In fact, more abstract thinkers believe that "despite their conditions of bondage or the social, political, and economic constraints that smother and confine them, the violent actor is liberated internally."[15] In other words, the pride and humanizing power of the revolt is itself enough to make the oppressed feel free. Even when not violently revolting against the white power structures of our nation, African Americans have often fantasized about rising up against oppression in a violent manner. These fantasies are clearly visible in "artistic expressions produced by African Americans from slavery through the present."[16] Even the earliest hip-hop-linked graffiti "taggers" viewed their art as "a reclaiming of urban space by its marginalized inhabitants."[17] In 1989, N.W.A. caused major news headlines with the release of its song of violent revolt, "F— the Police," and Spike Lee's film *Do the Right Thing* unflinchingly showed a riot following white police killing a black man. America clearly tried to make a connection between these artistic expressions and the three riots that happened in the same year, but most failed to understand that there was a societal cause for the animosity within the lyrics. And where white Americans might view N.W.A. member Ice Cube as simply trying to reject and undermine all authority, a discerning listener of "F— the Police" understands that Cube "first describes 'his' treatment by the police, along with 'his' objection to this treatment."[18] There is not an effect without a cause, and much of the rap music from the 1980s and 1990s carried the tone of revolt due in part to the oppression the rappers feel. Rhetorically, one has to wonder if hip-hop is a verbal violent revolt. Does rap music have both cathartic and instrumental value?

During the 1980s, a strong conservative government brought poor African American communities to their knees, due mostly to legislation cutting taxes, which forced massive cuts in all levels of public assistance programs and caused a rise in the unemployment rate. It has been argued that this recession, affecting so many families, helped spark the wildfire that is now the crack epidemic within the inner city. Why? Because this highly addictive substance became a way for deprived African Americans to earn money for survival. Thus an impossibly difficult economic situation and the advent of crack cocaine into troubled communities turned the birthplace and home of the hip-hop movement into a tough, hostile, unforgiving environment. Peter Katel, a CQ (*Congressional Quarterly*) researcher and staff writer, made the observation that "inevitably, popular culture, including hip-hop began to reflect the distressing, new inner-city realities."[19] Many hip-hop groups (such as Public Enemy) during this time period viewed rap as a "form of social and political commentary and activism," and viewed themselves as the activists for an African American brotherhood against a white society viewed as the source of the condition of the black community.[20] Although some artists have strayed from the initial message of social activism and reform, those presenting their art at the onset of gangsta rap were simply describing their condition and the social problems inherent with it, not celebrating lawlessness. Marc Lamont Hill, Assistant Professor of Urban Education and American Studies at Temple University, has spoken of the great strength that hip-hop gives the African American community. Hill believes that ". . . in addition to speaking truth to power, hip-hop like its cultural forebears, has enabled us to find joy, love and community in the midst of the most absurd circumstances."[21]

Against the odds, hip-hop artists have fought and continue to fight to strengthen the African American community, striving to make a difference within a white-controlled society that at best misunderstands them and at worst vilifies them. Michael Dyson, professor of humanities at the University of Pennsylvania and author of *Is Bill Cosby Right? Or Has the Black Middle Class Lost Its Mind,* struck a chord when he said, "Gangsta rappers are an easy target. We should be having a hearing on crime and on economic misery."[22] Supporters of rap argue that its primary goal is in fact social betterment. When speaking of inner-city youths, rapper Blitz the Ambassador has said that "hip-hop helps these kids cope with extreme environments they are born into," which has the effect of changing expectations and increasing the positive impact each of them may have on society.[23] Many artists within the hip-hop community, recognizing the political nature of their music, have spent considerable effort and finances within the political arena. In 2003, Sean "P. Diddy" Combs and hip-hop mogul Russell Simmons devoted time and money fighting for reform of the unreasonably harsh Rockefeller drug laws of New York. More recently, Combs and Simmons worked with their Hip-Hop Summit Action Network to convince American youth, both black and white, to register for and participate in the voting process. The next presidential election showed an increase of 4.3 million young American voters, half of whom were hip-hop's targeted African American and Latino audience.

In continuing, given the lack of drama and disinterest in things that go right, many individuals never learn about the good work by hip-hip organizations. Bakari Kitwana, cofounder of the National Hip-Hop Political Convention and former executive editor of *The Source* magazine, said that the real work in the communities is "off the radar . . . ; you're not going to see it on CNN."[24] Herein, there is a real tragedy; no matter how hard these organizations struggle to improve their own lives or the lives of those around them, their valiant efforts are rarely newsworthy.

Whether against governmental detractors trying to marginalize the positive impact that hip-hop activists have on the American culture or pundits directly opposing gangsta rap through accusations of misogyny and violence, hip-hop continues to fight for its community. In the footsteps of the graffiti artists taking back the neighborhoods for marginalized people, hip-hop activists and social reformers fight not only for the good of the African American community by encouraging a stance against injustice, but also by supporting them—in the lyrics of their music. Unlike the negative characterizations ingrained in the minds of a large percentage of Americans, many of these artists are champions of their society and should be lauded for the good work they do.

Although there are more than enough points of interest to illustrate how the hip-hop community shares experiences to make America, and thus the world, a better place, there are still those who call for major reform within the hip-hop genre. The media, which is often guilty of the same glorification of violence for which many opponents persecute rap, has fueled the anti-rap movement since the 1970s. The media has created stereotypes and "[failed] to challenge stereotypical expectations. How? By frequently establishing unconscious mental connections for whites (and others) so that perceiving a 'young man of color' stimulates *negative emotions* such as fear and anger."[25] Although almost always acting indirectly by generally misrepresenting what the hip-hop community is all about, the media has recently taken a much more active role in persecuting the outspoken lyricists. This antagonistic role is apparent in the media's use of a double standard with respect to the hip-hop community and white rock musicians.

Much of this antagonism may simply be the result of ignorance fueled by racial bias or xenophobia. As of 2005, there were 364 major newspapers that did not employ a single person of color in their newsrooms. A report released by the John S. and James L. Knight Foundation, an organization promoting excellence in journalism, found that this number could be even higher. According to a recent report, available on the web at www.powerreporting.com/knight/, it could be that up to 44 percent of all newsrooms in the country employ no minorities. With these numbers in mind, it becomes clear that characterizations of hip-hop within the media are often made with grand misunderstanding and erroneous assumptions about the genre. While a white musician can sing misogynistic lyrics and portray himself as a carefree and fanciful "rock star," the same lyrics rhymed by a black man become the target of media scorn, political activism, and even crucifixion by their own communities. The media conveys "impressions that whites occupy different moral universes from young men of color."[26] After a recent comment by rapper Cam'ron was obfuscated on *60 Minutes,* the rapper was subjected to an outcry of public ridicule and lambasted by one of the original gangsta rappers, Ice-T. In contrast, relatively little media attention was paid in 1999 to the disaster of Woodstock, where several women were raped during what Alona Wartofsky described in her July 1999 *Washington Post* article on the victims as a "three-day music festival in Upstate New York that disintegrated into a melee of vandalism and destruction."[27] During a performance by the rock band Korn, an off-duty volunteer saw "women who had been crowd-surfing—hoisted into the air and passed around above the heads of the tightly packed crowd—being forcibly pulled down into the [crowd]" and unfortunately in one case Wartofsky's article reports "there were five guys that were raping this girl and having sex with her."[28] Dana Williams, a staff writer for Tolerance.org points out that while the Rolling Stones, guilty of the same misogynistic lyrics as some rappers, "celebrates its classic rock 'n' roll status, hip-hop and rap . . . [have] become the whipping boys of the music industry."[29]

To find a potential reason to keep hip-hop in the news media, even when shed in a negative light, one only has to look at the most obvious of facts. The corporations that own these media outlets also own the movie studios that produce the films that capitalize upon the public's interest with the hip-hop culture. In some cases they own music labels that produce the hip-hop music itself. A perfect example of this pervasive control of the media is Viacom, which boasts revenues upwards of $20 billion. And Viacom owns the CBS network, 184 radio stations, and Paramount Pictures, which has produced movies such as the gangsta *Hustle and Flow* (2005), which culminates in the main character "making it big" while locked up in prison for committing a violent felony. Needless to say, this movie (and others) glorify the gangsta culture of the inner city. A casual observer might wonder how a media corporation could show stories negatively portraying the criminal life within the "ghetto" on the nightly news, while at the same time reaping "monetary benefits" off a society so entertained by the inner city. The easiest answer to this question is to consider the amount of money made by these media conglomerates. In the music industry alone, hip-hop music accounted for $131 million of the music-downloads business in 2006, coupled with two top-ten bestselling albums in 2005, resulting in over $33 billion in revenues. Consider that the companies owning the major music labels also own the major news corporations, television channels, radio stations, and motion-picture studios, and it is not difficult to imagine how $33 billion in profit might be the tip of the iceberg. Even Russell Simmons, who sold his Def Jam Records to Universal Music Group—owned by the same Vivendi Universal that jointly owns Universal Studios and NBC—has earned over of $325 million on clothing, jewelry, and television. With this much money at stake, the real question is not about what is socially acceptable or good for the African American community, but rather as rapper David Banner points out, "what does America want?"[30] He goes on to frankly describe gangsta rap as "a reflection of America,"[31] which in his opinion equates to a "sick" society that revels in NASCAR crashes and violent movies.

There can be little doubt as to why hip-hop maintains the image of the rebellious, violent, misogynistic art form that only seeks to further debase the dregs of society. With a news media that cannot hope to understand the origins and life of the art form, and global media conglomerations that exploit the negative images of the artists and African American population to sell more merchandise to an increasingly larger white audience, hip-hop may never truly get a fair representation. This is most unfortunate when the industry can't even rely on its own lineage for support and when Congress and the Federal Communications Commission are becoming increasingly bold in pursuing major media corporations for "inappropriate" content. Without anyone to help hip-hop artists champion their cause, and with this political pressure on the conglomerates that control the entire industry, there may be a day when controversial, thought-provoking lyrics are a thing of the past.

No genre of music has been so controversial, so vilified, so uplifting to its community, and so influential as hip-hop has been in the past thirty years. Often exploited by white-owned corporations that seek to use up their creativity, the hundreds of artists who have come and gone through the hip-hop community have all shared at least one common goal: They seek to tell the world about the realities of life in the inner city. Though not often characterized in a favorable light, they continue to make a difference in their communities by the giving of themselves and by the empowering messages within their music. The reality is that hip-hop does not, and has never, beaten down the African American people or caused them to perpetrate criminal activity. Through unflinching lyrics, the rapper holds up a mirror and forces society to take a look, even if the reflection is not always one that is easy to stomach. As African Americans, and more importantly as simply Americans, these men and women have the right to say what they feel. As Marc Hill wrote, "they should . . . feel empowered to produce art that reflects their own feelings, desires and beliefs about the world—uplifting or not."[32]

CRITICAL THINKING QUESTIONS

1. What is the irony behind the depiction of Woodstock and the imagery of hip-hop music?
2. Why has rap music been so vilified by the public? What are your thoughts about this characterization?
3. How does money factor into the overall the growth of the hip hop or gangsta rap industry?
4. Why have some black entertainers and celebrities decided to speak out against rap music? Is this the right way to proceed?
5. What does Michael Dyson, a black intellectual, suggest about hip-hop music?
6. Is there a place for hip-hop and gangsta rap music in America society? If so, why? If not, why not?

NOTES

1. Peter Katel, "Debating Hip-Hop," *CQ Researcher Online* 17, no. 23 (June 15, 2007): 529, http://library .cqpress.com/cqresearcher/cqresrr e2007061500.
2. Katel, "Debating Hip-Hop," 532.
3. Katel, "Debating Hip-Hop," 531.
4. Katel, "Debating Hip-Hop," 532.
5. Katel, "Debating Hip-Hop," 538.
6. Katel, "Debating Hip-Hop," 531, 533.
7. Katel, "Debating Hip-Hop," 533.
8. Ibid.
9. Ibid.

10. Heru Ofori-Atta, "At Issue: Should Hip-Hop Artists Produce Material That Is Socially Uplifting to African-Americans?" *CQ Researcher Online* 17, no. 23 (June 15, 2007): 545. http:// library.cqpress.com/cqre searcher/cqresrre2007061500.
11. Katel, "Debating Hip-Hop," 542.
12. Luther Campbell, "Banned in the U.S.A.," stanzas 3–4, 30–31.
13. Katel, "Debating Hip-Hop," 544.
14. Donn C. Worgs, "Beware of the Frustrated . . .": The Fantasy and Reality of the African American Violent Revolt," *Journal of Black Studies* 37 (2006): 21.
15. Worgs, "Beware," 27.
16. Worgs, "Beware," 23.
17. Katel, "Debating Hip-Hop," 536.
18. Worgs, "Beware," 36.
19. Katel, "Debating Hip-Hop," 540.
20. Katel, "Debating Hip-Hop," 541.
21. Marc Hill, "At Issue: Should Hip-Hop Artists Produce Material That Is Socially Uplifting to African-Americans?" *CQ Researcher Online* 17, no. 23 (June 15, 2007): 545. http:// library.cqpress.com/cqre searcher/cqresrre2007061500.
22. Katel, "Debating Hip-Hop," 546.
23. Katel, "Debating Hip-Hop," 547.
24. Katel, "Debating Hip-Hop," 537.
25. Robert Entman, "Young Men of Color in the Media: Images and Impacts," Report, Joint Center For Political and Economic Studies, 2006, 13.
26. Entman, "Young Men of Color,"6.
27. Alona Wartofsky, "Police Investigate Reports of Rapes at Woodstock," *Washington Post*, July 29, 1999, C1.
28. Ibid.
29. Dana Williams, "Beyond Rap: Musical Misogyny," 2003, http:// www.tolerance.org/news/article _tol.jsp?id=831 (accessed June 2008).
30. Katel, "Debating Hip-Hop," 532.
31. Ibid.
32. Hill, "At Issue," 545.

CHAPTER 10

Are Media Depictions of Crimes and Criminal Offenders Related to the Differential Treatment of Cocaine and Methamphetamine Offenders within America's Incarceration Binge?

Robyn Rosenthal

A disproportionate number of African Americans are currently incarcerated at great social, financial, and capital cost to American society; is it possible for researchers to connect depictions of crime and criminal offenders with disparate rates of incarceration?

Researchers in many disciplines have examined the growth in American incarceration rates and the disparate effects on certain communities. This article synthesizes research from several different social science fields in order to both present a richer and deeper understanding of the incarceration binge and to begin to explore one possible causal mechanism. Studies in sociology, criminology, public policy, law, political science, and other social science disciplines examine the same problem from different theoretical perspectives. Integrating these varied disciplines can help researchers expand their narratives and encourage the formation of new discourses about the unequal application of law in America. While the primary focus of this chapter is on the disparities between drug offenders who use cocaine and those who use methamphetamines, it is plausible that the themes explored here could be generalized to explain disparities in a larger segment of the American offender population.

WHAT IS THE AMERICAN INCARCERATION BINGE AND WHY SHOULD WE STUDY IT?

American rates of incarceration have risen every year since 1980, with one in every thirty-two Americans under correctional supervision (incarcerated, on probation, or on parole) at the end of 2005[1] and one percent of all Americans in jail or prison as of February 2008.[2] Although the chances of an individual becoming a victim of violent crime, always a rare event, have been steadily falling for years, fear of crime continues to rise.[3] This irrational[4] fear of crime and the fact that such a large segment of the American population has come within the purview of the criminal justice system makes the study of penal policies increasingly salient to both our understanding of American society and the overall public policy discourse.

The salience of criminal justice policies and theories that might explain public acceptance of these policies becomes increasingly evident when contextualized by the realization that in addition to the social and human capital costs, the direct financial cost of incarceration rose from 36 billion dollars in 1982 to 186 billion in 2006.[5] Although it is logical to expect taxpayers to be outraged that their tax dollars are going to support the prison industrial complex rather than their roads, hospitals, and schools, that is not the case. In order to understand how the United States has arrived at a point where we have the highest per capita incarceration rates in the world, yet there is not widespread public protest, one must understand these issues.

HAVE RESEARCHERS IDENTIFIED ANY CAUSES OF THE MASS INCARCERATION BINGE?

Although numerous theories have been proposed to explain this mass incarceration binge, many scholars associate the "war on drugs" with the three-decade-long increase in incarceration rates.[6] In 2004, 21 percent of persons held in state facilities and 55 percent of those in federal facilities were incarcerated as a result of drug offenses.[7] Of those persons under correctional supervision but not incarcerated, 28 percent of probationers and 37 percent of parolees are nonviolent drug offenders.[8]

ARE ANY GROUPS DISPROPORTIONATELY AFFECTED BY AMERICA'S INCARCERATION BINGE?

As large as these overall numbers might appear, the discrepancy between the American correctional population and America's entire population is vastly larger. According to the Bureau of Justice Statistics, in 2006 an estimated 4.8 percent of black men were in prison or jail, compared to 1.9 percent of Hispanic men and 0.7 percent of white men.[9] While these racial disparities are well documented,[10] it is interesting to note that the widespread use of incarceration, ostensibly as a means of crime control, was not always prevalent in the United States. In order to understand the incarceration binge that has taken place over the last thirty years, it must be considered within the context of its ahistorical nature.

While a salient feature of the current mass incarceration binge is racial inequity, racial disparities within the America criminal justice system have varied significantly since the early 1900s. In 1926, African Americans accounted for approximately 10 percent of the American population[11] and 21 percent of prison admissions.[12] By 1986 African Americans comprised almost 12 percent of the overall population[13] and 44 percent of the correctional population.[14] Between 1980 and 2003, the number of drug offenders in prison or jail increased by 1100 percent, rising from 41,100 in 1980 to 493,800 in 2003. Prior to the inception of the drug war in 1980, there were 684 African Americans per 100,000 arrested for drug offenses and 387 drug arrests per 100,00 white Americans; in between 1980 and 2003, black drug arrests rose by 225 percent and white drug arrests by 70 percent.[15]

Within the overall growth in the use of imprisonment, the social disparity in the incidence of imprisonment among certain groups has meant that some communities experience concentrated levels of incarceration.[16] It is important to remember that while crime rates among African Americans may explain some portion of incarceration rates, the interaction between race and class must also be considered. Since African American communities are more likely to be low income, as well as more likely to experience the disadvantages resulting from concentrated poverty than low-income whites, what may appear to be a race effect is often one of social class.[17] Therefore, any analysis of the demographics of crime and incarceration must include the structural factors of the community in order to be complete. The incarceration binge and its disproportionate effects in certain communities increases inequality and decreases access to opportunities and life chances for the members of those communities; this decrease in social capital disrupts relationships both within the community and between community members and the larger society.[18]

HAVE RESEARCHERS DISCOVERED ANY QUANTIFIABLE DIFFERENCES IN THE TYPES OF DRUG OFFENDERS INCARCERATED?

In 2007, 82.7 percent of those incarcerated for crack cocaine were black, 8.9 percent were white, and 8.5 percent were either Hispanic or a different group. In that same year, 2.5 percent of Americans convicted for methamphetamines offenses were black, 51.5 percent were white, and 40.1 percent Hispanic.[19] The United States Department of Health reports that .5 percent of African Americans have used crack cocaine and 4.4 of white Americans report having used crack cocaine. One tenth of one percent of African Americans reported using methamphetamines within the last twelve months, compared with almost 5 percent of white Americans or Americans who identify themselves as belonging to two or more races.[20]

For one particular type of offender, pregnant cocaine addicts, the typical classification of "criminal" rather than "addict" that took place within the context of America's war on drugs led to more than ten times as many pregnant African American women being referred for prosecution than pregnant white drug abusers, despite similar rates of drug use among pregnant African American and white women of equivalent socioeconomic status.[21]

According to a recent article in the *Congressional Quarterly Weekly*, some lawmakers attribute these differences to disparities between legislative activities concerning methamphetamines and those concerning crack cocaine.[22] While much of the legislative activity concerning crack cocaine consisted of the establishment of strict sentencing guidelines and mandatory minimum sentences and the use of harsh punitive sanctions, antimethamphetamines laws focus primarily on cutting off the supply of the chemical ingredients used to make the drug. According to a legislator quoted in that article, "There seems to be more of an emphasis on shutting down these meth labs and trying to figure out ways to treat these addicts and then get them back into flow of society . . . [W]e don't get for crack or heroin that kind of support for prevention, treatment and rehabilitation."[23]

ARE THERE ANY PLAUSIBLE THEORIES TO EXPLAIN THESE DISPARITIES?

While researchers have found that there is a clear and unequivocal inverse relationship between the representation of minorities within the custody and control of the criminal justice system and their social status,[24] there is not such a clear understanding of how and why that situation persists. One possible explanation is media framing of crime and criminal offenders. Framing, the process by which individuals either develop a personal conceptualization of or reorient their thinking about a specific issue,[25] can be affected by the language of the discourse concerning that issue.

Language can do more than describe events and situations, it can also help shape the way in which those events and situations are viewed. Language attributing social problems in disadvantaged neighborhoods to a "decline of a universal maternal instinct" resulting from the use of crack cocaine or "deviant values" which encouraged criminal activity also allows policy makers to shift the focus of policy discourse from the provision of needed social services to additional criminalization of addiction.[26] Once these frames have become internalized as a sociocultural meme, when new social problems arise, those frames allow the new problems to be viewed within the framework, or templates, of the existing social model by a public with little knowledge of or interest in the political process.[27]

During the height of the so-called "crack epidemic," media coverage, including CBS's special report "48 Hours on Crack Street" and cover stories in both *Time* and *Newsweek* magazines gave dire predictions of the impact of this "epidemic" and primed the public to believe that America was in the midst of an unprecedented crisis.[28] While similar language appears to be increasing concerning methamphetamine, such as seen in a recent article in the *British Medical Journal* which announced: "Methamphetamine epidemic hits middle America," there are subtle differences in the language used to describe the "meth epidemic." According to this article, while methamphetamines use is "overwhelming hospitals and police departments in the United States,"[29] the problem is primarily one of public health and an increased need for social services, rather than a need for increased criminal justice activities.

While there is no clear-cut causal relationship between media framing and criminal justice policies, there is evidence that television viewing is associated with misperceptions concerning crime, such as a belief that crime is increasing when in fact it is decreasing and that the nature of crime is becoming more violent.[30] Other researchers have collected evidence suggesting that while attitudes towards crime and criminality have become increasingly racialized, it is possible that negative depictions of blacks may have less of an effect on attitudes concerning criminal justice policies among more highly educated respondents with a larger exposure to norms prescribing racial equality.[31]

PUBLIC OPINION AND PUNITIVENESS

Although one would like to think that criminal justice policies are informed by science and responsive to evolving knowledge, that is not always the case. With the perspective afforded by the passage of two decades, it is clear that both the rise in cocaine use in the 1980s and the media-induced panic about its effects led to many policies based upon pandering to media-inflated public fears rather than upon scientific evidence.[32] Researchers have reported finding data that the public has very little accurate information about the criminal justice system, that they underestimate levels of punitiveness, and that they overestimate the ease with which offenders navigate the criminal justice system.[33] This lack of understanding of the realities of the criminal justice system leads to an ill-informed public, whose misinformation is reflected in polls presenting public views on the criminal justice system. This polling data, based on incorrect information, is then used by policy makers in combination with reports from industry lobbyists to determine the course of legislative action to follow.

Despite politicians' belief that the public is uniformly punitive when it comes to fighting crime and punishing criminals, researchers have provided evidence to the contrary. Public-opinion researchers report[34] that when public opinion is analyzed, support for punitive policies is "mushy" with the majority of respondents preferring a less punitive option when that option is provided. Although overall polling data shows Republicans to be more punitive and less forgiving than Democrats,[35] increasingly punitive policies have been legislated and implemented by both Republican and Democratic lawmakers.[36] These policies are frequently adopted with no apparent research, discourse, or motivation other than attempts to be seen as more "tough on crime" than the opposition candidates. Punitive policies, such as "three strikes" and other mandatory sentencing plans, and collateral consequences, such as removal of access to public housing, student loans, and professional certification, do nothing to either decrease crime or increase safety and serve no real purpose other than to provide a means by which elected officials can claim to have "done something about crime."[37]

MORAL PANICS, THE MASS MEDIA, AND PUBLIC OPINION

The current war on drugs is not unprecedented; there have been moral panics concerning various substances for many years, such as the "temperance movement" or "reefer madness."[38] By linking a dangerous substance with a "dangerous class" of person, these moral panics allow the demonization of the substance to serve as a proxy for the demonization of a group of people.[39] Some of these associations include Catholic working-class immigrants and alcohol, Chinese railroad workers and opium dens, African Americans with marijuana and cocaine, and women with all manner of illegal substances.[40] The common theme these moral panics share is the association of a social trend that scares the elites, such as growth of an ethnic group, with a "dangerous" substance that allows blame to be placed on the use of these substances rather than on the changes in society.[41]

When discourse concerning public policy is viewed through the frames provided by the language of crisis or war, that language distorts the resulting polices.[42] Reagan's war on drugs utilized both social inoculation tactics,[43] such as the infamous "Just Say No" campaigns, and harsh punitive sanctions.[44] The phrase "governing through crime"[45] has been used to describe the unprecedented amount of influence that crime has amassed over American institutions and legislative policies. Under this model as the fear of crime rises, communities become more accepting of increases in surveillance, securitization, and subjugations of civil rights.[46] Another model, proposed by Katherine Beckett, articulates that support for punitive crime measures is less related to fear of crime than to manipulations of those fears by the elites in government and industry. Beckett's model articulates punitive policies as being led by politicians instead of the public.[47] By transferring agency from the public to the politicians, Becket introduces a more cynical construct. Under this model, the issue of "law and order" was developed by Southern officials to discredit the civil rights movement[48] and the media coverage of each crime or drug "crisis" can be attributed to manipulation of the press by the elites to distract the public's attention from an injustice or to ensure that the patriarchal hegemony remains intact.

WHAT DO RESEARCHERS SAY ABOUT MEDIA INFLUENCES, PUBLIC OPINION, AND CRIME POLICY?

While racism within the criminal justice system, whether conscious or not, contributes to disproportionate incarceration via the use of racial profiling and disparities in decision making in plea bargaining and sentencing,[49] researchers studying racism have found that racist behaviors can be an unconscious reaction conditioned by social learning.[50] In order to combat these socially conditioned attitudes and behaviors, they must first be understood.

Researchers using cultivation theory to explain the persistent public belief that violent crime is a widespread national problem in the United States despite the actual decreases in crime found that viewing local television news in one local news area was related to increased fear of and concern about crime.[51] When studies conducted over a period of several decades were reviewed, a consistent increase in fear of crime due to media coverage emerged. A 1976 study[52] reported virtually no increased fear of crime due to newspaper coverage, a 1981 study of media coverage of crime reported a small increase in fear of crime[53] due to media coverage, and a 2003 study[54] reported a large increase in fear after exposure to media coverage of crime.

Several studies in California have found significant differences between media depictions of offenders and the facts. Researchers who conducted content analyses of random samples of news stories that ran in California during a two-year period discovered that whites were overrepresented as victims and underrepresented as offenders and that blacks were underrepresented as victims and overrepresented as offenders in comparison with crime statistics supplied by the California Department of Justice Supplemental Report for that jurisdiction.[55] Content analysis of "reality-based" entertainment television revealed similar results, with blacks being overrepresented as offenders and underrepresented as law enforcement officers.[56] Another study revealed that the racial imagery on local news stories formed a narrative discourse that effected changes in viewers' attitudes about both crime and race.[57]

Among studies examining news portrayals of poverty, blacks were found to be disproportionately represented among magazine portrayals of poverty. Blacks were further found to be especially overrepresented in negative stories on poverty and in those instances when the poor were presented with stereotypical traits that reinforce the notion that poverty is a result of either poor personal choices or values associated with a deviant subculture.[58] News coverage of poverty, and especially poor mothers, was found to inaccurately portray the typical family living in poverty as a single mother with an average of seven children, living in squalor due to laziness and drug use.[59]

WHAT DOES THIS ALL MEAN?

While there is not sufficient empirical evidence at this time to conclude that there is a causal relationship between media depictions of crime and criminal offenders and differential prosecutions of cocaine and methamphetamines users, there is a large body of evidence supporting the plausibility of that hypothesis. Disproportionate minority representation among offender populations and differential legal treatment of cocaine and methamphetamines users have been extensively documented. The question then becomes, what further research is necessary to gain a broader and deeper understanding of the effects of media framing of crime issues on these outcomes?

If framing, the process by which individuals either develop a personal conceptualization of or reorient their thinking about a specific issue,[60] can be affected by the language of the discourse concerning that issue, then language can do more than describe events and situations, it can also help shape the way in which those events and situations are viewed. When language attributing social problems in disadvantaged neighborhoods to the values of a deviant subculture allows policy makers to shift the focus of policy discourse from the provision of needed social services to additional criminalization of the effects of poverty[61] and to change the relationship between the government and certain communities, it should become an urgent social priority to develop solutions that are cost effective and add to, rather than detract from, the social capital in marginalized neighborhoods. Studying the relationship between media depictions of crime and criminal offenders and public support for America's war on drugs and the associated mass incarceration binge can provide a valuable tool for researchers to help formulate rational and evidence-based policy. While media outlets are privately held corporate entities, it is entirely possible that an understanding of the impact of their programming can help social scientists identify the types of therapeutic narratives that social-justice activists can use to ameliorate some of the harm resulting from years of negative portrayals and achieve some measure of reconciliation between the mainstream and marginalized communities.

CRITICAL THINKING QUESTIONS

1. Discuss the causes of America's mass incarceration binge.
2. What images are created with use of the metaphor "war on drugs"? Please explain.
3. What is the impact of public opinion on the development of punitive law?
4. How would you characterize media's coverage of the so-called crack epidemic?
5. What is the role of "moral panic" in the formation of public-opinion drug-use policies?

NOTES

1. L. Glaze and T. Bonczar, "Probation and Parole in the United States, 2005," *Bureau of Justice Statistics Bulletin*, NCJ215901 (2006), http://www.ojp.usdoj.gov/bjs/abstract/ppus05.htm.

2. http://www.pewcenteronthestates.org/initiatives_detail.aspx?initiativeID=31336.

3. D. Garland, *The Culture of Control: Crime and Social Order in Contemporary Society* (Chicago: University of Chicago Press, 2001), 3; K. Beckett, *Making Crime Pay: Law and Order in Contemporary American Politics* (New York: Oxford University Press, 1997); L. Bobo and V. Thompson, "Unfair by Design: The War on Drugs, Race, and the Legitimacy of the Criminal Justice System," *Social Research* 73, no. 2 (2006): 445–472.

4. Ibid.

5. J. Austin, W. Naro, and T. Fabelo, "Public Safety, Public Spending:

Forecasting America's Prison Population 2007–2011," *The Public Safety Project* (2007) http://www.pewpublicsafety.org/research.aspx 6.

6. K. Beckett, *Making Crime Pay,* 53; K. Beckett, "Setting the Public Agenda: 'Street Crime' and Drug Use in American Politics," *Social Problems* 41, no. 3 (1994): 425–447; L. Bobo and V. Thompson, "Unfair by Design"; D. Garland, *The Culture of Control,*" 132; K. J. Maschke, "Prosecutors As Crime Creators: The Case of Prenatal Drug Use," *Criminal Justice Review* 20, no. 1 (1995): 21–33; T. Meares, "Charting Race and Class Differences in Attitudes towards Drug Legalization and Law Enforcement," *Buffalo Criminal Law Review* 1, no. 1. (1997) 137–174; T. Ross, A. Khashu, and M. Wamsley, "Hard Data on Hard Times: An Empirical Analysis of Maternal Incarceration, Foster Care, and Visitation," *The Vera Institute of Justice*, New York, (2004), http://www.vera.org/publication_pdf/245_461.pdf.

7. C. Mumola, and J. Karberg, "Drug Use and Dependence, State and Federal Prisoners," *Bureau of Justice Statistics Bulletin*, NCJ213530, (2007), http://www.ojp.usdoj.gov/bjs/abstract/dudsfp04.htm.

8. Glaze and Bonczar, "Probation and Parole."

9. W. J. Sabol, H. Couture, and P. Harrison, "Prisoners in 2006," *Bureau of Justice Statistics Bulletin*, NCJ219416 (2007). http://www.ojp.usdoj.gov/bjs/pub/ascii/p06.txt.

10. Bobo and Thompson, "Unfair by Design"; Glaze and Bonczar, "Probation and Parole"; J. Hagan,

J. P. Coleman, "Returning Captives of the American War on Drugs: Issues of Community and Family Reentry," *Crime & Delinquency* 47, no. 3 (2001): 352–367; P. Harrison and A. Beck, "Prisoners in 2005," *Bureau of Justice Statistics Bulletin*, NCJ215092 (2006), http://www.ojp.usdoj.gov/bjs/abstract/p05.htm.

11. C. Gibson and K. Jung, "Historical Census Statistics on Population Totals by Race, 1790 to 1990, and by Hispanic Origin, 1970 to 1990, for the United States, Regions, Divisions, and States," *Population Division U.S. Census Bureau, Working Paper Series No. 56* (2002), http://www.census.gov/population/www/documentation/twps0056.html.

12. M. Mauer, "Racial Impact Statements As a Means of Reducing Unwarranted Sentencing Disparities," *Ohio State Journal of Criminal Law* 5, no. 19 (2008): 19–46.

13. Gibson, and Jung, "Historical Census Statistics."

14. Mauer, "Racial Impact Statements."

15. R. King, "Disparity by Geography: The War on Drugs in America's Cities," The Sentencing Project, (2008), http://www.sentencingproject.org/PublicationDetails.aspx?PublicationID=614.

16. T. R. Clear, D. R. Rose, J. A. Ryder, "Incarceration and the Community: The Problem of Removing and Returning Offenders," *Crime & Delinquency* 47, no. 3 (2001): 335–351.

17. Mauer, "Racial Impact Statements."

18. Clear, Rose, and Ryder, "Incarceration and the Community"; Hagan and Coleman, "Returning

Captives"; J. Travis, and J. Petersilia, "Reentry Reconsidered: A New Look at an Old Question," *Crime & Delinquency* 47, no. 3 (2001): 291–313.

19. United States Sentencing Report, 2007 Annual Report, http://www.ussc.gov/ANNRPT/2007/Chap5_07(optimized).pdf.

20. National Survey on Drug Use and Health (NSDUH), United States Department of Health and Human Services, Substance Abuse and Mental Health Services Administration, Office of Applied Studies, http://www.icpsr.umich.edu/cocoon/SAMHDA/DAS3/00064.xml.

21. A. Sachs, "Here Come the Pregnancy Police," *Time* (1989), http://www.time.com/time/magazine/article/0,9171,957711,00.html.

22. S. Stern, "Meth vs. Crack: Different Legislative Approaches," *CQ Weekly Online*, (2006): 1548–1554, http://library.cqpress.com/cqweekly/weekly report109-000002240935.

23. Ibid.

24. K. Dale and M. Tonry, "Gender, Race, and Sentencing," *Crime and Justice*, Vol. 22 (1997): 201–252. M. Mauer and M. Chesney-Lind, eds., *Invisible Punishment: The Collateral Consequences of Mass Imprisonment* (New York: New Press, 2002). M. Mauer, "Racial Impact Statements."

25. D. Chong and J. Druckman, "Framing Theory," *Annual Review of Political Science,* 10 (2007): 103–126.

26. N. D. Campbell, *Using Women: Gender, Drug Policy, and Social Justice* (New York: Routledge, 2000), 17.

27. R. Lau and R. Schlenginer, "Policy Frames, Metaphorical Reasoning,

and Support for Public Policies," *Political Psychology* 26, no. 1 (2005): 77–113.

28. Campbell, *Using Women*.

29. J. H. Tanne, "Methamphetamine Epidemic Hits Middle America," *British Medical Journal* 18, no. 332 (2006): 382–389.

30. R. K. Goidel, C. M. Freeman, and S. T. Procopio. "The Impact of Television Viewing on Perceptions of Juvenile Crime," *Journal of Broadcasting & Electronic Media* (2006); B. Barnett, "Guilty and Threatening: Visual Bias in Television News Crime Stories," *Journalism of Communication Monographs* 5 (2003): 105–155; R. W. Busselle, "Television Exposure, Perceived Realism, and Exemplar Accessibility in Social Judgment Process," *Media Psychology* 3 (2001): 43–68.

31. C. M. Federico and J. W. Holmes, "Education and the Interface between Racial Perceptions and Criminal Justice Attitudes," *Political Psychology* 26, no. 1 (2005): 47–75.

32. S. Walker, *Sense and Non-Sense about Crime and* Drugs (Belmont, CA: Thomson-Wadsworth, 2006), 261.

33. J. Robert, L. Stalans, D. Indermaur, and M. Hough, *Penal Populism and Public Opinion: Lessons from Five Countries* (New York: Oxford University Press, 2002), 23.

34. T. Flanagan and D. Longmire, eds., *Americans View Crime and Justice: A National Public Opinion Survey* (Thousand Oaks, CA: Sage, 1996); F. T. Cullen, B. S. Fisher, and B. Applegate, "Public Opinion about Punishment and Corrections," in *Crime and Justice: A Review of Research,* 27 ed. M. Tonry (Chicago:

University of Chicago Press, 2000).

35. R. M. Eisinger, "Partisan Absolution? Exploring the Depths of Forgiving," *International Journal of Public Opinion Research* 12, no. 3 (2000): 254–258; H. Erskine, "The Polls: Politics and Law and Order," *The Public Opinion Quarterly* 38, no. 4 (1975): 623–634.

36. Roberts, et al., *Penal Populism and Public Opinion*, 189.

37. Mauer and Chesney-Lind, *Invisible Punishment*, 12.

38. C. Reinarman, "The Social Constitution of Drug Scares," in *Deviance, the Interactionist Perspective*, eds. E. Rubington and M. Weinberg (Needham Heights: Simon and Schuster, 1996).

39. Ibid.

40. M. Keire, "Dope Fiends and Degenerates: The Gendering of Addiction in the Early 20th Century," *Journal of Social History* 31, no. 4 (1998): 809–822.

41. Ibid.

42. M. Sherman and G. Hawkins, *Imprisonment in America: Choosing the Future* (Chicago: University of Chicago Press, 1981), 18.

43. Richard Midford, "Does Drug Education Work?" *Drug and Alcohol Review* 19, no. 4 (2000): 441–446.

44. J. Hagan, and J. P. Coleman, "Returning Captives of the American War on Drugs: Issues of Community and Family Reentry," *Crime & Delinquency* 47, no. 3 (2001): 352–367.

45. J. Simon, "Introduction: Crime, Community and Criminal Justice," *California Law Review* 90, no. 5 (2002): 1415–1422.

46. J. Simon, "Megan's Law: Crime and Democracy in Late Modern America," *Law & Social Inquiry* 25, no. 4 (2000): 1111–1150.

47. K. Beckett, *Making Crime Pay: Law and Order in Contemporary American Politics* (New York: Oxford University Press, 1997).

48. Ibid.

49. Mauer, "Racial Impact Statements."

50. New York University, "NYU/Yale Research Team Explores Neural Basis of Racial Evaluation," *ScienceDaily* (September 18, 2000), http://www.sciencedaily.com/releases/2000/09/000913203757.htm.

51. Ibid.

52. J. E. Conklin, "The Impact of Crime," *Social Forces* 54, no. 4 (1976): 957–958.

53. W. B. Jaehnig, W. H. Weaver, and Frederick Fico, "Reporting Crime and Fearing Crime in Three Communities," *Journal of Communication* 31, no. 1 (1981): 88–96.

54. D. Romer, K. H. Jamieson, and S. Aday, "Television News and the Cultivation of Fear of Crime," *Journal of Communication* 53, no. 1 (2003): 88–104.

55. T. L. Dixon and D. Linz, "Race and the Misrepresentation of Victimization on Local Television News," *Communication Research* 27, no. 5 (2000): 547–573. Travis L. Dixon, Cristina L. Azocar, and Michael Casas, "The Portrayal of Race and Crime on Television Network News," *Journal of Broadcasting & Electronic Media* 47, no. 4 (2003): 498–523.

56. M. B. Oliver, "Portrayals of Crime, Race, and Aggression in 'Reality Based' Police Shows: A Content Analysis," *Journal of Broadcasting & Electronic Media* 38 (1994): 179–193.

57. F. D. Gilliam Jr. and S. Iyengar, "Prime Suspects: The Influence of Local Television News on the Viewing Public," *American Journal of Political Science* 44, no. 3 (2000): 560–573.

58. R. A. Clawson and R. Trice, "Poverty As We Know It: Media Portrayals of the Poor," *Public Opinion Quarterly* 64, no. 1 (2000): 53–64.

59. L. A Williams, "Race, Rat Bites, and Unfit Mothers: How Media Discourse Informs Welfare Legislation Debate," *Fordham Urban Law Journal* 22 (1995): 1159–1196.

60. Chong and Druckman, "Framing Theory."

61. N. D. Campbell, "Regulating 'Maternal Instinct': Governing Mentalities of Late Twentieth-Century U.S. Illicit Drug Policy," *Signs* 24, no. 4 (1999): 895–923.

CHAPTER 11

Crime in Prime Time

Nickie D. Phillips
Natasha A. Frost

This chapter provides an overview of crime as portrayed on cable television. Specifically, the chapter addresses both fictional and nonfictional representations of crime, including crime dramas, crime-based reality shows, news magazines, and 24-hour news networks. We describe the dramatization of crime on cable television and address the broader social implications of programming that more often than not misrepresents the crime problem at the expense of minorities.

The relationship between race, crime, and the media is a complex and contentious one. Since for most, day-to-day contact with and exposure to crime and criminal offenders is minimal, media outlets become one of the primary sources by which the public learns about crime, offenders, victims, and criminal justice agents. Too often, unfortunately, the media perpetuates stereotypes by overrepresenting people of color as criminal offenders, neglecting positive role models, and ultimately reinforcing generalizations that certain groups of people can and should be considered threats to public safety.

Despite tremendous growth in the type and number of media outlets, television remains the dominant provider of images of crime and justice that Americans consume. Although television is primarily a source of entertainment, an American Psychological Association task force on television and society has emphasized television's educative aspects: "[Television] is always more than mere entertainment. Even when it is not intentionally designed to teach, it carries messages about social interactions and about the nature and value of groups in the society that can influence attitudes, values, and actions among its viewers."[1]

The oft-repeated news mantra "if it bleeds, it leads," could similarly apply to television programming. The media is a consumer-driven industry—an industry that invests in research and development by closely monitoring viewer preferences and marketing accordingly. Given the proliferation of crime-focused programming in prime time, it appears that Americans have an almost insatiable appetite for crime and justice content.

Most Americans watch television regularly, sitting before the small screen in their living rooms for an average of four and a half hours per day.[2] Over the course of daily television viewing, the average consumer, irrespective of their programming choices, will be exposed to some level of crime and violence. Research suggests that by the time a typical child enters elementary school, s/he will have seen 100,000 acts of violence and as many as 8,000 murders.[3]

There is a vast literature outlining the ways in which the media distorts and exaggerates the "true" crime problem, misrepresents and often stereotypes offenders and victims, and offers overly simplified solutions to complex social problems.[4] In fact, Surette uses the concept of the "law of opposites" to describe that the media often presents the exact opposite of the "reality" of crime as measured by crime statistics.[5] Research, for example, has documented the media's tendency toward the sensational and its preference for focusing on extraordinary crime (murder, rape, etc.) rather than ordinary crime (larceny, shoplifting, etc.).[6] Of the violent crimes portrayed, murder is among the most common, although according to official statistics it is the most infrequently occurring violent crime. Minorities are generally underrepresented as victims, although official statistics indicate that minorities have higher victimization rates than whites. The extent and nature of juvenile crime is often misrepresented as primarily violent and irrational. Further, criminal offenders in general are all too frequently depicted as psychopathic predators on television. Even the run-of-the-mill offenders (pickpockets, petty thieves, etc.) are depicted as dangerous and unpredictable, preying on the vulnerable and poised to attack at the first sign of weakness. When offered, explanations for criminal offending tend to neglect any social factors that criminologists have linked to criminal behavior and instead raise the popular themes of individual choice and lack of conscience that tend to resonate with American values and viewers.[7]

The well-documented influence of the media suggests that we should think more critically about the ways in which it portrays crime to the average viewer. Katheryn Russell credits television with perpetuating many of the stereotypes that contribute to the erroneous assumption that "most black men are criminals."[8] Other research suggests that blacks in general, and black males in particular, are portrayed as particularly menacing across most television programming.[9] Blacks, it is argued, are overrepresented as offenders, underrepresented as victims, and depicted on television in ways that propagate and exacerbate racial stereotypes.[10]

The primary purpose of this chapter is to explore representations of race and crime on cable television. What is the significance of the convergence of entertainment and crime on racialized images of offenders and victims? Does crime-related programming perpetuate, and potentially even generate, fear of crime? To what extent do media representations (and misrepresentations) of crime contribute to development and perpetuation of stereotypes about crime, criminal offenders, and victims? What type of offender does cable television present as most dangerous? What type of victim is portrayed as most at risk?

These questions, important in their own right, assume more urgency given the role the media plays in the creation of cultural representations of crime and justice. Ferrell and colleagues suggest that the meaning of crime and crime control emerges "from a contested process of symbolic display, cultural interpretation and representational negotiation."[11] Media representations of crime and criminals are not static, but are constructed and reconstructed, informing and shaping our attitudes about crime and justice and our perspectives on policy.

THE EVOLUTION OF MASS MEDIA

Over the past few decades, drastic changes in mass media have occurred in both form and content. In addition to the general transition away from more traditional types of media such as print media and radio, the development of the Internet has transformed the media from a passive to an interactive medium. Despite the increasing trend toward Internet usage, television remains the dominant form of video consumption among Americans.[12] Along with changes in format, increasing media consolidation over the past several years continues to impact the dissemination of information to the general public. Currently, five large global corporations—News Corporation, TimeWarner, Viacom, Walt Disney Company, and Bertelsmann—together control most of the media in the United States.[13] Often referred to as "media conglomerates," these corporations own the companies that deliver television, radio, films, newspapers, and books, and therefore control the content.[14] Although anyone with an Internet connection has access to alternative and independent sources of information, concerns have arisen over the selective nature of content disseminated by merely a handful of media organizations and the consequences of that corporate dominance within a democratic society.[15]

Similarly, there has been much concern over the merging of entertainment with "hard news."[16] This shift toward tabloid-style journalism is apparent in television news programming that focuses on sensational news stories, celebrity trials, and other high profile cases. With the advent of 24-hour cable television news networks, there is round-the-clock opportunity for the media to focus on tabloid justice. Ironically, although Americans are increasingly exposed to crime-focused television networks and programs, including crime-focused "reality" shows, they are not necessarily more confident in the criminal justice system, nor more knowledgeable about how the criminal justice system works.[17]

MEDIA AND CRIME

Themes of crime and justice have become staples in nearly every form of mass media. Novels, comic books, and films have a rich history of detailing both fictional and nonfictional accounts of crime. For example, early crime-focused comic books during the 1940s and 1950s reveled in violence and gore with titles such as *Crime Does Not Pay, Crime SuspenStories,* and *Crimes by Women.* Bradford Wright describes the typical themes of "psychopathic personalities, self-destructive lifestyles, killing aplenty, and inevitable, though usually belated, retribution."[18] Though eventually tamed by the publisher's self-imposed Comics Code

Authority, comic book stories of crime and justice continue to inspire. Adding to the rich history of crime and justice themes in films, comic-book-inspired super-hero tales have been among the top grossing films of the past several years.

Similar to literature and films, television is replete with crime and justice focused programs. According to Nielsen Media Research, individuals watch approximately four and a half hours of television a day, reaching a "record high" of households with a television set tuned each day for an average of about eight hours.[19] Increasingly, cable television and the Internet are gaining in popularity over more traditional forms of media such as newspapers.

Cable television refers to the transmission of television signals via coaxial cable or satellite. Although earlier generations typically enjoyed only a handful of broadcast networks that could be received through their television's built-in antenna, most homes in America now have access to hundreds of channels transmitted through a cable or satellite provider. According to the National Cable and Telecommunications Association, over 64 million of the 112 million total households in the United States hold basic cable subscriptions. This has steadily grown from the 9.8 million recorded in 1975.[20] The proliferation of cable television has come at a significant cost to broadcast networks with cable channels "enjoying their highest ratings ever, while their broadcast brethren look back on their worst year ever."[21]

Viewers may subscribe to cable companies that provide a variety of channels. With "narrowcasting," cable companies do not need to worry about satisfying all viewers with a single choice in programming. Rather, channels are offered that are very specific in content and target niche groups.[22] There are channels targeting adolescents (Disney, Nickelodeon, The N), women (Lifetime, Oxygen), men (Spike), sports enthusiasts (ESPN, Versus), boomers (TV Land), gays and lesbians (Logo), and political junkies (C-Span). News junkies now have an assortment of channels to which they can turn for round-the-clock news coverage. Launched in 1980, CNN became the first 24-hours news network, followed sixteen years later by MSNBC and Fox News Channel.[23]

Cable television provides a wealth of programming focused on policing and investigation, the judicial process, and corrections. During the 2004–2005 television season, crime procedurals comprised one-third of the top 40 shows.[24] One only need consult the (now onscreen) *TV Guide* to witness the dominance of crime-related programming across cable television. The "longest running crime-drama," *Law and Order,* has multiple spin-offs: New York and Miami each enjoy their own versions of the popular program *Crime Scene Investigation* (*CSI*), and each year a slew of new crime dramas are piloted on broadcast and cable networks. The proliferation of crime dramas is only one piece of a much larger puzzle. In addition to these dramas, there are crime-focused reality shows and "news magazines."

Crime coverage is also a major component of the 24-hour news networks (CNN, MSNBC, and Fox News) and there are two cable television channels (truTV and ID) devoted entirely to crime content. Court TV, originally launched in 1991, was designed to provide live coverage of trials, largely criminal trials, in an effort to help "people realize that courtroom trials are not at all what they thought."[25] The emergence of Court TV helped usher in the era of "tabloid justice" described by Fox et al. that continues today.[26] Tabloid justice is described as the trend toward packaging news as entertainment with an overwhelming emphasis on sensational trials and criminal investigations. During the past decade, Court TV expanded beyond trial coverage to include shows featuring commentary by hosts such as Catherine Crier, Star Jones, and Nancy Grace, as well as premiering various crime-based reality shows. In the latest move to broaden its appeal, Court TV has since been supplanted by truTV, a cable channel self-described as "television's destination for real-life stories told from an exciting and dramatic first-person perspective and features high-stakes, action-packed originals" (trutv.com/about). The transition is described by the network as a move toward focusing on "real life situations" as opposed to "typical reality shows, which often involve contests or other highly staged events" (http://www .trutv.com/about/faq.html). Similarly, Discovery's recently launched Investigation Discovery Channel (known as ID) offers 24-hour programming devoted to crime issues, offering syndicated crime docudramas and original programming such as *Deranged, Life of a Crime,* and *Most Evil.*

CRIME-RELATED PROGRAMMING ON CABLE TELEVISION

There are essentially three categories of crime-related entertainment shows on cable television: crime dramas (*Law and Order, The Closer,* etc.), crime-focused "reality" shows (*COPS, The First 48,* etc.), and crime docudramas and newsmagazines (*Lockup,* A&E's *American Justice,* and *Investigative Reports,* etc.). Each of these categories is described in some depth in the sections that follow.

Crime Dramas—Fiction as Entertainment

Since *Dragnet* transitioned from radio to television in the early 1950s, broadcast television has long embraced crime and justice programming in fictional dramas.[27] The success of crime-related dramas is still riding high with top-rated shows such as *CSI: Crime Scene Investigation, CSI: Miami, CSI: New York, NCIS (Naval Criminal Investigative Service), Law & Order, Law & Order: Special Victims Unit, Law & Order: Criminal Intent, Boston Legal, Criminal Minds, Medium,* and *Without a Trace.* Cable television viewers have also witnessed a surge in programming specifically devoted to crime and justice. Fictional crime dramas on premium cable channels include such critical hits as *The Wire, The Sopranos, Oz* (which each enjoyed long runs on HBO), and *Dexter* (which is one of Showtime's most successful programs to date).

On the majority of crime drama shows, white males are cast as lead crime fighters, leaving peripheral roles for women in general and particularly for men and women of color. In their study of *Law & Order: SVU,* Britto and colleagues found that minorities tend to be underrepresented as both crime fighters and victims.[28] Similarly, in their study of *NYPD Blue* and *Law & Order,* Eschholz, Mallard, and Flynn found that African Americans offenders are 1.75 times as likely to be shown in handcuffs as white offenders, almost 5 times as likely to be shown as an offender than a victim, and 3.57 times as likely to be shown as an offender than an attorney.[29]

Baynes found that for *Law & Order*, casting is dependent on finding the right "type" for a particular role, and that generally, white is the default. In other words, generally for a person of color to be cast, race must be specified in the script.[30] The current casts of the various *Law and Order* programs feature predominantly white actors in the roles of crime fighters. The original *Law and Order* program has the most diverse cast of the three, with a number of minorities in prominent police roles. However, none of the regularly featured district attorneys on *Law and Order* are black. The other two *Law and Order* programs have predominantly white casts. Despite being set in diverse cities, two of which have large minority populations, the current casts of all three of the *CSI* programs are nonetheless predominantly white.

In contrast, *The Wire*, set in Baltimore, features predominantly black actors in lead roles, including in roles as crime fighters. Mark Bowden of *The Atlantic* describes the largely African American cast as ". . . painstakingly authentic, down to the uniquely slurred consonants and nasal vowel sounds of the local dialect, Balmerese."[31] Critically acclaimed, *The Wire* is notable due to its refusal to reduce the workings of the criminal justice system and the corresponding players to a mere "good vs. evil" morality play. Instead, the show presents the complexity of individual decisions made in the context of dysfunctional and repressive social institutions. In addition to bringing issues of race, crime, and justice to the forefront, *The Wire* was acclaimed for its critical portrayal of the war on drugs as a futile and often counter-productive strategy. In its final season, the role of the media became central to the storyline.

Showtime's *Dexter*, while more fantastical than HBO's *The Wire*, inverts some stereotypes while perpetuating others. The lead in the show *Dexter* is a white male in his 30s who holds a day job as a crime-scene investigator and moonlights as a serial killer. Dexter's sister, a white female, also works for the police department in the stereotypical role of the woman who means well but whose naiveté often leads to situations which require her rescue by one of the stronger male characters. Although the lead is a white male, a number of minority actors are featured in prominent law enforcement roles on the show. Four of the eight most frequently featured cast members are minorities, including a Latina as the homicide division head, black and Latino males in the roles of lead homicide detectives, and an Asian American male as (somewhat stereotypically) the forensic investigator.

Cable channels, including basic cable channels, are routinely producing crime programming and over the past few years have recruited top talent to star in their crime-related dramas. Kyra Sedgwick, Glenn Close, and Holly Hunter star in the cable hits *The Closer, Damages,* and *Saving Grace,* respectively. In 2005, TNT gained one of the largest audiences ever for a basic cable drama series with the premiere of the procedural *The Closer*—a show that features Kyra Sedgwick as a deputy police chief for the LAPD.[32] Although *Damages* is a "legal thriller" with the protagonist a civil lawyer, the show's first season involved unraveling a heinous murder. Finally, in *Saving Grace* Holly Hunter stars as a "fiery police detective" who employs a "no-holds barred" approach. These shows are notable in that they feature female leads that are in many ways breaking free from the stereotypes of female crime fighters that have so often been portrayed as sexually repressed sidekicks that eventually require saving by the male protagonist. Although the shows generally have a racially diverse cast, none feature a woman of color as female lead.

Crime-Based Reality Shows—Nonfiction as Entertainment

Crime-based reality programs are designed as an attempt to "present true stories about crimes, criminals, and victims."[33] Crime-based reality shows sell crime as entertainment by nicely packaging shows with theme songs and graphics similar to any other fictional entertainment show.[34] Fishman and Cavender point out that crime-based reality shows grew in popularity during the late 1980s, a conservative "tough-on-crime" era with an increasingly pronounced focus on maintaining social order. With their reliance on law enforcement agencies for source material, these shows arguably foster a conservative ideology and support for punitive crime control policies.[35]

Perhaps the most well known, and one of the longest running, crime-based reality show is *COPS*, which premiered in 1989. On location, the camera follows law enforcement officers on the street as they investigate crime "as it happens." The use of the shaky camera situated in the passenger seat, devoid of voice-over narration, leaves the viewer with the impression that she is in some ways enjoying a "ride along" and witnessing the "reality" of the crime and policing as it happens. Despite this "ride-along" impression, the video footage undergoes much manipulation before reaching the viewing public. In the creation of a *COPS* episode, as many as 120 hours of raw footage are selectively edited down to 22 minutes.[36]

Like many fictional programs, *COPS* underrepresents African Americans and Hispanics as crime fighters. In fact, Kooistra and colleagues found that about two-thirds of the "cops" on *COPS* were white while more than half of the suspects were minorities. The authors characterize the show as one in which "crime is a battle between white police officers and nonwhite violent offenders."[37] Moreover, although crime is generally intraracial and is depicted as such on the show, they found that in the few cases in which interracial crime was featured, the show depicted "nonwhite criminals claiming white victims."[38] The authors suggest the cumulative effect is the impression that criminals are "not like us," ultimately reinforcing the "criminal blackman" stereotype.[39]

Other reality shows include A&E's *The First 48*, in which cameras follow homicide detectives from various jurisdictions as they attempt to follow leads during the crucial first forty-eight hours after the murder. *SWAT*, also airing on A&E, follows members of elite paramilitary units located in Dallas, Kansas City, and Detroit as they carry out various missions including "routine" drug search warrants. The viewers are described by A&E as riding "shotgun as the teams execute high-risk drug busts, apprehend murder suspects, search for high-profile missing persons, and rescue hostages." Some shows, such as *Animal Precinct* and *Animal Cops*, focus on following law enforcement officers as they target wrongdoing against some of the most vulnerable in our society, beloved pets and other more exotic animals. Similar to *COPS*, each of these shows presents "reality" from the perspective of law enforcement agents.

Other reality-based shows feature compilations of "shocking" real-life scenes "caught on tape." For example, *The Smoking Gun Presents: World's Dumbest* airing on truTV, catalogs segments of not-so-bright criminals caught on video surveillance tapes. The truTV show features various celebrities and comedians providing commentary on the failed criminal escapades. The purpose of these "caught in the act" segments is to shame and humiliate, while at the same time providing comic relief.

Rather than educate the viewer about the reality of law enforcement, these crime-based reality shows merge crime and entertainment into "humiliation tv." Bennett, Johnson, and Triplett have previously argued that print media is often a source of disintegrative shaming of the offender.[40] Disintegrative shaming is the process of shaming offenders without any corresponding efforts to reintegrate the offender back into the fold. Crime-based reality shows could quite easily be accused of engaging in disintegrative shaming by airing segments with no other end than to ridicule and humiliate the offender. Given the popularity of these shows, viewers presumably take pleasure in watching all the "dummies" and "pervs" getting caught and publicly humiliated leaving one to wonder whether the sociologist Emile Durkheim might have described these shows as providing a way for society to reinforce boundaries by collectively observing the spectacle of losers being caught.

One of the most disturbing of these reality shows, *To Catch a Predator*, features Dateline NBC correspondent Chris Hansen confronting alleged child sex predators who have attempted to make contact with underage children in stings set up by the program in cooperation with local-law enforcement agencies. To date, NBC has run twelve of these *To Catch a Predator* specials, focusing on a different geographic area in each.

Unencumbered by *Miranda*, or any other legal protections that restrict law enforcement, Hanson revels in publicly humiliating each suspect that is lured into the decoy house by adults posing online as children. Considering the repugnant nature of the crime, there is understandably little sympathy by viewers for the suspect. However, there is also no sense that the suspect is innocent until proven guilty. Rather, the judge and jury is Hansen himself. Unfortunately, in one case, the humiliation led to tragedy. In 2006, the show ensnared fifty-six-year-old Bill Conradt, a Texas prosecutor. Conradt had engaged in sexually explicit online conversations with a person he believed to be a thirteen-year-old boy. During the ambush, as the SWAT team entered his house, Conradt shot himself. Later, a wrongful death suit filed by Conradt's family was settled for an undisclosed amount.[41]

The show's questionable tactics have at times drawn criticism. In fact, in 2007 the show's own producer, Marsha Bartel, sued NBC, arguing she was fired from the network for complaining about the show's unethical practices and its working relationship with civilian group Perverted Justice and law enforcement.[42] The district court ultimately ruled in favor of the network, stating that the twenty-one-year NBC veteran Bartel could be fired at will.[43]

The merging of crime and entertainment, specifically in the form of crime-based reality shows, raises many ethical considerations. For example, although these programs usually end with a statement that the accused is innocent until proven guilty, and occasionally provide a statement indicating the case outcome for particular individuals, many of the suspects may never be charged, prosecuted, or found guilty of the alleged crimes. Instead, the cameras shut down as soon as the arrests are made and viewers are left with images of irredeemable "bad boys." Scholars have argued that crime-based reality programs are not so much informing the audience as they are reinforcing existing stereotypes, presenting criminals as irrational, predatory "others" who can only be controlled by an increasingly punitive criminal justice system. To that end, such programming encourages "widespread surveillance, and revives the spectacle of punishment."[44]

As importantly, the role of law enforcement is transformed through crime-based reality programming with police becoming active participants in the commodification of crime as entertainment. Agencies are complicit in the filming of these programs and maintain editorial control over the final product and in the process strive to present themselves in the best light.[45] The viewer is presumed to be witnessing reality, but what is left on the cutting room floor may be just as telling as that which made it to air. In his examination of *COPS*, Doyle notes that the show "omits any portrayals of overtly racist behavior by police."[46] Similarly, Doyle points out *COPS* maintains a class bias by focusing on poor neighborhoods to the exclusion of weathly areas. Since the show is dependent on the cooperation of law enforcement, not surprisingly negative portrayals of police may jeopardize the future of the show. Doyle states *COPS* rarely airs material that would reflect negatively on police.[47]

There are a handful of shows designed to primarily "educate," rather than humiliate the viewer. For example, the Discovery Channel's *It Takes a Thief* employs the services of two formerly convicted thieves who break into homes to demonstrate the vulnerabilities that homeowners have overlooked. The break-in is "followed by a lesson in what steps to take to prevent such a violation from occurring again."[48] Similarly, truTV's *The Real Hustle* is designed to show how even the most hypervigilant can fall prey to street scams and con artists. A personal security consultant (and sleight-of-hand artist), psychology specialist (and magician), and actress join forces to con unsuspecting New Yorkers. Although these shows sell themselves as providing consumer education around crime prevention, the value of the "education" they provide is questionable.

Crime Docudramas and Newsmagazines

Crime docudramas and newsmagazines give the audience insight into either an unsolved crime or a crime that has already been investigated and processed through the criminal justice system, perhaps many years after the fact. These shows, such as *City Confidential, The New Detectives,* and *Cold Case Files,* often focus on the reenactment of cases, often building a "who-dun-it" suspense narrative for the viewer. They typically present a particular criminal event challenging the viewer to piece together the facts of the case before a twist reveal at the conclusion.

In 2000, the Oxygen network was launched, primarily targeted toward female viewers. With *Snapped,* Oxygen contributes its own crime docudrama by focusing on the stories of female murderers. Although some episodes address the previous victimization experiences of the women featured that so often contributes to the ultimate act of violence, the show basically reduces the motivations of all murders, regardless of circumstances, to the individual "snapping" (i.e., losing control). On its website, the show claims that the "shocking but true stories turn common assumptions about crime and criminals upside down, and prove that even the most unlikely suspects can be capable of murder."[49] By focusing on females as violent offenders, the show is unfortunately contributing to the very myths that it seeks to disprove. If the common assumption is that most murders are committed by men, then that is a correct assumption. In fact, women are far less likely to commit crimes than men, and when women do commit crime, they (like men) are far more likely to engage in nonviolent property crimes than murder.

Currently, women account for approximately seven percent of the overall prison population.[50] Minorities generally, and African Americans in particular, are vastly overrepresented in prison populations, including among populations of women prisoners. Close to 45 percent of females in prison are women of color (28 percent black and 17 percent Hispanic) and the incarceration rate for black women is three times the rate for white women. Many of these women are incarcerated for drug offenses and only about one-third of them have been sentenced to prison following a conviction for a violent crime. Over the past few decades, the war on drugs has been largely responsible for the vast increase in the size of the prison population generally and particularly for the dramatic increase in female prison populations. While less than 20 percent of male prisoners are serving sentences for drug convictions, almost 30 percent of the women in prison are doing time for a drug offense. Like other crime-focused entertainment, *Snapped* forgoes serious discussion of criminal justice policies—such as the war on drugs—that lead to the mass incarceration of females, in favor of individual profiles of the very unusual women who kill. In the sixth season of *Snapped,* four of the twenty-two profiles on the show's website featured African American females.

Other news magazines provide a documentary-style examination of various crime and justice issues, such as *American Justice* or MSNBC's prison-focused *Lockup. Lockup* provides a view of jail and prison life "on the inside." Since the correctional system tends to be the most overlooked component of the criminal justice system by the media, it is laudable to give some much needed attention to incarceration.[51] However, the perspective given on the shows is rarely that of the inmates, but rather the perspective of outsiders looking in. The inmates become a spectacle, human refuse to be forgotten at the end of the hour. Viewers are exposed to situations in which unremorseful inmates are at odds with each other and the system, are frequently engaged in violence, and doomed to recidivism. These shows tend to completely ignore the social context from which the prisoners have emerged. The viewer is merely left with images of caged (usually black and brown) inmates. Although the show is providing a pseudorealistic look at the facility under examination and the show sometimes includes experts to discuss the problems confronted in prisons, the criminal justice system itself is not critiqued in any meaningful manner. Criminal behavior is reduced to a problem of individual responsibility, totally neglecting the social and economic forces that impede successful reentry for these offenders.

Crime in the News—24-Hour News

In addition to crime-related entertainment shows, the convergence of crime and entertainment has perhaps been most apparent on the 24-hour news networks. In one of the most comprehensive examinations of television news coverage of crime and justice related issues, Fox and colleagues documented the merging of news and entertainment into the now ubiquitous "tabloid justice."[52] Tabloid justice refers to increased interest in investigation and trials by mainstream journalists, elevating unusual, sensationalist stories to national significance.[53] The vast majority of the crime stories have little relevance to each of our daily lives. It is, for example, not clear why the murder of a pregnant woman by her husband in a small California town has any relevance to the lives of Americans living in the South or in New England. Still, the murder of Laci Peterson made for national headline news for the better part of a year. Fox and colleagues points out that of the eleven top-covered tabloid justice stories since 1991, only two seemed to have direct relevance of national concern.[54]

The emergence of 24-hour cable news provides a forum for hours of dissection and punditry. The news programs package a particular trial, complete with catchphrases and graphics, and sell it to the consuming public. Unfortunately, as has been documented elsewhere, this style of broadcasting has contributed to the distortion and exaggeration of the crime problem.[55] This exaggeration has been particularly pronounced in the area of missing and abducted children generally and missing white girls and women specifically.

Missing White Girls and Women   During 2002, cable news channels featured numerous stories on child abductions.[56] During that year, the media disproportionately focused on the abduction of three girls, two of whom were subsequently murdered. A search on LexisNexis of 2002 television transcripts revealed 1,336 references across the three 24-hour news networks to just three missing girls: 513 references were made to Danielle Van Dan (a missing seven-year-old white girl from San Diego, California, who was kidnapped and ultimately murdered by a neighbor), 333 references to Samantha Runnion (a missing five-year-old white girl from Riverside County, California who was abducted, sexually assaulted, and killed by a man who had previously been charged, but acquitted of a sexual offense), and 490 pertaining to Elizabeth Smart (a fourteen-year-old missing white girl abducted from her home in Salt Lake City, Utah, and ultimately found in the company of her kidnappers nine months later).

The "theme" of child abductions that year resulted in an exaggeration and distortion of the problem of missing children.[57] The extensive coverage of these cases created the impression that most missing persons are young girls, stranger abductions are frequent, and that missing children are likely to be murdered. According to the Department of Justice, in 1999 there were approximately 797,000 missing children. Of the children reported missing, 84 percent ran away or were reported as missing as the result of a misunderstanding between the child and the caretaker of where the child should have been.[58] The report concludes, "only a small minority of missing children were abducted, and most of these children were abducted by family members."[59]

Although young missing white girls dominate media coverage, there is no shortage of stories around missing adult women. These women, typically college-aged women, are also almost exclusively white. Indeed, one common thread among the coverage of missing persons was the fact that nearly every missing child or adult that received national coverage was white. The disproportionate focus by the media on missing girls, specifically missing white girls, has led to criticism, even from journalists themselves. MSNBC, in an article in the "Crime & Courts" section by Alex Johnson, reports "If you're missing, it helps to be young, white, and female."[60] Other journalists have addressed the apparent bias in the coverage of missing persons. Some of the reasons given for the lack of coverage of missing nonwhite persons were that the stories were "extraordinary," therefore warranting coverage, or that local news coverage drives the national coverage, or that there was unconscious bias at work rather than conscious manipulation of the news.[61]

Whatever the explanation, the "missing white girl" phenomenon has real consequences including the potential to mislead the public around the nature of the problem, exaggerate the extent of the problem, and ratchet up fear of crime. Although their stories are often tragic, focusing only on missing white girls and women who have been abducted gives the impression that these girls and women are in fact representative of all individuals that are missing. In 2007, according to the FBI National Crime Information Center (NCIC) report, there were over 800,000 missing persons, very few of whom had been abducted and even fewer of whom received national media coverage.[62] Approximately 78 percent of those missing are under eighteen years of age. Of those, 56 percent are female. Further, of those missing who are under eighteen years of age, 61 percent are white and 33 percent are black.[63] In other words, blacks (who make up approximately 13 percent of the U.S. population) are disproportionately represented among missing-person populations yet are almost never the focus of media coverage of missing persons. The exclusion of persons of color from media coverage devalues their plight, allocating the majority of resources to one particular group of people who fit the typical, innocent American concept of a true victim.

MEDIA DISTORTION: RACE AND CRIME

Much of the criticism of media portrayals of crime and justice focuses on the presence of racial stereotypes. Although research has found that blacks are often underrepresented as offenders on fictional programs, they are frequently over-represented as offenders on news and reality-based programming.[64] Although some might suggest that blacks are overrepresented as offenders in the news media simply because they are overrepresented as offenders in official crime data, research has demonstrated that even higher arrest rates for blacks cannot explain the frequency with which they appear as offenders in news coverage.[65] In other words, although there are clear and pronounced racial disparities in crime data and across the criminal justice system more generally, these dispari-ties are exaggerated further still in news coverage. In his study of the effects of the overrepresentation of blacks as criminals on news programs, Dixon found that "exposure to blacks' overrepresentation as criminals on local news pro-gramming was positively related to the perception of blacks as violent."[66]

Pager recently argued that media coverage of crime perpetuates and aggra-vates racial stereotypes by emphasizing the "racialized context" in which criminal events are depicted. Citing studies that demonstrate that blacks are more likely to be shown in mugshots or handcuffs being escorted under the direct control of (usually white) police officers, she argues that not only are blacks more likely to be depicted as offenders in news coverage, but the context in which they are depicted is also skewed.[67] Chiricos and Eschholz, for example, found that on local television news programs in Orlando, although blacks were not overrepresented as suspects, they were more likely to be portrayed in a "threatening" manner than white suspects, such as a mug shot, stranger victimization, or interracial victim-izations.[68] The images of black offenders tend to be more "menacing" with blacks all too frequently depicted as "dangerous, violent, and criminal."[69]

In an examination of the "dangerous black criminal" stereotype, Dixon and Maddox examined the effects of the skin tone of the perpetrator on television news viewers. The authors found that, particularly among heavy television users, dark-skinned perpetrators elicited more emotional concern, or "worry about the story," than white perpetrators. Participants found the white perpe-trators to be the least memorable compared to dark-skinned perpetrators. Fur-ther, they found that victims of black perpetrators, regardless of skin tone, were viewed more favorably than victims of white perpetrators.[70]

Moreover, according to Anthony Thompson, these media images of the black criminal exacerbate the problem of racial stereotyping because white Americans are for the most part residentially segregated from black Americans and experience limited direct personal interaction with them.[71] Due to the lack of significant direct contact, most of what whites typically know about blacks is gleaned from the media.[72] Thompson points out that all blacks, criminal or otherwise, are affected by these media portrayals, and "the lack of contact be-tween whites and most persons of color has made it virtually impossible to break down the large and diverse racial stereotypes promulgated in the media and politics."[73]

Representations of crime and justice from the news media, crime-focused "reality shows," and fictional dramas inform the construction of our social reality. In fact, Holbrook and Hill found that viewers of television crime dramas were more likely to perceive crime as "as one of the most important issues—if not *the* most important issue—facing the nation."[74] The authors argue that crime dramas are as significant as the news media in potentially increasing the salience of crime as a political issue.

THE MEDIA, PUBLIC OPINION, AND PUBLIC POLICY

Criminologists have long recognized the importance of the media in shaping public opinions and, at least indirectly, influencing public policy.[75] Some have argued that public opinion drives public policy; others argue that public policy shapes and directs public opinion, while a sizeable number believe that the relationship is far more complex and almost certainly reciprocal in nature. Proponents of all three perspectives reserve a role for the media. Those who describe a reciprocal relationship between public opinion and public policy argue that public opinion plays an important role in the development of public policy and that political posturing undoubtedly affects public opinion. Katherine Beckett, for example, has argued that the media act as the crucial middlemen in the development of public policies related to crime. According to Beckett, when reporting on crime and punishment, the media rely heavily on government sources because they make good 'official' sources and tend to package information in ways that are useful for dissemination. Through an overreliance on government sources, the media allows these sources, or "claims-makers" as Beckett refers to them, to shape the nature of the conversation about crime, criminals, and appropriate punishments. In her groundbreaking study, Beckett was able to demonstrate that public concern about various crime problems followed, rather than preceded, media coverage of those problems.[76]

David Garland similarly argues that "public knowledge and opinion about criminal justice are based upon collective representations rather than accurate information; upon a culturally given experience of crime, rather than the thing itself."[77] According to Garland, cultural representations of crime and justice inform our sense of what is right or wrong and our ideas of justice and punishment. And while Garland also credits the media for its contributions to these cultural representations, he ultimately argues that "it is a mistake to infer . . . that the voting public is easily and infinitely malleable, that mass support for law and order policies can be conjured up from nothing, or that newspapers and television can create and sustain a mass audience for crime stories without certain social and psychological conditions being already in place."[78]

Regardless of its source, public opinion regarding crime and punishment is complex and often contradictory. An abundance of previous research has demonstrated that the American public knows very little about the actual extent of crime or about the nature of sentencing and punishment.[79] Cullen and colleagues note this "lack of knowledge about crime is not an isolated domain of ignorance" and cite Kinder (1998) in arguing that the public is "awash in ignorance" about most policy issues.[80] The public usually thinks criminal justice policies are not punitive enough but also frequently lacks knowledge with regard to how punitive those policies actually are. Even where there is some knowledge, Roberts points out that very few people have had direct experience with the criminal justice system, and so most of the knowledge that the public does have about crime is secondhand.[81]

CONCLUSION

Cable television has become one of our most influential sources of both fictional and nonfictional representations of crime and justice in the twenty-first century. Given the extent to which the media both reflects and shapes our social lives, it is imperative that we develop a better understanding of the ways in which the media generally and cable television more specifically portray crime and justice. Unfortunately, the media provides images that misrepresent and distort the crime problem through the demonization or marginalization of minorities. Through our examination of crime-related cable television programming we attempt to recognize and challenge those images.

CRITICAL THINKING QUESTIONS

1. What is the role of cable television in the production of crime?
2. How are minorities presented in crime dramas on cable television? Are there any identifiable trends?
3. Discuss research findings as they relate to crime-based reality shows. What is the impact of these shows?
4. Do you agree or disagree with the authors' findings as they relate to crime docudramas and news magazines?
5. How do the media and prime-time television manage to instill fear and to reinforce negative stereotypes?

NOTES

1. Aletha Huston, Edward Donnerstein, Halford Fairchild, Norma Feshbach, Phyllis Katz, John Murray, Eli Rubinstein, Brian Wilcox, and Dianna Zuckerman, *Big World, Small Screen: The Role of Television in American Society.* (Lincoln, NE: University of Nebraska Press, 1992), 6.

2. Nielsen Media Research, "Nielsen Reports Television Tuning Remains at Record Levels," October 17, 2007, http://www.nielsenmedia .com/nc/portal/site/Public/menu item.55dc65b4a7d5adff3f659361 47a062a0/?vgnextoid=13280e5b2 cea5110VgnVCM100000ac0a260a RCRD.

3. Huston et al., *Big World, Small Screen.*

4. Gregg Barak, *Media, Process, and the Social Construction of Crime* (New York: Garland, 1995); Victor Kappeler and Gary Potter, *The Mythology of Crime and Criminal Justice,* 4th ed. (Long Grove, IL: Waveland Press, 2005); Jessica Pollak and Charles Kubrin, "Crime in the News: How Crimes, Offenders, and Victims Are Portrayed in the Media," *Journal of Criminal Justice and Popular Culture* 14, no. 1 (2007): 59–83; Clinton Sanders and Eleanor Lyon, "Repetitive Retribution: Media Images and the Cultural Construction of Criminal Justice," in *Cultural Criminology,* ed. Jeff Ferrell and Clinton Sanders (Boston: Northeastern University Press, 1995), 25–44. Ray Surette, *Media, Crime, and Criminal Justice: Images, Realities, and Policies* (Belmont, CA: Wadsworth, 2007).

5. Ray Surette, "The Media, the Public, and Criminal Justice Policy," *Journal of the Institute of Justice & International Studies.* Papers from the November 2002 Crime, Media, & Public Policy Symposium, 2003, 39–52.

6. Victor Kappeler and Gary Potter, *The Mythology of Crime and Criminal Justice,* 4th ed. (Long Grove, IL: Waveland Press, 2005). Ray Surette, *Media, Crime, and Criminal Justice: Images, Realities, and Policies* (Belmont, CA: Wadsworth, 2007).

7. Gregg Barak, *Media, Process, and the Social Construction of Crime;* Sarah Eschholz, Matthew Mallard, and Stacy Flynn, "Analysis of *NYPD Blue* and *Law & Order,*" *Journal of Criminal Justice and Popular Culture,* 10 no. 3 (2004): 161–180; Pollak and Kubrin, "Crime in the News," Surette, *Media, Crime, and Criminal Justice.*

8. Katheryn Russell, *The Color of Crime* (New York: New York University Press, 1998), 3.

9. Devah Pager, *Marked: Race, Crime, and Finding Work in an Era of Mass Incarceration* (Chicago, IL: University of Chicago Press, 2007).

10. Leonard Baynes, "White Out: The Absence and Stereotyping of People of Color by the Broadcast Networks in Prime Time Entertainment Programming," *Arizona Law Review,* 45 (2003): 293–369.

11. Jeff Ferrell, Keith Hayward, Wayne Morrison, and Mike Presdee, eds., *Cultural Criminology Unleashed* (London: Glasshouse Press, 2004), 4.

12. Brian Stelter, "Whichever Screen, People Are Watching," *New York Times,* July 8, 2008, Media & Advertising section.

13. Ben Bagdikian, *The New Media Monopoly* (Boston, MA: Beacon Press, 2004).

14. Ibid.

15. Ibid.; Mark Miller, "What's Wrong with This Picture?" *The Nation,* January 7, 2002, http://www.thenation.com/doc/20020107/miller.

16. Thomas Patterson, "Doing Well and Doing Good: How Soft News and Critical Journalism Are Shrinking the News Audience and Weakening Democracy—And What News Outlets Can Do About It" (Cambridge, MA: President and Fellows of Harvard College, 2000).

17. Richard Fox, Robert Van Sickel, and Thomas Steiger, *Tabloid Justice: Criminal Justice in an Age of Media Frenzy,* 2nd ed. (Boulder, CO: Lynne Rienner Publishers, 2007).

18. Bradford Wright, *Comic Book Nation: The Transformation of Youth Culture in America* (Baltimore, MD: The Johns Hopkins University Press, 2001), 81.

19. Nielsen Media Research, "Nielsen Reports Television Tuning Remains at Record Levels," October 17, 2007, http://www.nielsen media.com/nc/portal/site/Public/menuitem.55dc65b4a7d5a dff3f65936147a062a0/?vgnextoid =13280e5b2cea5110VgnVCM1000 00ac0a260aRCRD.

20. National Cable and Telecommunications Association, Statistics, 2007, http://www.ncta.com/Statistic/Statistic/Statistics.aspx.

21. Brian Stelter, "Cable Networks Trying to Building on Their Gains in Ratings," *New York Times,* May 26, 2008, http://www .nytimes.com/2008/05/26/business/media/26cable.html?_r=1 &oref=slogin.

22. Edwin Vane and Lynne Gross, *Programming for TV, Radio, and Cable* (Boston: Focal Press, 1994).

23. Fox et al., *Tabloid Justice.*

24. Manuel Mendoza, "For Network and Cable TV, Crime Does Pay," *The Boston Globe,* July 5, 2005, http://www.boston.com/ae/tv/articles/2005/07/05/for_network_and_cable_tv_crime_does_pay/.

25. Dennis Cauchon and Tony Mauro, "Tonight, Real-Life Courtroom Drama Opens Its Case on TV: Viewers See 'L.A. Law' Isn't Real Law," *USA Today,* June 21, 1991, p. 1A.

26. Fox et al. *Tabloid Justice.*

27. Surette, *Media, Crime, and Criminal Justice.*

28. Sarah Britto, Tycy Hughes, Kurt Saltzman, and Colin Stroh, "Does

'Special' Mean Young, White and Female? Deconstructing the Meaning of 'Special' in *Law & Order: Special Victims Unit,*" *Journal of Criminal Justice and Popular Culture,* 14 no. 1: 39–57.

29. Eschholz, Mallard, and Flynn, "Analysis."

30. Baynes, "White Out," 311.

31. Mark Bowden, "The Angriest Man in Television," *The Atlantic,* Jan/Feb 2008, http://www.theatlantic .com/doc/200801/bowden-wire.

32. Mendoza, "For Network and Cable TV, Crime Does Pay."

33. Mark Fishman and Gray Cavender, *Entertaining Crime: Television Reality Programs* (New York: Aldine de Gruyter, 1998), 3.

34. Marianna Valverde, *Law and Order: Images, Meanings, Myths* (New York: Rutgers, 2006).

35. Fishman and Cavender, *Entertaining Crime.*

36. Fox Press Release, "'COPS' Warrants an Arresting 20th Season Milestone and Celebrates its 700th Episode This Fall on Fox," http://www.foxflash.com/div.php/main/page?aID=1z2z2z49z2z8&ID=3613.

37. Paul Kooistra, John Mahoney, and Saundra Westervelt "The World According to 'COPS,'" in *Entertaining Crime: Television Reality Programs* (New York: Aldine de Gruyter, 1998), 141–158, p. 153.

38. Ibid, 153.

39. Ibid, 155.

40. Katherine Bennett, Wesley Johnson, and Ruth Triplett, "The Role of the Media in Reintegrative Shaming: A Content Analysis," in *Popular Culture, Crime & Justice* (Belmont: Wadsworth, 1998), 142–156.

41. Luke Dittrich, "Tonight on Dateline This Man Will Die," *Esquire*, August 2, 2007, http://www.esquire.com/features/predator.

42. Marcus Baram, "Turning the Tables on 'To Catch a Predator,'" *ABC News*, June 5, 2007, http://abcnews.go.com/US/story?id=3235975&page=1.

43. Zach Lowe, "Winston & Strawn Helps NBC Squash Ex-Dateline Producer's Firing Suit," *The AmLaw Daily*, September 11, 2008, http://amlawdaily.typepad.com/amlawdaily/2008/09/ex-nbc-producer.html.

44. Gray Cavender, "In 'The Shadow of Shadows': Television Reality Crime Programming," in *Entertaining Crime: Television Reality Programs* (New York: Aldine de Gruyter, 1998), 79–94; Pamela Donovan, "Armed with Power of Television: Reality Crime Programming and the Reconstruction of Law and Order in the United States," in *Entertaining Crime: Television Reality Programs* (New York: Aldine de Gruyter, 1998), 117–137.

45. Surette, *Media, Crime, and Criminal Justice.*

46. Aaron Doyle, "'COPS': Television Policing as Policing Reality," in *Entertaining Crime: Television Reality Programs* (New York: Aldine de Gruyter, 1998), 106.

47. Ibid, p. 105.

48. Discovery Channel, "About the Show," *It Takes a Thief*, http://dsc.discovery.com/fansites/ittakesathief/about/about.html.

49. Oxygen, "About the Show," *Snapped*, http://www.oxygen.com/TvShows/Detail.aspx?code=SNP&view=about.

50. William Sabol, Heather Couture, and Paige Harrison, *Prisoners in 2006* (Washington, D.C.: U.S. Department of Justice, 2007).

51. Surette, *Media, Crime, and Criminal Justice.*

52. Fox et al., *Tabloid Justice.*

53. Ibid.

54. Ibid.

55. Ibid. Kappeler and Potter, *The Mythology of Crime and Criminal Justice;* Nickie Phillips and Natasha Frost "Punditry on Parade: Crime Reporting on Cable News," presented at the American Society of Criminology, 59th Annual Meeting. Atlanta, GA, 2007. Surette, *Media, Crime, and Criminal Justice.*

56. Leon Harris, "Cases of Kidnapped, Missing Children Dominate Headlines," *CNN Live Today*, transcript, August 29, 2002, http://transcripts.cnn.com/TRANSCRIPTS/0208/29/lt.09.html.

57. Kappeler and Potter, *The Mythology of Crime and Criminal Justice.*

58. Andrea Sedlak, David Finkelhor, Heather Hammer, and Dana Schultz, *National Estimates of Missing Children: An Overview* (Washington, D.C.: Office of Juvenile Justice and Delinquency Prevention).

59. Ibid, p. 10.

60. Alex Johnson, "Damsels in Distress: If You're Missing, It Helps to Be White," MSNBC, July 23, 2004, http://www.msnbc.msn.com/id/5325808/.

61. Associated Press, "Media under Fire on Missing Persons," MSNBC, June 15, 2005, http://www.msnbc.msn.com/id/8233195/; Eugene Robinson, "(White) Women We Love," *Washington Post*, June 10, 2005, A23.

62. National Crime Information Center (NCIC), "Missing Person and Unidentified Person Statistics for 2007," http://www.fbi.gov/hq/cjisd/missingpersons.htm#missingfilereport.

63. Ibid.

64. Travis Dixon, "Crime News and Racialized Beliefs: Understanding the Relationship Between Local News Viewing and Perceptions of African Americans and Crime," *Journal of Communication* 58 (2008): 106–125; Mary Oliver and Blake Armstrong, "The Color of Crime: Perceptions of Caucasian's and African American's Involvement in Crime," in Fishman & Cavender *Entertaining Crime: Television Reality Programs*, eds. Mark Fishman and Gray Cavender (New York: Aldine De Gruyter, 1998).

65. Travis Dixon and Daniel Linz, "Overrepresentation and Underrepresentation of African Americans and Latinos as Lawbreakers on Television News," *Journal of Communication* 50, no. 2 (2000): 131–154; Daniel Romer, Kathleen Jamieson, and Nicole deCouteau "The Treatment of Persons of Color in Local Television News: Ethnic Blame Discourse or Realistic Group Conflict?" *Communication Research* 25, no. 3 (1998): 286–305.

66. Dixon, "Crime News and Racialized Beliefs," p. 117.

67. Pager, *Marked: Race, Crime, and Finding Work in an Era of Mass Incarceration*.

68. Chiricos and Eschholz, "The Racial and Ethnic Typification of Crime and the Criminal Typification of Race and Ethnicity in Local Television News," p. 415.

69. Pager, *Marked*, 95.

70. Travis Dixon and Keith Maddox, "Skin Tone, Crime News, and Social Reality Judgments: Priming the Stereotype of the Dark and Dangerous Black Criminal," *Journal of Applied Social Psychology*, 35 (2005): 1555–1570.

71. Anthony Thompson, *Releasing Prisoners, Redeeming Communities: Reentry, Race, and Politics* (New York: NYU Press, 2008).

72. Baynes, "White Out."

73. Thompson, *Releasing Prisoners*, 20.

74. R. Andrew Holbrook and Timothy G. Hill, "Agenda-Setting and Priming in Prime Time Television: Crime Dramas as Political Cues," *Political Communication* 22 (2005): 291.

75. Katherine Beckett, *Making Crime Pay: Law and Order in Contemporary American Politics* (New York: Oxford University Press, 1997); Todd Clear and Natasha Frost, "Rules of Engagement: Criminology & Criminal Justice Policy," *Criminal Justice Matters* 72, no. 1 (2008): 37–38; Todd Clear and Natasha Frost, "Informing Public Policy," *Criminology & Public Policy* 6, no. 4 (2007): 633–640; David Garland, *The Culture of Control: Crime and Social Order in Contemporary Society* (Chicago, IL: University of Chicago Press, 2001).

76. Beckett, *Making Crime Pay*.

77. Garland, *The Culture of Control*, p. 158.

78. Garland, *The Culture of Control*, p. 146.

79. Julian Roberts, "Public Opinion, Crime and Criminal Justice," *Crime and Justice: A Review of Research* (Chicago: University of Chicago Press, 1992), 99–180;

Julian Roberts and Loretta Stalans, *Public Opinion, Crime and Criminal Justice* (Boulder, CO: Westview Press, 1997); Francis Cullen, Bonnie Fisher, and Brandon Applegate, "Public Opinion about Punishment and Corrections," in *Crime and Justice: A Review of Research*, ed. M. Tonry (Chicago: University of Chicago Press, 2000), 1–79.

80. Cullen et al., "Public Opinion about Punishment and Corrections," 4.

81. Roberts, "Public Opinion, Crime and Criminal Justice."

CHAPTER 12

The Presentation of Race in Crime Stories

Steven Chermak
Jeffrey Gruenewald
Jesenia Pizarro

The murder of JonBenet Ramsey was one of the most celebrated crime events of the last twenty years. There were many factors that increased the appeal of this case, including that the murder occurred in an affluent suburb and that it remains unsolved, due in part to investigatory foul-ups and power struggles between law enforcement agencies pursuing this case. Moreover, the primary suspect status of the victim's wealthy parents and widely distributed photographs of JonBenet's involvement in child beauty pageants opened a window to a strange world that certainly fueled the celebrated nature of this case. Although all of these factors have melded together to produce a long-running front-page story and widespread public recognition of the case, perhaps the most important variables that contributed to its high-profile coverage were that the victim was a child and white.

Horrible crimes are especially salacious when a child is the victim, but all children, and all victims, are not treated equally by the news media. White victims are significantly more newsworthy than minority victims. Would the Jon-Benet Ramsey murder case have been nearly as newsworthy if she had been black or Hispanic? Lee Bey of the *Chicago Sun-Times* concluded that it would not have been an important news story. He compared the coverage of Ramsey to a young, black girl who was raped, poisoned, brutally beaten, and left for dead with gang symbols written on her body in a Chicago housing project.[1] Although there was local news coverage of the girl who would become known as Girl X, the case did not generate national outrage. Bey wrote: "The Cabrini-Green rape would be widely known had the victim been white. Then it would have been news. Some legislator would have pushed for tougher laws against brutalizers of children . . . But the deafening silence in the wake of the girl's attack has a lot to do with the fact that society has blind spots when it comes to realizing bad

141

guys and their victims come in all colors and classes. A vicious crime against a child is a breach of moral decency—whether it happens in the projects or the penthouse, whether the criminal is black or white."[2]

The study of race in the media, especially how race is presented in crime stories, is important for several reasons. First, people consume an incredible amount of media imagery. Although the numbers appear to be declining, the average news consumer spends over 3,500 hours in media interactions in a typical year.[3] More specifically, in a 24-hour period, adults spend on average over 260 minutes watching television, 125 minutes on radio, 85 minutes on the Internet, 20 minutes with newspapers, and 16 minutes with magazines.[4] Children and teenagers are also deeply embedded within the media culture of society. In a 2005 research symposium hosted by Nickelodeon called the "New Normal," participants highlighted that 70 percent of children have television in their bedrooms, watch almost a full day of television in a typical week, and use multiple media simultaneously.[5] New technologies have also influenced how we interact with the "objective world." A November 2007 Harris Public Opinion Poll indicated that the number of adults online and the amount of time spent online has increased. Nearly 80 percent of adults are online for just over eleven hours per week. In comparison, only 9 percent of adults reported that they went online in 1995.[6] The growth of other media outlets, although not frequently studied, certainly is contributing to additional changes to the media landscape.

Second, images and ideas presented in the media are critically important to how an individual thinks about and interacts with the social world. Several researchers who have discussed the social construction of reality have provided a good framework for thinking about the potential influence of the media.[7] These studies, and other related research, indicate that an individual's ideas, actions, interactions, and opinions are influenced by a multitude of factors, including objective and symbolic conditions, such as their personal experiences and exposure to mass media. It is important to note that as an individual's objective interactions with the social world decrease, the influence of symbolic conditions increase. So, for example, media consumers are much more strongly influenced by what they read and view about crime when their experiences with crime and the criminal justice system are minimal. It is for these reasons that criminal justice organizations and other key social control organizations invest considerable resources in preparing to work with the media to strategically influence what is publicly known about these organizations.

Third, racism remains one of the United State's most challenging social issues. There is a general belief that some progress has been made in the last thirty years in the fight against racism. One example of this progress is how "overt acts" and "explicit forms" of racism have significantly declined. Shanto Iyengar and Kyu Hahn discuss how "racial bias is no longer explicit because most Americans, having been socialized in the post–civil rights era, accept the norm of racial equality and are unwilling to express overt racial prejudice." Similarly, there has been a significant effort by news organizations to directly confront racism in newsroom and racist content by hiring minority journalists, attempting to present issues that are particularly salient to minority communities, and critically thinking about how race is covered in the news. These conclusions do not mean that racism has been eliminated, but that it has been transformed into more "implicit forms of racial prejudice."[8] Evidence of this implicit racism comes from research on how the coverage of crime influences public opinion. Gilliam and Iyengar, for instance, examine the various elements of the "crime news script," comparing the importance of the type of crime with characteristics of the suspect.[9] Using a series of laboratory experiments, they found that when elements of the story are "racialized," public support for harsher sentences, such as mandatory minimums and the death penalty, increases.[10]

It is important to examine the existing research that describes the presentation of blacks and Hispanics in contemporary crime stories. In this chapter, we explore more deeply the presentation of race/ethnicity in crime stories. Our focus is primarily on the presentation of race/ethnicity in the news, but we also highlight how these findings are consistent with research examining other mediums, such as popular films, prime-time television, and commercials. In order to lay the foundation for our discussion, we begin by highlighting the extant research on crime in the news. We then discuss literature on how blacks and Hispanics are presented in the news and influence the coverage of crime. In the final section, we provide some notable explanations that attempt to explain why race is presented as it is in the news.

THE PRESENTATION OF CRIME IN THE NEWS

Research has clearly established that crime is an important news topic.[11] Depending on the medium studied and what is counted as a crime story, research estimates that between 10 to 75 percent of all news stories discuss crime incidents. The popularity of crime as a news topic does not appear to correspond to crime rates and/or public concern about crime. Crime has historically been presented as a top news topic, and even when the United States has experienced significant declines in crimes, such as in the middle 1990s, the coverage of crime increased. Moreover, when a particularly noteworthy crime event happens, the news coverage of the facts, circumstances, and related stories can dominant national attention for a substantial period of time. Crime events, such as the September 11th attacks, the Oklahoma City bombing, the murders of Nicole Brown Simpson and Ronald Goldman by accused former NFL running back O. J. Simpson, the assassination of John F. Kennedy, and the kidnapping of Charles Lindbergh's baby, are just a few examples of events that resonated with the public in various historical eras.

Crime gets considerable media attention for several reasons. First, it is a topic that is dramatic and emotional, and one that captivates the public. The public has an appetite for it, fascinated by the mystery, suspense, and consequences of crime events. Second, crime stories are relatively easy to put together. There is a consistent stream of events that are available to reporters. Reporters have access to police and court documents related to these events and have established relationships with key criminal justice sources in order to have easy access to the information needed to write a story. These sources are motivated to provide the information necessary because it provides them the opportunity to manage the nature of news coverage about their organization. Third, although obvious, it is important to note that crime is a significant social problem that most communities must struggle to manage and that the public is deeply concerned about it. In addition, the management of crime involves discussions about key political and social institutions, such as schools and businesses. Terrorism, for example, has a long history of being a significant social problem, but responding to terrorism only became a significant policy issue because of the September 11th attacks. What is interesting is that these attacks not only impacted how local, state, and federal criminal justice agencies respond to crime in society, but has also influenced other social institutions and policy arenas contributing to significant social change.

It is a fact, however, that even though there are an increasing number of channels and venues for the dissemination of information about crime, only a small percentage of crime incidents are ever presented to the public as news. In short, editors and reporters have considerable discretion to decide which of the available crime incidents warrant a public presentation of the facts. One consistent conclusion is that violent crimes, especially the types of crime that are least likely to occur, are significantly more likely to be presented in the news. Some studies estimate that over 30 percent of local crime news in cities with significant crime rates discuss murder.[12] Rape, robbery, and aggravated assault may be presented to the public, but coverage of such crimes depends on the unavailability of more serious crimes. Property crimes, white-collar crimes, and drug crimes are not as likely to be presented in the news absent other interesting circumstances.

Violent crimes, especially murders, are high priority news items, but decisions have to be made about how prominently the incident should be discussed in the news. Should the event be on the front page? Be the lead story in an evening broadcast? How much space should be provided? For example, in cities like Detroit or Miami, many homicides will be covered but some have to be excluded. Chermak argues that other characteristics of a crime incident determine which events increase the likelihood of news coverage.[13] Crimes involving "Knowns" are much more likely to be covered than crimes of "Unknowns."[14] A politician, high school principal, or television news anchor matter more because they are familiar to the community. Certain demographic characteristics, such as the age, gender, and occupation of the victim and/or suspect, can increase the likelihood that a crime event is presented to the public. Crimes that can be related to other events also increase coverage. For example, Mark Fishman's interesting work on crime waves discusses how a few assaults against elderly victims resulted in events not typically covered being presented prominently in the news.[15] Finally, race of the victim and of the defendant are also predictors of the importance of a crime event.

THE PRESENTATION OF RACE IN THE NEWS

In this section we review studies that comparatively analyze representations of crime participants in news stories to their representations in other social domains (e.g. crime statistics), focusing our discussion primarily on findings related to the race/ethnicity of crime participants. Studies on this topic have taken two general forms that are differentiated by (1) the type of media examined, and (2) how crime news stories are linked to official crime reports. The first type of study compares television news representations of perpetrators and victims to their statistical representations in other areas, like crime, employment, and population.[16] The second type of study examines the relationship between actual crime (usually homicide), perpetrator, and victim characteristics, and news media coverage of crime occurrences.[17] The latter approach is unique in that it links specific homicide incidents, perpetrators, and victims to local print-news media coverage. Scholars utilizing this approach examine which elements of crime occurrences are most influential in evaluations of homicide newsworthiness, and by extension, how news media coverage misrepresents or distorts the reality of homicide in particular locations and time periods.

We first consider studies that examine how television news representations of crime participants compare to official counts of victims and offenders. Utilizing this approach, among others, Dixon and Linz compared representations of racial/ethnic minorities found in a representative sample of news broadcasts aired by Los Angeles television stations to crime reports provided by the State of California Justice Department. Dixon and Linz hypothesized that whites would be overrepresented, while blacks and Hispanics would be underrepresented as victims in television crime news when compared to crime reports. In brief, they found that whites were overrepresented, Hispanics were underrepresented, and that blacks were neither overrepresented nor underrepresented as homicide victims on television news broadcasts when compared to crime reports. On the other hand, in terms of images of perpetrators, blacks were overrepresented, Latinos were underrepresented, and whites were neither overrepresented nor under-represented as crime perpetrators. Thus, in Los Angeles the manner in which racial/ethnic minorities were misrepresented depended on their portrayal as perpetrators or victims. Rather than comparing crime news media portrayals of racial/ethnic minorities to crime statistics, other studies compare news representations to alternative statistical information in a number of social realms, such as employment and population.[18] Dixon and Linz, for instance, relied on employment records in their study to show that blacks were overrepresented as lawbreakers, while Hispanics and whites were underrepresented as lawbreakers on television news broadcasts. On the other hand, as law defenders, Dixon and Linz found that whites were overrepresented, and Hispanics were underrepresented. Blacks, on the other hand, were not significantly misrepresented as polices officers (law defenders) compared to employment records.[19]

In another study of racial typification of crime perpetrators in Orlando, Florida, crime news stories, Chiricos and Eschholz asked whether presumed criminals on local television news were disproportionately shown to be black or Hispanic compared with black and Hispanic proportions of the general population. Interestingly, they found that blacks were not overrepresented among television news crime suspects, while Hispanics were slightly overrepresented in relation to their share of general population.[20]

Linking Crime Participants to Local Newspaper Coverage

While Dixon and Linz and others have relied on television news broadcasts to study misrepresentations of racial/ethnic minorities, others have studied misrepresentations of particular crime participants in local news print media coverage.[21] This type of study begins with a compilation or "universe" of crime incidents, usually homicide incidents. Scholars then compare the elements of homicides that receive news media coverage with those that do not.[22] This type of study examines what homicide characteristics are important in determining whether homicides are covered (i.e., salience of coverage) and to what extent homicides are covered (i.e., prominence of coverage). Johnstone and colleagues relied on this approach to link specific homicide incidents to Chicago newspaper coverage of the incidents. They began by compiling a list of homicide incidents and the people involved in them based on data from the Chicago Police Department. Then, they examined if and how specific homicides were presented in two Chicago newspapers (the *Tribune* and *Sun-Times*).[23]

Studies like this one allow scholars to assess whether newspapers overemphasize or de-emphasize homicides involving minority perpetrators and victims in their local coverage of crime. For instance, they found that homicides involving black or Hispanic victims were less likely to receive print news media coverage compared to homicides involving white victims.[24] Sorenson and colleagues, who examined print news media coverage of homicides in Los Angeles, also found that homicides of blacks and Latinos received significantly less coverage than homicides of whites.[25] In addition, a number of studies have found that homicides involving victims that are white are more likely to be reported by news media[26] and covered prominently.[27] One explanation of this phenomenon is that news media sources tend to report on types of homicide cases that occur relatively infrequently. That is, because homicides involving white victims are relatively rare in some large U.S. cities, they are more likely to be reported in the newspaper. However, this explanation for why some homicides receive disproportionate media attention is problematic given other findings related to race and media coverage of homicide incidents.[28] For instance, Lundman found that homicides involving white offenders in Columbus, Ohio, never received significantly more news media coverage than homicides involving nonwhites. This is an interesting pattern given that in most highly populated U.S. cities homicides involving white offenders are relatively rare. Linking newspaper coverage of Columbus homicides occurring between 1984 and 1992, Lundman found that homicides involving victims and offenders who did not conform to race and gender-based stereotypes of crime victims and offenders received only average or significantly less than average news media attention.[29] In sum, this small but growing body of literature on media coverage of homicides shows that there is more than one way to examine how news media distort or misrepresent the "reality" of homicide and other crimes. Whether due to novelty or race- and gender-based cultural typifications, past research in this area makes it clear that print-news media sources oftentimes distort the reality of homicide in particular contexts, in many cases overpresenting whites as victims of crime and racial/ethnic minorities as crime perpetrators.

Racial/Ethnic Group Status and Perpetrators, Victims, and Police Roles

So far we have reviewed comparative analyses of crime news and employment, population, and crime statistics, as well as police homicide reports. Next, we review findings from studies that utilize other comparative techniques to examine possible misrepresentations of crime and crime participants, focusing primarily on racial/ethnic minorities. In particular, we review findings from studies that examine the relationship between minority groups and various character roles (i.e., perpetrator, victim, and police) in television news media crime stories. Before reviewing this literature, we provide a brief overview of Gerbner and associates' cultivation hypothesis, from which many of the scholars working in this area draw to theoretically link media's misrepresentation of minorities to increased perceptions of risk, fear of crime, and the reification of minority stereotypes.[30]

The "Mean World Syndrome" The cultivation hypothesis suggests that how media sources communicate information about the social world shapes audiences' views and beliefs about the social world. That is, beliefs and perceptions about the social world are cultivated over time by repeated consumption of mediated messages.[31] Moreover, because the majority of the public has little direct exposure to crime, most of what people know about crime and crime participants is based on media portrayals of crime.[32] Therefore, representations of crime and justice in various media outlets could have a very real influence on how audiences view criminals, causes of crime, and appropriate responses to crime. Supporting their hypothesis, Gerbner and associates found that portrayals of crime/violence on television resulted in increased fear of crime and perceptions of danger among consumers, otherwise known as the "mean world syndrome," especially among heavy consumers.[33] Recent studies have confirmed the cultivation hypothesis. For example, Chiricos, Eschholz, and Gertz surveyed residents of Tallahassee, Florida, and found that fear increases among older white females and those living in economically disadvantaged African American neighborhoods as their news consumption increases.[34] Chiricos, Gertz, and Padgett, surveying over twenty-two hundred Florida residents, found that the frequency of news consumption has a positive relationship with fear of crime. Thus, the more news watched by the resident, the more fearful the resident became. The notion of the "mean world syndrome" has been incorporated into the work of other scholars who have examined the relationship between race, crime, and media.[35]

Robert Entman and colleagues have published widely on racialized images of crime participants in the media. Entman and Rojecki, for instance, recently examined the content of Chicago's local evening/nightly television news and concluded that local television news depicts American life as filled with violence and danger, and that images of crime likely lead whites to increasingly link blacks to danger and violence.[36] Blacks were shown to be represented disproportionately in criminal roles, making them seem especially threatening, while whites were represented disproportionately as crime victims.[37] Furthermore, Entman found in comparisons of racial/ethnic groups that television news stories about blacks were more likely to include mug shots and images of perpetrators in jail clothes and were less likely to have their names identified in news stories, making them appear threatening, and immediately guilty, and robbing them of their individual identities. It is argued that such racial disparities in television news representations stereotype blacks' cultural status.[38]

Other studies that have incorporated interrole (i.e., racialized images of perpetrators, victims, and police) and intergroup (e.g., criminalized images of whites, blacks, and Hispanics) analyses of images among crime participants have found similar results. Dixon and Linz's comparative analyses of crime participants in news stories in two California counties suggest that blacks and Latinos are more likely to be portrayed as criminals than as victims, and vice versa for whites.[39] In a follow-up study Dixon and Linz relied on employment records to show that blacks were overrepresented as lawbreakers, while Hispanics and whites were underrepresented as lawbreakers on television news broadcasts. On the other hand, as law defenders, Dixon and Linz found that whites were overrepresented, Hispanics were underrepresented, and blacks were not significantly misrepresented as polices officers (law defenders) compared to employment records.[40]

In another study, Chiricos and Eschholz found somewhat different findings from those of Dixon and Linz after conducting a content analysis of three weeks of local television news on three network affiliates in Orlando during 1998. Chiricos and Eschholz asked whether presumed criminals on local television news were disproportionately shown to be black or Hispanic compared with black and Hispanic proportions of the general population. Interestingly, they found that blacks were not overrepresented among television news crime suspects, while Hispanics were slightly overrepresented in relation to their share of the general population. However, when the analysis was isolated to violent crimes only, blacks and Hispanics were more likely to be presented as the perpetrators. In addition, when comparing positive and negative roles, they found that blacks were more likely to appear in television news in police than in suspect roles, though blacks were also just as likely to be portrayed in television programs as role models as they were as suspects.[41] However, Latinos were underrepresented as police and role models compared to representation as suspects, leading Chiricos and Eschholz to conclude that typification of Hispanics is both stronger and more consistent than for blacks. Moreover, comparing portrayals of suspects among racial/ethnic groups, they found that blacks and Hispanics were not overrepresented as crime suspects compared to whites.[42]

Hispanics in the News

While some studies examining the relationship between race, media, and crime have compared multiple racial/ethnic categories,[43] the majority of studies in this diverse literature have followed the lead of Entman and his associates by focusing on black and white comparisons only. Entman and Rojecki provide a number of reasons why research has tended to consider only blacks as a racial minority group: First, they suggest that blacks have been the most visible subjects of political discourse and potent political symbols based on the consistent documentation of antiblack sentiment. Second, no other racial/ethnic group has endured discrimination in the same way as blacks. Finally, available methods for scholarly inquiry allow for a more reliable study of blacks compared to other racial/ethnic groups.[44]

One ethnic group deserving of more research by scholars is Hispanics. Relative to the examination of how blacks are portrayed in the media, very few studies have examined the presentation of Hispanics. Such an examination is important for three reasons. First, and most importantly, Hispanics are the fastest growing ethnic minority in the United States.[45] Hispanics comprise a little under 15 percent of the U.S. population with approximately forty-five million residents. According to census statistics, Hispanics have surpassed African Americans as the largest minority group in the country. These statistics also suggest that the Hispanic population in the United States is continuing to grow at a fast pace.

A second reason why it is important to examine the presentation of Hispanics is that overall the few studies that have examined their representation in the media do not show very positive findings. Similar to African Americans, news stories that focus on Hispanics are more likely to depict them as offenders and not as victims.[46] A recent content analyses of news stories on *CBS Evening News*, *ABC World News Tonight*, *NBC Nightly News*, and *CNN News Night* found that Hispanics were portrayed in less than 1 percent of the stories aired in 2002.[47] Specifically, of the approximately 16,000 stories that aired on these networks during the study period only 120, or .75 percent, were about Hispanics. Similar to Entman's study on African Americans,[48] the authors found that when news about Hispanics was aired, the majority (66 percent) dealt with crime, terrorism, or illegal immigration. Furthermore, Hispanics were more likely to be depicted as the perpetrator of a crime in 89 percent of these stories.

Other types of media also depict Hispanics negatively. For example, Mastro and Robinson show that unlike blacks and whites, 77 percent of Hispanic portrayals are in crime dramas.[49] On the other hand, whites are more likely to be discussed in shows about business and professional issues, and blacks in business, relationship, and leisure stories. Thus, the overall presentation of Hispanics seems more negative than that of blacks. In one of the first studies of its kind, Greenberg and Baptista-Fernandez examined prime-time programming during the mid-1970s and found that Hispanic characters were most likely to be featured in episodes that centered on illegal immigration and crime. Furthermore, their content analyses showed that when Hispanics were portrayed in television dramas their most likely vocation was that of a criminal.[50] Based on the examination of prime-time crime dramas in four major networks from 1992 to 1994, Lichter and Amundson also found that Hispanics were more likely to play the roles of criminals when compared to whites and blacks.[51] This pattern is also evident in reality police shows. Portales showed that when compared to the overall presentation of Hispanics in reality-based police shows 45 percent of all the Hispanic characters were shown committing crimes compared to 10 percent of all whites presented in these shows. His findings also suggest that whites were most often shown enforcing the law and minorities breaking them.[52]

Similar to the portrayals in the news and prime-time television, the representation of Hispanics in popular Hollywood films also leaves something to be desired. In one of the first studies of its type, Castro found throughout history Hispanics are almost always presented in stereotypical roles by the film industry. Specifically, his analyses showed that Latinos are often portrayed as liars, bandits, or criminals when showed on screen. Latinas are also more likely to be portrayed in a negative light. Latinas are often characterized as being sensual and seductive, and as having bad tempers.[53] In a more recent study Eschholz, Bufkin, and Long found very similar results in their content analyses of fifty popular films that were released in 1996. Of the 147 lead characters in the films they examined, only 20 percent were African American or Hispanic. When the data were disaggregated by race, the findings showed that Hispanics, Native Americans, and Asians were almost entirely missing from the 1996 popular lineup.[54]

Finally, and related to aforementioned points, the negative representation of Hispanics by the media may impact the perceptions of whites and other ethnic groups about Hispanics. One can infer based on studies by Gerbner and colleagues[55] and Entman[56] that similar to blacks the media representation of Hispanics has contributed to negative connotations, such as fear. In addition, the negative representation of Hispanics could contribute to current immigration debates and bias crimes against the group. Indeed, recent hate crime statistics compiled by the Federal Bureau of Investigation show that bias crimes against Hispanics (specifically Mexican Americans) have doubled since 2003.[57] Although no direct relationship currently exists between the increase in bias crimes and the representation of Hispanics in the media, one can infer based on prior research that the negative connotations presented in the media have increased levels of hate and fear toward Hispanics.

Images of Racial/Ethnic Minorities in Prime-Time and Reality-Based Police Shows

To provide an overview of studies that link race and media crime images, we have primarily focused thus far on studies of portrayals of minority crime participants in television news broadcasts and newspapers. Nonetheless, other studies have examined this relationship in other media forms, such as prime-time television, reality police shows, modern film, television commercials, and academic textbooks. These studies too are concerned with issues such as misrepresentations of racial/ethnic minorities, as well as the qualitative context in which minorities are portrayed. Thus, we turn now to a selective review of studies that address portrayals of racial/ethnic images in other various media outlets.

In their study of portrayals of racial/ethnic minorities in prime-time television, Mastro and Robinson collected a two-week sample of television shows in the fall of 1997 to examine issues of race and aggression in their analysis of police officers and perpetrators. Interestingly, they found that police were significantly more likely to use excessive force against perpetrators when they were young racial/ethnic minorities.[58] Grounded in the cultivation theory, Mastro and Robinson also conclude that these images may lead prime-time television audiences to believe that police need to control minorities by any means necessary.[59]

In addition to prime-time television, some scholars have examined portrayals of racial/ethnic minorities on popular reality-based police shows such as *COPS* and *America's Most Wanted*. Also building off of the cultivation hypothesis, these studies suggest that reality-based police shows may also work to maintain racist stereotypes of crime, criminals and victims, and criminal justice responses to crime. In one important book on this topic, Cavender and Fishman suggest that reality-based police shows are difficult to categorize as they are similar to news in that they cover the facts of crime, but are also similar to other entertainment television formats because they air in prime time alongside other completely fictional programs.[60] Moreover, Cavender and Fishman argue that reality-based police programs have flourished in the U.S. since the 1970s because of a social context defined by popular sentiments and ideologies which view crime as a serious problem deserving policy attention.[61]

One study that directly addresses this topic includes content analyses of five reality-based police shows, *America's Most Wanted*, *COPS*, *Top Cops*, *FBI: The Untold Story*, and *American Detective*, and found that blacks and Hispanics were more likely to be portrayed as criminals than as police officers.[62] Oliver's findings related to reality-based police shows are similar to Mastro and Robinson's findings that police officers were more likely to act aggressively against criminal suspects if the suspects were black or Hispanic.[63] In another study, Oliver and Armstrong tested for cultivation effects of consuming reality-based television on the public's beliefs about crime and justice, and found that consumption of reality-based police shows results in higher estimates of African American crime.[64]

Other Media Portrayals of Racial/Ethnic Minorities

Moving from television to the big screen, other scholars have focused on the portrayal of racial and ethnic minorities in modern film. One relevant example is a study by Eschholz and colleagues that examined the demographic composition of the leading characters in the top fifty grossing films in 1996 in the United States. Analyzing fifty films and 147 lead characters, Eschholz and colleagues found that black characters over time have increased in American films.

However, the occupational prestige of black characters is still low compared to white characters, and movies with black lead actors were usually films in which the entire cast was black. In terms of other racial/ethnic minorities, they found that Hispanics, Native Americans, and Asians were almost entirely missing from the 1996 popular films. Although not directly addressing images of criminals or law abiders, other scholars have approached the examination of representations of racial/ethnic minorities in other mediums, such as television commercials and textbooks.[65]

Overall studies in this area have found that minorities are underrepresented in television commercial, newspaper ads, and educational textbooks. For instance, content analysis of television commercials between 1992 and 1994 by Coltrane and Messineo showed that whites (and males) were more prominent and exerted more authority than blacks and females. Supporting findings from research on images in other forms of media, Coltrane and Messineo found that Latinos were largely underrepresented. Overall, when considering both race and sex, they found that white males were portrayed as sex objects, African American men as aggressive, and African American females as inconsequential.[66] Other studies support their conclusions, finding that Latinos, as well as Asians and Native Americans, have been underrepresented in television commercials.[67] These studies have also shown that oftentimes when minorities are presented in advertisements they were more likely to be associated with certain products (i.e., Hispanics and African Americans with restaurants and food, and Asian Americans with technology associated products).

Finally, although also not directly addressing the issue of race and crime in the media, other scholars examine how racial/ethnic groups are portrayed in textbooks. In one study, for example, Shaw-Taylor and Benokraitis examined twenty best-selling marriage and family textbooks published between 1986 and 1990. They found that this type of textbook still largely ignored minorities. Indeed, racial/ethnic minorities were disproportionately underrepresented compared to their representation in the general population. In addition, racial/ethnic minority families were found to be portrayed from a culturally deviant perspective.[68]

CONCLUSION

The prior literature review suggests that overall racial and ethnic minorities in the United are misrepresented by the mass media. First, the bulk of studies that have examined this issue have found that minorities are depicted in news stories as offenders and not as victims. In particular, research indicates that race is a key predictor influencing whether a homicide receives coverage by the press, but more importantly it determines how much coverage a homicide receives. Crime reporters are less interested and devalue homicides when the victim is African American or Hispanic. Murders of whites, on the other hand, receive significantly more coverage. Second, films and television programming still depict Hispanics and African Americans in stereotypical roles, such as those of the crime perpetrator, and perpetuate racial myths. Finally, analyses of media advertisement and educational materials still show that minorities are under-represented. As a result one has to inquire why. Why are racial and ethnic minorities in the United States depicted in such a negative light? In the concluding section of this chapter, we explore this question in detail.

Our explanation for the differences in coverage begins with the acknowledgement of the important bureaucratic routines inherent to the construction of the news.[69] Reporters are line-level employees of bureaucratic organizations and rely primarily on bureaucratically affiliated officials for the information contained in news stories.[70] When a reporter is charged with constructing a crime story about the beginning stages of the criminal justice process, he or she gathers information provided by police officials.[71] The basic mandate of news organizations is to summarize the most important events of every single day in a profitable way. Crime is a desirable topic since multiple new crime events are available each day, and crime is generally believed to be entertainingly pleasing to the public. Research confirms that crime is a topic of high priority.[72]

We believe that the organizational realities of news production provide a good understanding of why crime is such an important news topic and why certain types of crime (e.g., personal crimes like homicide) are preferred over other types of crime. White collar and other organizational crimes are simply too complex and are unlikely to come to the attention of a reporter whose primary source of information is local police officials. However, these organizational realities do not completely account for the racial differences in news coverage, as well as the consistent finding that these differences exist in multiple types of media. Our contention is that a reporter's and other media workers' discretion, as well as the organizational processes others have argued limit that discretion, are influenced by the cultural frames that the public use to evaluate and interpret the importance of specific events. These frames, which are reflective of the racial divisions of society, influence how reporters describe a crime incident to the public.

Research, for example, examining criminal justice decision making discusses how criminal justice personnel rely on typifications to structure their work. Such typifications help these bureaucrats easily respond to a variety of complex social situations. For example, John Van Maanen discusses how police officers use terms like "asshole," "know nothing," and "suspicious person" to categorize and decide how best to handle a situation.[73] David Sudnow's early work on court processes describes how attorneys develop an understanding of "normal crimes,"[74] and similarly in research by Eisenstein, Flemming, and Nardulli, it is discussed how members of the courtroom workgroup dispose of individual cases based on a shared understanding, or the "going rate," for a particular type of crime. Workgroup members identify a "slam dunk" or a "garbage case" and then use these signposts to decide the appropriate disposition.[75] Corrections research also discusses the importance of typifications to the completion of work assignments. Richard McCleary's work on parole decision making, for example, discusses how parole officers use typifications like "dangerous men" to decide how much trouble to expect from a new parolee. Such typifications help criminal-justice personnel transform complex individual and unique events into standard operating decision-making procedures. Once a recognizable category can be applied to an individual event or a specific case, then a standard set of outcome procedures can be applied using established patterns of disposal.[76]

Media personnel also use shorthand classification schemes to place events into known categories or likenesses when organizing their occupational world. Research discusses the "frames" used by media personnel to classify events or the "framing" of an event.[77] Frames are "schemata of interpretation that enable individuals to locate, perceive, identify, and label" events.[78] Snow and colleagues refer to these frames as "unifying devices" that first provide meaning to an event,[79] and then they organize experience and guide action. Although the media worker's *immediate* goal is the production of a news story and the criminal justice worker's goal is the processing of a case, the reliance on specific frames serve the same purpose: They provide an efficient means to organize their work and provide an easy way to decide the work pattern that flows from that categorization.[80]

The frames that reporters use to categorize their world can seep into their language and are used as convenient shorthands to communicate the significance of an event to others. For example, all types of news story can have "legs." These stories are celebrated events, and reporters follow through on these stories completely, exhausting all potential angles because of the importance attached to these incidents.[81] Gitlin, however, also establishes that frames can be "unspoken and unacknowledged," and "organize the world both for journalists who report it and, in some important degree, for [those of] us who rely on their reports."[82]

The incidents consistent with a reporter's frames for significant events are provided increased space. The most important aspect of how reporters organize their world and assign salience to an event is through this framing process, which is afflicted with ideological significance.[83] Entman states that "by providing, repeating, and thereby reinforcing words and visual images that reference some ideas but not others, frames work to make some ideas more salient in the text, other less so, and others entirely invisible."[84] Both explicit frames, like homicides resulting from a "drug deal that went bad" or "it's an ordinary homicide," and implicit frames, like ignoring murders occurring in inner-city neighborhoods, have significant implications for the presentation of race in crime stories. Frames such as these ensure that certain types of homicide, specific elements of each incident, and certain individuals will be emphasized or marginalized.

Specific frames are also influenced by the larger historical and cultural themes and processes operating in a community. Many scholars argue that individual frames are particularly significant and strike a "responsive chord" when they are able to resonate with larger cultural frames that exist in society.[85] For example, Binder states that "a frame has a much greater chance of success if it draws on some conscious or subconscious, unified or disorganized belief held in the culture at large."[86] Similarly, Fair and Astoff discuss how "the process of

assigning racial meaning to acts of violence is part of a larger ideological practice of classification and marginalization,"[87] and Swart highlights how a "frame
is thus defined by its resonance with the cultural, political, or historical milieu
in which it emerges."[88]

There are three areas of research that are relevant to understanding how
cultural context infiltrates individual decision making in the use of race in various media products. First, earlier we discussed the important work by Iyengar
and Hahn, which emphasizes the implicit decisions that reflect racial bias in
society. It appears that when most of the public thinks about crime, they are also
thinking about race.[89] Thus, scholars argue that the nature of news construction
in society contributes to a "racist mythology."[90]

Second, the marginalization of minorities as crime victims is consistent
with larger cultural understandings of "ideal victims." "Ideal victims" are
viewed as being completely innocent. The public can easily see and understand
the harm caused by a crime when the victim's "status" is consistent with this
frame. Cavender, Bond-Maupin, and Jurik, in their analysis of gender in reality crime-television programs, provide a good understanding of the cultural
construction of "ideal." They discuss how "ideal victims" are viewed in society
as being legitimate and given status as real victims. It is difficult for media personnel to consistently assign minority homicides significant amounts of space
because the perception of those minority victims are not "ideal."[91] Throughout
history, it has been difficult to afford minorities full victim status because they
are more likely to be thought of deserving of their fate. In Omi and Winant's
important book on how constructions of race are formed, they state: "In the
past white supremacy was so thorough that it located all nonwhites in positions of comprehensive subordination. Racially defined minorities at one time
lacked even victim status . . . Today less than ever does minority status cor-
relate with victim status."[92] Similarly, Randall Kennedy provides an excellent
historical analysis clearly establishing the unequal and racially selective underprotections afforded minorities. He discusses how the withholding of protections has "its roots in slavery" and can be seen in the failure to protect slaves
from murder, assault, and rape in antebellum America. He demonstrates that
these underprotections have existed from the Civil War and include the lack
of legislative protections from lynching and differences in contemporary
criminal-justice case processing procedures used when the victim is black
rather than white. His argument is easily extended to the representation of
minorities in the media crime stories.[93]

Third, in many ways minorities are also seen as "ideal offenders." Where
the murder of minorities and issues affecting minority communities are generally ignored, images of minorities as offenders are frequently presented.[94] In
Entman's analysis of local television news, he finds "violent crimes committed
by blacks was the largest category of local news."[95] In addition, he found that
blacks are presented in the news as being more dangerous and hostile than
whites. Using Kennedy's work again, he discusses how police officers and the
public see race as a proxy for an increased risk of criminality. That is, there is an
expectation that minorities are likely to be involved in crime. He states that race

serves as a "sorting device used by police and others to demarcate groups of persons who, because of their race, are viewed more risky than other persons."[96] This discussion is also consistent with research examining minorities as social threats. The social threat hypothesis was originated by Blalock in 1967 and based on a conflict theoretical framework. Specifically, it starts with the assumptions that societal groups must compete with each other for control of valuable commodities, such as politics, the economy, and the status quo. Consequently, the group that has dominance over these commodities feels threatened when minority groups increase in numbers and power. That is, as minority groups in society increase so does the perceived threat attributed by the dominant groups who control these various commodities due to fear of losing the dominant status. This threat is due to fear that the minority group could become dominant. Interestingly, this theory poses that those who are less privileged (i.e., working class and undereducated) in the dominant group are the most likely to perceive this threat, particularly because they are the ones that have to directly compete for such economic means as employment with the growing minority groups.

Due to this perceived threat, the dominant group, in order to maintain its power, consciously or unconsciously acts in ways that will permit them to retain their control. One of these ways is by perpetuating stereotypes of the growing minority groups through media imagery. The perpetuation of ethnic and racial stereotypes increases fear of crime, especially the fear of being victimized by these groups. As a result, the general public becomes more likely to support social-control campaigns, especially those that are related to crime and justice, against these groups in order to control the perceived "social threat."[97]

When the dominant frame or expectation is for minorities to be offenders in the news, and this frame is consistent with more general notions of who the "ideal offender" is and who is a risk to the community, it is difficult for reporters and their audiences to accept minorities as being significantly harmed from victimization. News organizations are sometimes applauded for the significant strides that they have made to eliminate blatant examples of racism from the newsroom.[98] Carolyn Martindale, when comparing pre– to post–civil rights coverage of blacks, concludes that the "old stereotypes of black Americans are beginning to lose their sway."[99] The number of minorities employed by news organizations has increased, and one might think that such a change would result in a more diverse range of images presented in the news. However, it appears that the media still contributes to the racial stratification of society in this country in the devaluation of minority victims and an overemphasis of minority offenders in the media.

CRITICAL THINKING QUESTIONS

1. How would you characterize or compare Hispanic versus black coverage in the media? Explain the differences.
2. Explain the over- or underrepresentation of racial/ethnic groups in U.S. media outlets.

3. What does the data reveal about the reporting of homicides by the media?
4. Discuss the impact of media coverage of violent crimes upon society.
5. Describe and discuss the black-white dichotomy in media news coverage.

NOTES

1. Julie Grace and Elizabeth Gleick, "Belated Outrage for Girl X," *Time.com*, 2001, http://www.time.com/time/magazine/article/0,9171,1101970224-137315,00.html (accessed December 31, 2008).

2. Lee Bey, "Take Responsibility for This 9-Year-Old Girl," *Chicago Sun-Times*, January 25, 1997.

3. Joe Mandese, "Time Spent with Media Falters, Digital Spawns Shorter Attention Spans," *Media Daily News*, 2007, http://publications.mediapost.com/index.cfm?fuseaction=Articles.san&s=65295&Nid=33017&p=204904 (accessed December 31, 2008).

4. John Eggerton, "TV Shines in TVB Study," *Broadcasting & Cable Online*, http://www.broadcastingcable.com/article/CA6326694.html?display=Breaking+News (accessed December 31, 2008).

5. Betsy Rogers, "Captivating Kids," *Washington University in St. Louis Magazine*, 2007, http://magazine.wustl.edu/Spring07/nickelodeon.htm (accessed December 31, 2008).

6. Harris Interactive, "The Harris Poll #108," November 5, 2007, http://www.harrisinteractive.com/harris_poll/index.asp?PID=827 (accessed December 31, 2008).

7. See Peter L. Berger and Thomas Luckmann, *The Social Construction of Reality* (New York: Anchor Books, 1967); Richard Quinney, *The Social Reality of Crime* (Boston: Little, Brown and Company, 1970).

8. Shanto Iyengar and Kyu S. Hahn, "Natural Disasters in Black and White: How Racial Cues Influenced Public Response to Hurricane Katrina," *WashingtonPost.com*, June 8, 2006, http://www.washingtonpost.com/wpdyn/content/article/2006/06/07/AR2006060701177.html (accessed February 20, 2008).

9. Franklin D. Gilliam and Shanto Iyengar, "Prime Suspects: The Influence of Local Television News on the Viewing Public," *American Journal of Political Science* 44, no. 3 (2000): 560–573.

10. Jon Hurwitz and Mark Peffley, "Public Perceptions of Race and Crime: The Role of Racial Stereotypes," *American Journal of Political Science* 41, no. 2 (1997): 375–401.

11. Steven M. Chermak, *Victims in the News: Crime in American News Media* (Boulder, CO: Westview Press, 1995); Doris Graber, *Crime News and the Public* (New York: Praeger Publishers, 1980); Paul Klite, Robert A. Bardwell, and Jason Salzman, "Local News: Getting Away with Murder," *Harvard International Journal of Press/Politics*

2, no. 2 (1997): 102–112; Brendan Maguire, Diane Sandage, and Georgie Ann Weatherby, "Crime Stories as Television News: A Content Analysis of National, Big City and Small Town Newscasts," *Journal of Criminal Justice and Popular Culture* 7, no. 1 (1999): 1–14.

12. Chermak, *Victims in the News.*

13. Ibid.

14. Herbert Gans, *Deciding What's News: A Study of CBS Evening News, Newsweek and Time* (New York: Pantheon Books, 1979).

15. Mark Fishman, *Manufacturing the News* (Austin, TX: University of Texas Press, 1980).

16. For example, see Chermak, *Victims in the News*; Ted Chiricos, Sarah Eschholz, and Marc Gertz, "Crime, News and Fear of Crime: Toward an Identification of Audience Effects," *Social Problems* 44, no. 3 (1997): 342–357; Doris Graber, *Crime News and the Public.*

17. For example, see John W. C. Johnstone, Darnell F. Hawkins, and Arthur Michener, "Homicide Reporting in Chicago Dailies," *Journalism Quarterly* 71 (1995): 860–872; David Pritchard, "Race, Homicide and Newspapers," *Journalism Quarterly* 62 (1985): 500–507.

18. Travis L. Dixon and Daniel Linz, "Race and the Misrepresentation of Victimization on Local Television News," *Communication Research* 27, no. 5 (2000a): 547–573.

19. Travis L. Dixon and Daniel Linz, "Overrepresentation and Underrepresentation of African Americans and Latinos as Lawbreakers on Television News," *Journal of Communication* 50, no. 2 (2000b): 131–154.

20. Ted Chiricos and Sarah Eschholz, "The Racial and Ethnic Typification of Crime and the Criminal Typification of Race and Ethnicity in Local Television News," *Journal of Research in Crime and Delinquency* 39 (2002): 400–420.

21. Dixon and Linz, "Race and the Misrepresentation of Victimization," 547–573; Dixon and Linz, "Overrepresentation and Underrepresentation," 131–154.

22. See David Pritchard, "Race, Homicide and Newspapers," *Journalism Quarterly* 62 (1985): 500–507.

23. Johnstone, Hawkins, and Michener, "Homicide Reporting in Chicago Dailies," 860–872.

24. Ibid.

25. Susan B. Sorenson, Julie G. P. Manz, and Richard A. Berk, "News Media Coverage and the Epidemiology of Homicide," *American Journal of Public Health* 88 (1998): 1510–1514.

26. Johnstone, Hawkins, and Michener, "Homicide Reporting in Chicago Dailies," 860–872; Derek J. Paulsen, "Murder in Black and White," *Homicide Studies* 7 (2003): 289–317; Moira Peelo, Keith Soothill, Jayn Pearson, and Elizabeth Ackerly, "Newspaper Reporting and the Public Construction of Homicide," *British Journal of Sociology* 44 (2004): 256–275; Sorenson, Manz, and Berk, "News Media Coverage and the Epidemiology of Homicide," 1510–1514.

27. Richard J. Lundman, "The Newsworthiness and Selection Bias in News about Murder: Comparative and Relative Effects of Novelty and Race and Gender Typifications on Newspaper Coverage of Homicide," *Sociological Forum* 18, no. 3 (September, 2003): 357–386;

Paulsen, "Murder in Black and White," 289–317; David Pritchard and Karen D. Hughes, "Patterns of Deviance in Crime News," *Journal of Communication* 47 (1997): 49–67; Alex Weiss and Steven M. Chermak, "The News Value of African-American Victims: An Examination of the Media's Presentation of Homicide," *Journal of Crime and Justice* 21 (1998): 71–88; William Wilbanks, *Murder in Miami: An Analysis of Homicide Patterns and Trends in Dade County (Miami) Florida, 1917–1988*, (Lanham: University Press of American, Inc, 1984).

28. Lundman, "The Newsworthiness and Selection Bias in News About Murder," 357–386; Pritchard and Hughes, "Patterns of Deviance in Crime News," 49–67.

29. Lundman, "The Newsworthiness and Selection Bias in News About Murder," 357–386.

30. George Gerbner and Larry Gross, "Living with Television: The Violence Profile," *Journal of Communication* 26 (1976): 173–199; George Gerbner, Larry Gross, Michael Morgan, and Nancy Signorielli, "Living with Television: The Dynamics of the Cultivation Process," in *Media Effects: Advances in Theory and Research*, ed. Jennings Bryant and Dolf Zillmann (Hillsdale, NJ: Lawrence Erlbaum, 1986), 17–40.

31. Gerbner and Gross, "Living with Television: The Violence Profile," 173–199; Gerbner, Gross, Morgan, and Signorielli, "Living with Television: The Dynamics of the Cultivation Process," 17–40.

32. Ray Surette, *Media, Crime, and Criminal Justice: Images, Realities, and Policies*, 3rd ed. (Belmont, CA: Thomson Wadsworth, 2007).

33. Gerbner, Gross, Morgan, and Signorielli, "Living with Television: The Dynamics of the Cultivation Process," 17–40.

34. Ted Chiricos, Sarah Eschholz, and Marc Gertz, "Crime, News and Fear of Crime: Toward an Identification of Audience Effects," *Social Problems* 44, no. 3 (1997): 342–357.

35. Ted Chiricos, Marc Gertz, and Kathy Padgett, "Fear, TV News, and the Reality of Crime," *Criminology* 38, no. 3 (2000): 755–785.

36. Robert M. Entman and Andrew Rojecki, *The Black Image in the White Mind: Media and Race in America* (Chicago: University of Chicago Press, 2000), 78.

37. Entman and Rojecki, *The Black Image in the White Mind*, 81.

38. Robert M. Entman, "Modern Racism and the Images of Blacks in Local Television News," *Critical Studies in Mass Communication* 7 (1990): 32–45.

39. Dixon and Linz, "Race and the Misrepresentation of Victimization," 547–573.

40. Dixon and Linz, "Overrepresentation and Underrepresentation," 131–154.

41. Chiricos and Eschholz, "The Racial and Ethnic Typification of Crime," 400–420.

42. Chiricos and Eschholz, "The Racial and Ethnic Typification of Crime," 416.

43. For example, see Chiricos and Eschholz, "The Racial and Ethnic Typification of Crime," 400–420; Dixon and Linz, "Race and the Misrepresentation of Victimization," 547–573; Dixon and Linz, "Overrepresentation and Underrepresentation," 131–154.

44. Entman and Rojecki, *The Black Image in the White Mind*, xi–xii.

45. Census 2007.

46. For example, see Chiricos and Eschholz, "The Racial and Ethnic Typification of Crime," 400–420; Dixon and Linz, "Race and the Misrepresentation," 547–573.

47. Serafin Mendez-Mendez and Diane Alverio, *Network Brown-out 2003: The Portrayal of Latinos in Network Television News, 2002*, (National Association of Hispanic Journalists, 2003).

48. Entman, "Modern Racism and the Images of Blacks," 32–45.

49. Dana E. Mastro and Amanda L. Robinson, "Cops and Crooks: Images of Minorities in Primetime Television," *Journal of Criminal Justice* 28 (2000): 388.

50. Bradley Greenberg and Pilar Baptista-Fernandez, "Hispanic-Americans: The new minority on television," in *Life on Television: Content Analysis of U.S. TV Drama*, ed. Bradley Greenberg (Norwood, NJ: Ablex Publishing, 1980), 3–13.

51. Robert S. Lichter and Daniel R. Amundson, *Don't Blink: Hispanics in Television Entertainment* (Washington DC: National Council of La Raza, 1996).

52. Marco Portales, "Hispanics and the Media," in *Chicanos, Latinos, and Cultural Diversity: An Anthology*, ed. Dionne Espinoza, Ester E. Hernandez, Richard T. Rodriguez, and Lionel A. Maldonado (Dubuque, Iowa: Kendall/Hunt Publishing Company, 2004), 29–35.

53. Diego O. Castro, "Stereotyping by the Media 'Hot Blood and Easy Virtue': Mass Media and the Making of Racist Latino/a Stereotypes," in *Images of Color, Images of Crime*, ed. Coramae Richey Mann and Marjorie S. Zatz (Los Angeles: Roxbury Publishing: 1998), 134–144.

54. Sarah Eschholz, Jana Bufkin, and Jeremy Long, "Symbolic Reality Bites: Women and Racial/Ethnic Minorities in Modern Film," *Sociological Spectrum* 22 (2001): 299–334.

55. Gerbner, Gross, Morgan, and Signorielli, "Living with Television," 17–40.

56. Entman, "Modern Racism and the Images of Blacks," 32–45.

57. FBI 2007.

58. Dana E. Mastro and Amanda L. Robinson, "Cops and Crooks: Images of Minorities on Primetime Television," *Journal of Criminal Justice* 28, no. 5 (2000): 385–396.

59. Mastro and Robinson, "Cops and Crooks," 394.

60. Mark Fishman and Gray Cavender, eds. *Entertaining Crime: Television Reality Programs* (New York: Aldine de Gruyter, 1998), 3.

61. Mark Fishman and Gray Cavender, *Entertaining Crime: Television Reality Programs*, 5–7.

62. Mary Beth Oliver, "Portrayals of Crime, Race, and Aggression in 'Reality-Based' Police Shows: A Content Analysis," *Journal of Broadcasting & Electronic Media* 38 (1994): 179–192.

63. Mastro and Robinson, "Cops and Crooks," 385–396.

64. Mary Beth Oliver and G. Blake Armstrong, "The Color of Crime: Perceptions of Caucasians' and African-Americans' Involvement in Crime," in *Entertaining Crime: Television Reality Programs*, ed. Mark Fishman and Gray Cavender (New York: Aldine de Gruyter, 1998), 19–35.

65. Eschholz, Bufkin, and Long, "Symbolic Reality Bites," 299–334.

66. Scott Coltrane and Melinda Messineo, "The Perpetuation of Subtle Prejudice: Race and Gender Imagery in 1990s Television Advertising," *Sex Roles* 42, no. 5/6 (2000): 363–389.

67. Hae-Kyong Bang and Bonnie B. Reece, "Minorities in Children's Television Commercials: New, Improved, and Stereotyped," *The Journal of Consumer Affairs* 37, no. 1 (2003): 42–67; Bradley Greenberg and Jeffrey Brand, "Minorities in the Mass Media: 1970s to 1990s," in *Media Effects: Advances in Theory and Research*, ed. Jennings Bryant and Dolf Zillmann (Hillsdale, NJ: Lawrence Erlbaum, 1994), 273–314; Meredith Li-Vollmer, "Race Representation in Child Targeted TV Commercials," *Mass Communication & Society* 5, no. 2 (2002): 207–228; Ellen Seiter, *Sold Separately: Children and Parents in a Consumer Culture* (New Brunswick, NJ: Rutgers University Press, 1995); Charles B. Taylor and Barbara Stern, "Asian Americans: Television Advertising and the 'Model Minority' Stereotype," *Journal of Advertising* 26 (1997): 47–61; Robert E. Wilkes and Humberto Valencia, "Hispanics and Blacks in Television Commercials," *Journal of Advertising* 18, no. 1 (1989): 19–25.

68. Yoku Shaw-Taylor and Nijole V. Benokraitis, "The Presentation of Minorities in Marriage and Family Textbooks," *Teaching Sociology* 23, no. 2 (1995): 122–135.

69. Gans, *Deciding What's News*; Gaye Tuchman, "Making News by Doing Work: Routinizing the Unexpected," *American Journal of Sociology* 79, no. 1 (1973): 110–131.

70. For example, see Jesenia Pizarro, Jeffrey A. Gruenewald, and Steven M. Chermak, "Juvenile 'Super Predators' in the News: A Comparison of Adult and Juvenile Homicides," *Journal of Crime and Popular Culture* 14, no. 1 (2007), http://www.albany.edu/scj/jcjpc/ (accessed December 31, 2008).

71. Chermak, *Victims in the News*; Steven M. Chermak, "The Presentation of Drugs in the News Media: News Sources Involved in the Construction of Social Problems," *Justice Quarterly* 14, no. 4 (1997): 687–718; Richard V. Ericson, Patricia M. Baranek, and Janet B. L. Chan, *Representing Order: Crime, Law, and Justice in the News Media* (Toronto: University of Toronto Press, 1991); Sandford Sherizen, "Social Creation of Crime News: All the News Fitted to Print," in *Deviance and Mass Media*, ed. Charles Winick (Beverly Hills, CA: Sage Publishing, 1978), 203–224.

72. Chermak, *Victims in the News*; Ericson, Baranek and Chan, *Representing Order*.

73. Jon Van Maanen, "The Asshole," in *Policing: A View from the Street*, ed. Peter K. Manning and Jon Van Maanen (New York: Random House, 1978).

74. D. Sudnow, "Normal Crimes: Sociological Features of the Penal Code in a Public Defender's Office," *Social Problems* 12 (1965): 255–276.

75. James Eisenstein, Roy B. Flemming, and Peter F. Nardulli, *The Contours of Justice: Communities and Their Courts* (New York: University Press of America, 1999).

76. Richard McCleary, *Dangerous Men: The Sociology of Parole* (New York: Harrow and Heston, 1992).

77. Amy Binder, "Constructing Racial Rhetoric: Media Depictions of Harm in Heavy Metal and Rap Music," *American Sociological Review* 58 (1993): 753–767; Robert M. Entman, "Framing U.S. Coverage of International News: Contrasts in Narratives of the KAL and Iran Air Incidents," *Journal of Communication* 41 (1991): 6–27; William A. Gamson and Andre Modigliani, "Media Discourse and Public Opinion on Nuclear Power: A Constructionist Approach," *American Journal of Sociology* 95, no. 1 (1989): 1–37; Todd Gitlin, *The Whole World Is Watching* (Berkeley, CA: University of California Press, 1980); David A. Snow, E. Burke Rochford, Steven K. Worden, and Robert D. Benford, "Frame Alignment Processes, Micromobilization, and Movement Participation," *American Sociological Review* 51 (1986): 464–481.

78. Erving Goffman, *Frame Analysis* (Cambridge, MA: Harvard University Press, 1974), 21.

79. Snow, Rochford, Worden, and Benford, "Frame Alignment Processes, Micromobilization, and Movement Participation," 464–481.

80. For example, see Binder, "Constructing Racial Rhetoric, 753–767.

81. Robert Blau, *The Cop Shop: True Crime on the Streets of Chicago* (New York: Addison Wesley Publishing Company, 1993).

82. Gitlin, *The Whole World Is Watching*, 7.

83. Binder, "Constructing Racial Rhetoric," 753–767; Entman "Framing U.S. Coverage of International News," 6–27.

84. Entman "Framing U.S. Coverage of International News," 7.

85. Binder, "Constructing Racial Rhetoric," 753–767; Jo Ellen Fair and Roberta J. Astroff, "Constructing Race and Violence: U.S. News Coverage and the Signifying Practices of Apartheid," *Journal of Communication* 41, no. 4 (1991): 58–74; Gitlin, *The Whole World Is Watching*; William A. Gamson and Andre Modigliani, "The Changing Culture of Affirmative Action," *Research in Political Sociology* 3 (1987): 137–177; Gamson and Modigliani, "Media Discourse and Public Opinion on Nuclear Power," 1–37; David A. Snow and Robert D. Benford, "Ideology, Frame Resonance and Participant Mobilization," *International Social Movement Research* 1 (1988): 197–217; William J. Swart, "The League of Nations and the Irish Question: Master Frames, Cycles of Protest, and 'Master Frame Alignment,'" *Sociological Quarterly* 36, no. 3 (1995): 465–482; Rhys H. Williams, "Constructing the Public Good: Social Movements and Cultural Resources," *Social Problems* 42, no. 1 (1995): 124–144.

86. Binder, "Constructing Racial Rhetoric," 755.

87. Fair and Astroff, "Constructing Race and Violence," 58.

88. Swart, "The League of Nations and the Irish Question," 469.

89. Iyengar and Hahn, "Natural Disasters in Black and White."

90. Christopher Campbell, *Race, Myth and the News* (Thousand Oaks, CA: Sage Publications, 1995).

91. Gray Cavender, Lisa Bond-Maupin, and Nancy C. Jurik, "The Construction of Gender in Reality Crime TV," *Gender and Society* 13, no. 5 (1999): 645.

92. Michael Omi and Howard Winant, *Racial Formation in the United States: From the 1960s to the 1990s* (New York: Routledge Press, 1994), 158.

93. Randall Kennedy, *Race, Crime, and the Law* (Pantheon Books: New York, 1997).

94. Campbell, *Race, Myth and the News*.

95. Entman, "Modern Racism and the Images of Blacks in Local Television News," 33.

96. Entman, 1997, 138.

97. David L. Altheide and Sam R. Michalowski, "Fear in the News: A Discourse of Control," *The Sociological Quarterly* 40 (1999): 475–503; Raul Damacio Tovares, "Influences on the Mexican American Youth Gang Discourse on Local Television News," *The Howard Journal of Communications* 11 (2000): 229–246.

98. For example, see David Croteau and William Hoynes, *Media Society: Industries, Images, and Audiences* (Thousand Oaks, CA: Pine Forge Press, 2000).

99. Carolyn Martindale, "Changes in Newspaper Images of Black Americans," *Newspaper Research Journal* (Winter 1990): 48.

CHAPTER 13

Real Crime and News Coverage Involving Race: Impressions of Media Newspaper Reporting

Linn Washington Jr.

The confluence of race and crime in newspaper coverage continually sparks controversies across America. Such controversies roil despite sincere efforts by many in the news business since the late 1960s toward improving the content and the construction of crime coverage. A consistent concern about racial issues in crime coverage—dating from colonial times—is its impact on individuals and institutions.

This concern arises from the fact that negative imagery does influence attitudes and actions. For example, experts and activists argue that news coverage about America's crime-mired crack cocaine epidemic in the mid-1980s—coverage tainted by racial bias and factual flaws—heavily influenced congressional passage of laws mandating extraordinarily lengthy sentences for all crack-cocaine crimes, including simple possession by addicts. "Many of the stories were racist," one federal judge declared in a 1994 ruling critical of legislators using "these media accounts as informational support for the enactment" of stiff sentencing laws.[1] Enforcement of anti–crack cocaine laws resulted in the imprisonment of tens of thousands of minorities but curiously few whites despite federal government documentation of comparable crack use by whites and nonwhites. A year after the 1994 court ruling, a U.S. Sentencing Commission report on crack cocaine also faulted mid-1980s media coverage, stating "some assertions made in [those] reports were not supported by data at the time and in retrospect were simply incorrect."[2] The Code of Ethics of the Society of Professional Journalists in its first section urges testing the "accuracy of information from all sources and exercise care to avoid inadvertent error. Deliberate distortion is never permissible."[3]

This chapter examines racial controversies in newspaper crime coverage. A prism for this examination is observations and recommendations about race-related news media coverage contained in the 1968 Kerner Commission Report. The Kerner Report expressed deep concern that the America's news media had not fulfilled its "responsibility to tell the story of race relations . . . with the wisdom, sensitivity, and expertise it demands."[4]

THE MORE THINGS CHANGE . . .

The front page of the August 22, 2002, edition of the *Philadelphia Daily News* provoked a firestorm of controversy for the feisty tabloid newspaper. This controversy included a large protest outside the newspaper's office building a few blocks from Philadelphia's City Hall. A front-page collage containing mug shots of seventeen murder suspects then sought by Philadelphia police sparked this controversy. That front page carried a typical tabloid-style headline stating: "Fugitives among Us."

At the same time this story dominated the second largest daily newspaper in Pennsylvania's biggest city, daily newspapers in New York City, the nation's largest city, faced their own controversy arising from the same subject: crime coverage. New York's problem centered principally on the slant of coverage about a major development in a thirteen-year-old crime that had dominated the news across the nation for months in 1989. This controversy renewed criticisms about how mainstream New York City newspapers covered the vicious April 1989 sexual assault dubbed the "Central Park Jogger Case."

Those twin controversies in New York City and Philadelphia shared more than public complaints about how newspapers handle crime stories. At the core of both of these controversies was the contentious issue of race—specifically, renewed charges against newspapers in both cities alleging "racist coverage." All of the mug shots in the *Philadelphia Daily News* collage were nonwhites, some of whom were wrongfully identified as fugitives. The development in the New York City case was that five black teens had been wrongfully convicted of rape.

Criticisms

Critics in both New York City and Philadelphia lambasted newspapers for what they considered ongoing patterns of crime news coverage containing distinctions discernible by race. Many critics argued that crime coverage too often inflamed, more than it informed—a criticism disputed by newspaper officials. These criticisms of coverage perceived as racist in two major American cities echo persistent findings about failings in newspaper coverage. Criticisms arising from those controversies in New York City and Philadelphia mirrored concerns contained in the 1968 Report of the National Advisory Commission on Civil Disorders. This commission was an investigative body appointed by then U.S. President Lyndon Johnson to examine 1960s-era urban riots. This report from what is now known as the Kerner Commission contained an insightful yet rarely referenced analysis of news media coverage of African Americans.

Chapter 15 of the Kerner Report, titled "The News Media and the Disorders," listed the news media's failure to "analyze and report on racial problems in the United States" as one of the commission's "fundamental criticisms" of news practices.[5] The commission felt news media failings on race coverage were inexcusable "in an institution that has the mission to inform and educate the whole of our society."[6] These failings, the commission noted, intensified "white prejudices" and fed "alienation" among blacks.[7] A major problem in news coverage cited by the Kerner Commission was perspective, and it stated that the "media reports and writes from the standpoint of a white man's world."[8] This issue of perspective—the focus and framing of coverage—was the point of contention for those 2002 protests against newspapers in New York City and Philadelphia.

THE CRIME IS COVERAGE

Crime is a staple of newspaper coverage. The more violent and lurid the crime, the more likely it receives front-page positioning, often with sensationalist treatment. Sensationalist trial coverage of two millionaire playboys charged with murder bracketed both ends of the twentieth century: the 1907–1908 New York City trials of Harry Thaw and the 1995/1997 Los Angeles trials of O.J. Simpson. Sensationalism easily transcends color lines. Thaw was white. Simpson is black.

There have been persistent criticisms about newspaper crime coverage that portrays black men as creatures permeated with criminal proclivities. Many critics (including the author) feel newspaper coverage too often fertilizes this mythical boogeyman image—implicitly and/or explicitly. This embedded image of the criminally bent black boogeyman frequently gives traction to false allegations that garner headline grabbing coverage—charges, for example, like those falsely leveled by Susan Smith in 1994 and Charles Stuart in 1989.

Smith's claim that a black man kidnapped and killed her two young sons received widespread coverage. This coverage, fanning the stereotype of the marauding black male, continued until evidence uncovered by police investigators prompted a confession from Smith that she killed her sons to enhance her relationship with her lover.

Similarly, the October 1989 allegation of Charles Stuart that a black man fatally shot his pregnant wife and wounded him received widespread coverage. Enraged and incessant newspaper coverage of Stuart's claims triggered

Boston police to unleash a dragnet that targeted black men throughout the city, particularly in poorer neighborhoods. Leaks from police and/or prosecutors resulted in newspapers playing up one black man as the prime suspect—coverage that continued despite police never arresting this man.

Revelations from Charles Stuart's brother eventually led police to shift their investigative focus from black men to Charles Stuart. Charles Stuart committed suicide in January 1990 after learning police considered him the prime suspect for his wife's murder. Black leaders in Boston criticized that city's mainstream newspaper managers for allowing stereotypes about the inherent dangers in black urban neighborhoods to block following-up on logical leads for coverage like the substantial inconsistencies in accounts Charles Stuart provided police about the crime. The Society of Professional Journalists Ethics Codes states in its first section that journalists should "avoid stereotyping by race . . . geography . . . or social status."[9]

One of the faults cited in the Kerner Commission's analysis was that newspapers nationwide inadequately presented the significant reality that race-based "slights and indignities are part of [blacks'] daily lives."[10] This assessment in the Kerner report also noted that those slights and indignities came from the "white press"—an institution that reflects "the biases, paternalism [and] indifference of white America."

One of those indignities is pervasive poverty—a known contributor to crime. Another indignity is "injustice" in the justice system. Injustice includes the racist attitudes frequently found underlying policing, prosecution, and imprisonment practices. News coverage frequently overlooks the fundamental fact that while racism is neither *the* reason for crime nor a blanket excuse for crime, it is among factors fueling the dynamics of crime.

RACE AROUND RACE

Missing frequently from contemporary crime coverage, critics argue, are references to the recurring race-based inequities adversely impacting crime, the nation's criminal justice system and the society at-large. These inequities range from police abuses like false arrests to crime-spawning poverty caused in part by discriminatory practices in employment and education. These inequities discolor if not destroy the "American Dream" for nonwhites. The Kerner Commission found "pervasive discrimination and segregation in employment, education and housing" as key ingredients sparking major 1960s riots.[11] Those riots, the Commission stated, erupted following an incident of police brutality.

Many feel these inequities receive sporadic media attention because they ravage nonwhites, a factor the Kerner Commission attributed to "white racism." The Kerner Commission also found that the media reports and writes "from the standpoint of a white man's world." One of the dozen grievances the Kerner Report found existing in each of the cities it examined was "discriminatory administration of justice."[12] The Kerner Report stated "there were significant grievances growing out of beliefs that the courts administer justice on a double, discriminatory standard . . ."[13]

The 2008 sentencing in Georgia involving two white females dubbed the "Barbie Bandits" provided examples of double standards in both court procedures and news coverage. This duo of attractive, young blondes smiled and wore designer sunglasses while executing a weaponless bank robbery netting $11,000. The Bandits had conspired with two black men: the mastermind who planned the crime and a bank teller who facilitated the robbery by releasing money after receiving a demand note from the women. A point for critics was that mainstream news coverage about the sentencing focused predominately on personal matters involving the "Barbie Bandits," examining their plight and quoting their relatives and supporters.[14] This coverage contrasted sharply with the flat, matter-of-fact, they're-guilty accounts about their male accomplices and reduced the men's story to a mere tangent to the media's portrayal of a tragedy impacting the "Barbie Bandits." The bank teller in this scheme received a five-year sentence, while the mastermind received a ten-year sentence. The culpability of the bank teller and the two Bandits was arguably comparable in this nonviolent crime, yet coverage of the sentencing did not extend beyond uncritical reports that the bank teller received a prison sentence more than twice as long as the two-year term for the lone Bandit sent to prison. The second Bandit received probation. The disparate sentences meted to the Bandits and the bank teller resulted in charges of double standards from civil rights groups, including the NAACP in Georgia.[15]

Does the news media do the public a disservice by presenting day-to-day crime coverage that minimizes or excludes examinations of discriminatory inequities pervading the justice system? The Kerner Commission stated that "If what the white American reads in the newspapers . . . conditions his expectations of what is ordinary and normal in the larger society, he will [not] understand the black American."[16]

CONTROVERSIES AND CONUNDRUMS

Contemporary critics feel newspapers nationwide continue crime coverage practices that too often perpetuate stereotypes about minorities. These practices persist despite marked improvements in newspaper coverage of minorities since the late 1960s when the Kerner Commission conducted its analysis. Coverage that compounds the stereotyping of nonwhites is certainly the type of slights and/or indignities the Kerner Report stated blacks endure.

Concerns about the perpetuation of stereotypes drove those August 2002 barbs directed at the *Philadelphia Daily News* from prominent black leaders in that city.[17] Many black readers reacted angrily to the fact that all of the suspects presented in a front-page collage of fugitives were nonwhites. Black leaders and other critics claimed this collage and the accompanying article reinforced racial stereotypes regarding crime and minorities, particularly the image of the criminally bent black male.

The article the *Daily News* published accompanying the mug shot collage centered on a black man murdering his employer, an elderly white man.[18] The rub for critics was the fact that this article focused primarily on an interracial crime, when the overwhelming number of homicides in Philadelphia are intraracial. In Philadelphia, during the year prior to that front-page controversy, 90 percent of the 309 homicides were blacks killing other blacks. Nationwide, the majority of murders are intraracial crimes where members of one race kill other members of their race. One federal study found that between the years 1976 and 2005, whites killed 86 percent of the white murder victims nationwide, while 94 percent of black victims were killed by blacks.[19] That study also noted that whites commit more "workplace" homicides than blacks—70.5 percent vs. 26.7 percent—another informative fact missing from crime coverage of workplace violence.[20]

Critics of the *Daily News* coverage felt the paper could have included a single-sentence explanation in its long article to clarify that interracial crimes are not the norm. Critics felt providing this informational tidbit could help counter the perpetuation of the stereotype of blacks murderously rampaging against whites. Contrary to inferences in much newspaper crime coverage, statistics compiled by the federal government consistently reveal that whites experience violent crimes at rates far less than blacks.

Critics did concede the validity of a defense *Daily News* editors offered about the collage: that nonwhites were the only persons on the Philadelphia police department's most-wanted list at that time.

The *Philadelphia Daily News* did respond ethically to criticisms about the collage by issuing a public apology for the collage. Public apologies by the press are rare despite the SPJ Ethics Code provision that journalists should "admit mistakes and correct them promptly."[21] That apology stated that after "much soul-searching" it became apparent that "the front page photos . . . sent the message to some readers that only black men commit murder . . . That was a mistake."[22] Credit is due to the *Philadelphia Daily News* for its apology given the newspaper industry's paucity of introspectively probing public concerns about the confluence of crime coverage and racial issues.

In contrast, Philadelphia's mainstream news media ignored concerns from blacks about that media's failure to identify the race (white) of three teens arrested for the rape of an eleven-year-old (black) girl at the city's major-league baseball stadium in August 2000. Critics cited numerous instances of the mainstream media routinely identifying the race of nonwhite juvenile suspects in other high-profile cases. The identification of the suspects' race in this rape case came out weeks after the crime and only through coverage in the city's black-owned print and broadcast media.[23] An October 30, 2000, feature article in the *Philadelphia Inquirer* referenced "outrage" felt by some in the black community toward media coverage of that case.[24] However, aside from this brief reference in the second paragraph of the article, the remaining thirty paragraphs of the feature contained neither examination nor explanation of media conduct. The Society of Professional Journalists Code of Ethics in its "Be Accountable" section calls on journalists to "explain news coverage and invite dialogue with the public over journalistic conduct."[25]

Errors Aplenty

Differences over perceptions of the "fugitive" collage by the *Philadelphia Daily News* were not the only problems the paper encountered. The collage itself contained major errors.[26] Four of the people pictured in the collage were actually already in police custody and awaiting trial on August 22, 2002, when the *News* ran its front page, meaning they weren't fugitives. Additionally, three of the other photos in that collage were different images of the same person. *Philadelphia Daily News* editors later acknowledged these errors, calling them inexcusable.

Curiously, the *Daily News* provided no coverage when one of the so-called "fugitives" was acquitted of all charges fifteen months later. *News* editors apparently saw no "story" in the acquittal of a man their newspaper had mistakenly identified as a fugitive[27] and saw no duty to report this significant development in the life of a man it had fingered as a murderer. However, news existed in the exoneration of a person who faced murder charges—especially since matters related to that murder charge became a wider new story. The SPJ's Ethics Code, in its "Minimize Harm" section, urges journalists to "show compassion for those who may be affected adversely by news coverage." The code, in its "Be Accountable" section, also urges journalists to correct mistakes "promptly,"[28] but in the case of a black man acquitted of murder, journalists failed to honor their code.

FOGGED FOCUS

One constant criticism of newspaper crime coverage is that it affords greater attention and emphasis to crimes against whites than crimes against other racial groups. The crime coverage of the "Central Park Jogger" case caused controversy because the news media gave more attention to matters involving whites than nonwhites. In that case, a group of black teens was convicted of raping and brutally beating a white female jogger in Central Park. Over a decade after the horrific 1989 crime against the investment banker, a serial rapist confessed that he alone assaulted the jogger. DNA conclusively confirmed the accuracy of the sudden confession from the rapist. At the time of his confession, the rapist was imprisoned for four rapes and one murder in New York City—most of those crimes occurring after the Central Park incident. This confession exonerated the five black teens from convictions they didn't deserve.

Critics faulted New York City newspapers for their 2002 coverage focusing (subtly yet incessantly) on reputation-saving attempts by various (white) authorities to defend their false convictions of the (nonwhite) teens.[29] Some police and prosecutors reinvestigated the case feverishly seeking links between the newly confessed rapist and the falsely convicted teens. These reinvestigations never established links beyond authorities professing "gut feelings" about the teen's guilt—speculation dutifully reported in news accounts. "The newspapers have been filled with statements of those who insisted that the evidence that they had gathered . . . convinced them . . . the young black men were guilty," stated a caustic December 2002 assessment of the case published in the black-owned *New York Amsterdam News* by that paper's publisher emeritus.[30] Critics questioned why mainstream New York newspapers did not engage in substantive coverage of possible misfeasance by the police and prosecutors that produced the injustice that stuffed teens into adult prison cells. Much of the probative postconfession coverage focused on dynamics that cause false confessions, with most of that coverage devoid of serious examination of the race prejudice rife in the police, prosecutorial, and news media practices of the Central Park case.

Coverage critics were not mollified by this admission in an October 16, 2002, *New York Times* editorial: "The hysteria that surrounded the case may have contributed to a grave injustice."[31] That hysteria—fanned significantly by news media coverage, particularly by the city's tabloid *Daily News* and *Post*—contributed to news coverage in 1989 and 1990 that downplayed salient facts. Flaws in this case occurred with law enforcement, prosecutors, and media coverage of the story. First, police produced no forensic or physical evidence conclusively linking the teen suspects to the crime. Then, media coverage brushed aside the fact that prosecutors proceeded through the trial despite FBI reports that confirmed that DNA evidence recovered from the victim did not match any of the defendants. Further, the media bannered the confessions by four of the teens, even though these confessions were quickly recanted under claims of police coercion. Jurors found the confessions compelling evidence of guilt, evidence seemingly sufficient to overcome the lack of standard trial evidence like forensics and eyewitness identifications. Coverage of the confessions sidestepped the fact that not one defendant admitted his role in raping the victim. Another point critics found alarming was that most of the 2002 coverage about the confession that cleared the falsely convicted quintet did not receive the same kind of banner coverage given to events in 1989.

A Double Standard

News coverage of the Central Park case injected the terms "wilding" and "wolf pack" into American lingo as monikers for out-of-control, menacing minority youths. Such inflammatory language referencing the black and Hispanic teens in the Central Park case contrasted sharply with polite language used in news coverage of four white male teens charged with sexually assaulting a mildly retarded seventeen-year-old white girl in an affluent town near New York City in March 1989, weeks before the Central Park Jogger attack. Critics saw double standards in the tone of the language referencing the suspects in the Glen Ridge, New Jersey, assault case ("sports heroes" and "members of respected families").[32] Critics also saw double standards in the fact that many newspapers refrained from naming the two youngest Glen Ridge suspects, contending they were juveniles under eighteen years old. This practice contrasted with full media exposures for the Central Park–case juveniles (four under 16), which included listing home addresses of these teens.

Some of the 1989 coverage by mainstream New York City newspapers did examine contextual aspects around the Central Park case. A frequently cited *New York Times* article published weeks after the crime reported that twenty-eight other rapes and attempted rapes occurred across New York City the same week of the Central Park attack, each eliciting little if any coverage. According to that April 28, 1989, *New York Times* article, "Nearly all the rapes reported during that April week were of black or Hispanic woman. Most went unnoticed by the public."[33] For example, the brutal beating and rape of a black woman in Brooklyn days after the Central Park attack raised few news coverage eyebrows, despite the gruesomely unusual aspect of assailants throwing this victim off a four-story roof after their brutal assault.

LESSONS NOT LEARNED

It's not surprising those bitter 2002 controversies over crime coverage centering on race occurred in the particular cities of New York and Philadelphia. It is a fact that controversies over race coverage of crime and other race-impacted topics have arisen consistently in both of these cities for centuries.

In 1794, two prominent black leaders in Philadelphia published a detailed rebuttal to the "willful lies [and] slanders" contained in a white journalist's accounts of petty crimes committed by blacks while they serviced the sick and dying during a devastating yellow fever epidemic that killed 10 percent of Philadelphia's population the previous year.[34] The two prominent black ministers authoring this rebuttal bemoaned the lack of context in the white journalist's accounts. "That there were . . . black people guilty of plundering we acknowledge [yet] we know as many whites who were guilty of it; but this is looked over, while the blacks are held up to censure," stated this rebuttal.[35] The authors of that rebuttal, legendary figures Richard Allen and Absalom Jones, posed a question still applicable to crime coverage today: "Is it a greater crime for a black to pilfer, than for a white to privateer?"[36]

The March 1827 founding of *Freedom's Journal*—America's first black-owned newspaper (in New York City)—was a reaction to an influential New York City newspaper "which made the vilest attacks upon the Afro-Americans" according to a seminal yet rarely referenced book on the Black Press published in 1891.[37] The founders of *Freedom's Journal* sought to counter incessant support from newspapers for what scholars now consider one of the worst crimes in history: slavery in America. (The author of that 1891 book on Black Press history, I. Garland Penn, made this relevant historical observation, "Many who hated the Afro-American, published papers attacking the free Afro-American as well as the poor slave.")[38] The first editorial published in *Freedom's Journal* (March 16, 1827) began with declaring an objective of countering "misrepresentations" about blacks perpetrated by newspapers of that era.[39] This editorial noted that "our vices and our degradation are ever arrayed against us, but our virtues are passed by unnoticed."[40]

Charges of "vile" depiction animated February 2009 criticisms against the *New York Post*, a newspaper heavily criticized for racially inflammatory coverage of the Jogger case. The *Post*'s publication of an editorial cartoon (2/17/09) featuring police fatally shooting a chimpanzee sparked national outrage that crossed color lines.[41] While *Post* editors saw the cartoon as legitimate parody, critics saw race prejudice, citing the cartoon's construction around the chimp image with text copy referencing a recent legislative action associated with U.S. President Barack Obama, the first black American to hold the office of the presidency. Historically, linkages of blacks and primates (apes, monkeys, etc.) accounted for some of the most overtly racist depictions in all forms of American media prior to the 1960s–era civil rights movement. A scholarly study published in February 2008 stated "data suggests that ape like representations of black Americans persist in the press . . ."[42] This study found that often subliminal associations of blacks and apes in press coverage adversely impacted how police and other elements of the criminal justice system deal with blacks.

A lot of the mistrust among minorities for mainstream newspapers as an institution arises from coverage perceived as focusing inordinately on crime and other negative aspects of black life. In January 1908 a University of Pennsylvania doctorial candidate published the results of his one-month-long content analysis of coverage of blacks in Philadelphia mainstream newspapers. This researcher found that ". . . articles referring to the crimes of [blacks], their weakness, and other shortcomings . . . took up 87 percent of the newspaper space of the month, with articles referring to the good side of [black] life taking up only 5 percent of this space."[43]

In June 1987, the *Columbia Journalism Review* published an article regarding a month-long monitoring of newspaper coverage of two black neighborhoods in Boston. This report revealed coverage filled with "commonly held stereotypes about blacks and the poor."[44] The report stated while two black Boston neighborhoods accounted for only 7 percent of crime news, "59 percent of all the news about these two black neighborhoods was about crime."[45]

The researcher authoring that 1908 Philadelphia analysis—a noted black newspaper editor in Philadelphia—decried detrimental influences of newspaper coverage heavy with crime. "People get ideas damaging to the race but do not know where they got them. They often think them based upon facts, while they too often have their basis . . . [in] the reporting of proportionately more crimes, with greater emphasis on [blacks] than whites."[46] That 1987 study by an editor and University of Massachusetts–Boston researcher reached conclusions similar to his 1908 counterpart: "Stories featuring crime and violence dominate . . . The tacit message is that while all criminals may not be black, most inner-city blacks are criminals . . . [T]he media send powerful unspoken messages."[47]

MORE RIGHT THAN WRONG

Recurring controversies over newspaper coverage involving the often pernicious convergence of crime and race form an enigma. Despite evidence of flaws in coverage, much of what the public knows about race-related problems and/or racism comes from news media coverage, principally newspaper coverage. Newspaper industry leaders take pride in embracing recommendations contained in the Kerner Commission's Report, particularly the recommendation that mainstream newspapers hire more minority reporters and editors.[48] The *Philadelphia Daily News*, for example, has a commendable record of employing minorities. That newspaper in 2005 elevated its then managing editor, an African American, to the top post of editor, a position no black held at that time at any newspaper in the nation's five largest cities.

CONCLUSION

Given the persistence of controversies arising from crime coverage involving race, obviously more efforts toward improvement are necessary. Without change, an observation of the Kerner Commission will remain: "[O]ur evidence shows that the so-called white press is at best mistrusted and at worst held in contempt by many black Americans."[49]

Critics of media coverage must realize that the constitutional right of press freedom permits newspapers to be insensitive, raucous, and even wrong. Journalists must embrace the fact that the precious right to press freedom carries responsibilities to inform and to also hold those in power accountable—the watch-dog role of journalism. The responsibilities implicit in press freedom include holding public and private sector officials accountable for addressing racial inequities in American society. That accountability includes persistent coverage probing racial inequities.

CRITICAL THINKING QUESTIONS

1. If, in fact, as the author of this chapter explores, nonwhites commit the majority of crimes in America, why do you think the face of crime in newspaper coverage is persistently a person of color?
2. Discuss whether minorities are frequently excluded from newspaper coverage that does not relate to poverty-related pathologies, civil rights, crime, sports and entertainment. Cite examples in support of your position.
3. The author cites intense criticism of media coverage in Philadelphia and New York centering mainly on two recurring themes. Discuss and cite examples of these two recurring themes.
4. Discuss how the Society of Professional Journalists' Code of Ethics statement to "avoid stereotyping by race . . ." should be reflected in media coverage of minorities.
5. Discuss the statistics in relation to their respective coverage in the media: 65 percent of all annual, drug-related murders in the United States are committed by blacks while 70.5 percent of all work-place murders are committed by whites.
6. What role, if any, did the New York media play in the conviction of five black teens in the "Central Park Jogger" case?
7. The author raises the question of the New York media's double standard by citing the race of rape victims during the same week-long period of the infamous "Central Park Jogger" case. Discuss the lack of media coverage of these related crimes from the perspective of the media and from the perspective of the African American, Hispanic, and Asian communities.

NOTES

1. *US v. Clary*, 846 F. Supp 768 (E.D. Mo. 1994) at 783.
2. United States Sentencing Commission, *Special Report to the Congress: Cocaine and Federal Sentencing Policy*, February 1995, 122.
3. Society of Professional Journalists, "Code of Ethics," www.spj.org/ethicscode.asp.
4. The National Commission on Civil Disorders, "The News Media and the Disorders," report [Kerner Report], March 1, 1968. 211.
5. Ibid., 203.
6. Ibid.
7. Ibid., 211.
8. Ibid., 203.
9. Society of Professional Journalists, "Code of Ethics."
10. National Commission on Civil Disorders, 203.
11. Ibid., "Summary," 5.
12. Ibid., 81.
13. Ibid., 81–82.
14. See generally, Tom Opdyke, "One 'Barbie Bandit' Sentenced to 2 Years, the Other Probation," *The Atlanta Journal-Constitution*, March 24, 2008.
15. Tom Opdyke, "NAACP Alleges Racial Bias in Barbie Bandits Sentences," *The Atlanta Journal-Constitution*, April 7, 2008.
16. National Commission on Civil Disorders, 211.
17. Kia Gregory and Jonathan Valania, "Front Page News," *Philadelphia Weekly*, May 7, 2003, www.philadelphiaweekly.com/articles/5540/cover-story; see also, William Bunch, "Coalition Calls for Editor's Resignation," *Philadelphia Daily News*, August 30, 2002, 6.
18. Mark Angeles, "Fugitives Among Us—Sometimes, Murder Suspects Hide In Plain Sight: On the trail of a Pair of Killers," *Philadelphia Daily News*, August 22, 2002, 3.
19. U.S. Department of Justice Bureau of Justice Statistics, "Homicide Trends in the US—Trends by Race," http://www.ojp.usdoj.gov/bjs/homicide/race.htm.
20. Ibid.
21. Society of Professional Journalists, "Code of Ethics."
22. Ellen Foley, "To Our Readers: An Apology," *Philadelphia Daily News*, August 30, 2002, 6; see also, Ellen Foley, "Apologize When You've Offended," ASNE.org, September 21, 2002, www.asne.org/index.cfm?ID=4005.
23. Michael J. Rochon, "Teens Get House Arrest; Bias Seen," *The Philadelphia Tribune*, September 5, 2000, 1.
24. Maria Panaritis, "For Some, Race Plays a Role in the Veterans Stadium Rape Case," *The Philadelphia Inquirer*, October 30, 2000, B-1.
25. Society of Professional Journalists, "Code of Ethics."
26. Deborah Bolling, "The Fugitive Fumble: The Story behind the Daily News' Infamous Fugitive Cover," *Philadelphia City Paper*, November 27–December 3, 2002, www.citypaper.net/articles/2002-11-27/cover.shtm.
27. See Deborah Bolling, "Fumble Recovery: One of the Daily News' Faux Fugitives Goes Free," *Philadelphia City Paper*, December 25–31, 2003, www.citypaper.net/articles/2002-12-12/cb.shtml.

28. Society of Professional Journalists, "Code of Ethics."

29. See generally, Elombe Brath, "Lessons from the Central Park Jogger Case: A Miscarriage of Justice," *Everybody's* (Brooklyn), December 13, 2002; also Trinicenter.com, June 25, 2002, http://trinicenter.com/cgi-bin/selfnews/viewnews.cgi?newsid1024991284,31618,.shtml; Michael Wilson, "Protests Swirl around Jogger Case," *New York Times,* October 16, 2002, B8.

30. Wilbert A. Tatum, "A Will and Testament for Robert Morganthau," *NewYork Amsterdam News,* December 5, 2002, 12.

31. "Justice in the Central Park Jogger Case," *New York Times,* October 16, 2002, A22.

32. See generally, Dan Rouse, "Some See Double Standard in Park, Glen Ridge Sex Cases," *New York Amsterdam News,* January 2, 1993, 16.

33. Don Terry, "In Week of an Infamous Rape, 28 Other Victims Suffer," *New York Times,* May 29, 1989, Section 1, 25.

34. Thomas R. Frazier, *Afro-American History: Primary Sources,* 2nd ed. (Chicago, IL: Dorsey Press, 1988), "A Narrative of the Proceedings of the Black People during the Late Awful Calamity in Philadelphia," 27–38.

35. Frazier, *Afro-American History,* 31.

36. Ibid.

37. I. Garland Penn, *The Afro-American Press and Its Editors,* (Springfield, Mass.: Wiley, 1891), 28.

38. Ibid.

39. Milton Meltzer, *The Black Americans: A History in Their Own Words 1613–1983,* (Harper & Row 1987), 11.

40. Ibid., 12

41. See generally, Richard Prince, "N.Y. Post Chimp Cartoon Draws Outrage," Richard Prince's Journalisms, February 18, 2009, www.mije.org/richarprince/ny-post-chimp-cartoon-draws-outrage.

42. Richard Atiba Goff, Melissa J. Williams, Jennifer L. Eberhardt, and Matthew Christian Jackson, "Not Yet Human: Implicit Knowledge, Historical Dehumanization, and Contemporary Consequences," *Journal of Personality & Social Psychology* 94, no. 2 (2008): 304.

43. Richard R. Wright Jr., "The Newspapers and the Negro," *The Review* (African Methodist Episcopal Review), January 1908, 267.

44. Kirk A. Johnson, "Black and White in Boston: A Researcher Documents Disturbing Biases in Mainstream Coverage of Blacks," *Columbia Journalism Review,* June 1987, 50.

45. Ibid., 51.

46. Richard R. Wright Jr., "The Newspapers and the Negro," *The Review* (African Methodist Episcopal Review), January 1908, 270.

47. Johnson, 50–51.

48. The National Commission on Civil Disorders, 211.

49. Ibid., 210.

CHAPTER 14

Media Frames:
The Impact of
Public Opinion on
the Death Penalty

L. Elaine Sutton Mbionwu

The penalty of death for a crime was first etched into law in the Code of Hammurabi of Babylon in about 1800 BC. Throughout seventh century BC, the death sentence was the only punishment for crimes under the draconian code of Athens. Executions were imposed by stoning, drowning, burning, dismembering, and crucifixion. Hanging and beheading became common methods of execution in Europe by the ninth century AD, and colonial America brought from the Old World the punishment of death for serious crimes against social and religious rules. In 1692, Massachusetts sent nineteen men and women to the gallows because they were thought to be witches. During early colonial times, a perpetrator could be executed for over two hundred crimes, including horse theft, trading with Indians, and adultery.

In early America, hanging day was a popular event, often drawing thousands to an execution to witness the gruesome spectacle. In 1934, Pennsylvania became the first state to move executions inside prison walls, out of public view. Seeking humane and "painless" execution, a wooden chair with electrodes at head and foot was developed and connected to an electric generator manufactured by Mr. George Westinghouse of Pittsburgh. In August 1890, William Kemmler, a New York state inmate, became the first convict executed by electrocution.

For the next seven decades, hundreds of condemned prisoners were put to death by electrocution for murder, treason, and other crimes. In one of the nation's most famous cases, Julius and Ethel Rosenberg were electrocuted in 1953 at Sing Sing for selling A-bomb secrets to the Communists.[1] Death sentences have continued since that time. Today the trend is toward greater use of lethal injection.

An estimated 14,000 Americans have been executed since the inception of the death penalty. The United States remains the only advanced Western democracy that does not recognize capital punishment as a profound human rights violation and as a frightening abuse of government power.[2]

The media has played a role in the overall shaping and influencing of public opinion on many matters, including the death penalty. We begin our examination of this role with an evaluation of whether the news the public receives is "real news" or sensationalized, pre-packaged news frames for the purpose of entertainment.

THE POWER AND PREVALENCE OF MEDIA FRAMES

A frame is a psychological devise that offers a perspective and manipulates salience in order to influence subsequent judgment.[3] The impact of a frame can vary with the individual. As an example, consider a picture frame of your mother, one in which the picture has a nice finish and vibrant colors. Looking at the picture, you are drawn to memories of the figure in the frame and you want to proudly display its contents. On the other hand, a visitor to your home may mostly notice a "not-so-glossy" finish and a scratch on the frame. The visitor is not emotionally attached to the figure in the picture, nor does the visitor hold precious memories of the individual in the picture. It is only you and perhaps other family members who have wonderful memories of your mom and all she has done. The visitor's perspective of the framed picture is limited to a critical examination of the external frame in which the contents are housed and is void of any knowledge that would intimately connect that person to the individual for whom you have reserved a special place. The point to be made here is that we all look and see things through different lenses.

Now, suppose you were to replace the picture of your mother with one that did not have redeeming qualities. Your opinion of the picture and your connection to it would likely change. Next, consider the *media frame,* the media story with a clear bias intended to influence opinion, and how the media may influence public opinion about capital cases. How the media frames the case impacts greatly how the public responds to it. An old adage says, "A picture is worth a thousand words." In the case of media framing, a manipulated frame is worth a thousand pictures.

Media framing exists in many forms, often without public knowledge. The Center for Media and Democracy (CMD) has documented the pervasive use of media framing in the form of video news releases (VNRs). Over a ten-month period, the Center documented television newsrooms' use of thirty-six VNRs, a small sample of the thousands produced each year. CMD identified seventy-seven television stations, from those in the largest to the smallest markets, that aired these VNRs or related satellite media tours (SMTs) in ninety-eight separate instances without disclosure to viewers. Collectively, these seventy-seven stations reach more than half of the U.S. population. The VNRs and SMTs whose broadcasts the Center documented were produced by three broadcast public relations firms for forty-nine clients, including General Motors, Intel, Pfizer, and Capital One. In each case, these television stations actively disguised the sponsored content, creating the impression that the reporting was their own. In almost all cases, the television stations failed to balance the clients' messages with the independently gathered footage or basic journalistic research. More than one-third of the time, stations aired the prepackaged VNR in its entirety.

According to the Center for Media and Democracy, more than three-quarters of U.S. adults rely on local TV news, and more than 70 percent turn to network TV or cable news on a daily basis. The Center has also found that the quality and integrity of reporting by the media significantly impacts the public's ability to objectively evaluate a news item.[4] Thus, with widespread use of VNRs in all types of media outlets, the reliability and accuracy of the content to which the general public is exposed and from which the public ultimately formulates an opinion is questionable.

THE DEATH PENALTY AND THE MEDIA FRAME

A media frame has three roles.[5] These roles include the following:

1. It offers perspective by managing the viewer's exposure to a particular topic.
2. It manipulates salience by directing the viewer to consider only certain parts of a story.
3. It influences judgment as the frame precedes a persuasive argument on a certain position.

Why is framing important in the death penalty debate? Framing by the media serves the purpose of shaping, guiding, and directing public opinion on a particular topic in a manner that causes the viewer, reader, or listener to consider specific points of the frame, while ignoring other aspects of the frame. For example, media stories that highlight certain elements of a crime story involving a person of color, where the victim is white, will often shape a perspective for their audience by elevating the report around the perceived "dark features" of the framed story (e.g., black male, impoverished background, criminal history, etc.).

Some news directors argue that their mission is first and foremost to report facts, and if only racial or ethnic characteristics are available, there is still reason to go on the air with what is known. If, for example, police are looking for a "black male, six-foot-three, in blue jeans," and a reporter had just seen a six-foot, three-inch white male in blue jeans in the area, this meaningless lead would not be part of the news report or frame. Sometimes skin color is the only description given. It is obviously a judgment call requiring editorial sensitivity.[6] However, some stories clearly indicate media bias.

An example of media bias hails from a well-known 1998 ABC 20/20 special called "Hollywood's Unlikeliest Hero," which focused on the case of U.S. political dissident Mumia Abu-Jamal. In the late 1960s and early 1970s, Abu-Jamal was a Black Panther and the victim of illegal surveillance and harassment by the FBI and the Philadelphia police as part of J. Edgar Hoover's COINTELPRO (Counter Intelligence Program) operations. Sam Donaldson, 20/20's investigative reporter, was quoted in the *Philadelphia Inquirer* on December 9, 1998, the eve of his 20/20 report on Mumia, as saying: "The people who support his [Mumia's] release don't do so from a position of knowledge . . . They either oppose the death penalty or they're campus rebels or they're African-American activists who believe that a black man was railroaded and will continue to believe it, no matter what's presented to them." Donaldson's show presented a clear bias.[7] It illustrated how the media uses its power to effectively influence public opinion by manipulating the presentation of information through a bias. Given this powerful influence on the public, can most individuals today form opinions independent of media bias or are they opinions of a frame presented to them?

The program "Framing an Execution: The Media & Mumia Abu-Jamal," narrated by Danny Glover, examines how Donaldson's framing of the case stands up to the available facts and how it measures up to basic journalistic standards of fairness, balance, and accuracy, but it also raises disturbing questions about media and judicial ethics.[8] As of 2008, Mumia's legal appeals remained unsettled and he remained a prisoner at a state prison near Waynesburg, Pennsylvania.

Research conducted in December 2006 by Fabrizio, McLaughlin and Associates, for the Culture and Media Institute revealed the significance of media influence on Americans. The polling company interviewed two thousand adults (one thousand by telephone and one thousand through the Internet) for its research. The survey revealed the following results:

- 64 percent of Americans believe the media is the most important, or one of the most important, influences on American values.
- 74 percent believe American values are weaker than they were twenty years ago.
- 68 percent of Americans believe the media has a negative impact on moral values in the country.
- 56 percent of those who watch four hours or more of television per evening never volunteer, compared to 27 percent of those who watch one hour or less.
- It was revealed that heavy TV viewers are significantly more likely to support the death penalty.
- Overall, 19 percent of Americans say the death penalty is wrong, 26 percent say it's right, and 52 percent say it depends on the situation, for a combined total of 78 percent who can accept the death penalty in certain cases.
- 71 percent of light viewers will support the death penalty in certain cases, compared to 80 percent of heavy viewers.

These findings suggest that television viewing may impact how one feels about capital punishment. They also point toward how the use of frames impact public opinion about the death penalty.

THE MORALITY DEBATE FRAME

The media may also present what is referred to as the morality debate, which asks the question: Is this right or wrong? In other words, the debate is a challenge of belief systems. Challenging belief systems is a cognitive activity in which many are not prone to engage, especially if there is a possibility that their foundation of attitudes, perceptions, and ways of thinking are unstable. For example, personality traits, values, self-interest, group attitudes, and historical events significantly shape and impact public opinion. In 1950, Theodor Adorno and his colleagues introduced the concept of an "authoritarian personality." They defined authoritarian personality as a set of personality traits, including submissiveness to authority, a desire for a strong leader, general hostility, cynicism toward people, strict adherence to conviction, and a belief that people should be roundly punished if they defy those conventions. These traits appear most often in people exposed to strict and rigid child-rearing practices.[9]

Karen Stenner followed up on Adorno's study in 2005. Stenner believes an authoritarian personality is an individual predisposition concerned with the appropriate balance between group authority and uniformity as opposed to individual autonomy and diversity. Stenner categorizes authoritarian personalities as those who value conformity to group norms and libertarians as those who value diversity and individual freedom. An analysis of Stenner's research reveals that authoritarians were found to be more punitive than libertarians. They are more likely to support the death penalty, believe that the courts are too soft on criminals, support wiretapping, and gun ownership.[10]

Stenner's research raises myriad questions for consideration. For example, if the media's main interest is the presentation of entertaining and sensationalized news stories, would it not stand to reason that media conglomerates are also well schooled in the predispositions of their audiences? Would it then not also follow that much of the content disseminated as news is developed based upon the predisposition of an audience rather than developed to simply present facts for public consumption, so that the public might develop well-informed and unbiased opinions?

Another question is whether this same predisposition applies to the professionals reporting the news. I would say that it does! Are journalists realistically capable of minimizing their own predispositions when reporting the news? Going a step further, can corporations, often dictated by self-interests, limit the influence of their predispositions on the media outlets they own and from which we have chosen to extract our news? Corporate conglomerates call the shots by which the journalists must play, resulting in our inability to discern what's real and what's not. I suggest that the layers of their influence run deep and wide.

I do believe that the media is not tasked with the responsibility of shaping public opinion or coercing the public into a particular lane of thought. However, with the influx of 24-hour news coverage, fierce competition to "scoop" the latest news story, and the stiff competition for advertising dollars, the media's interest in adequately informing the public likely ranks at the bottom of the list of journalistic priorities.

In the next section, we will explore the outcomes of a media that is committed to strict adherence to core tenets that govern balanced and impartial journalism versus a media left to its own discretion.

THE INNOCENCE FRAME

The debate over the death penalty has historically centered around four issues: whether it is morally correct to kill; whether the death penalty serves as a deterrent; whether the penalty is applied fairly across racial, social, and economic classes; and whether the irrevocability of the penalty is justified considering possible new evidence or future revelations of improper conduct by the state. The following synopsis of case examples are offered as a foundation for further examination into the possibility of potential outcomes of death penalty cases when the media aggressively pursues an interest in exposing the truth.

Case Example #1

More than a decade after his capital conviction, new evidence casting doubt on Gary Graham's guilt caught the attention of the public via media outlets throughout the United States and around the world. Though Texas reporters had covered the case since Graham was charged in 1981, a highly publicized 1993 complaint filed with the U.S. Department of Justice by the NAACP Legal Defense Fund spawned a new wave of media coverage based on the issue of Graham's possible innocence. The Legal Defense Fund's (LDF) complaint, filed just days before Graham's first scheduled execution date, maintained that Graham was on death row as a direct result of widespread racial discrimination within the Texas criminal justice system and the denial to adequate assistance of counsel for indigents facing criminal charges in Texas. The LDF claimed that the injustices in Graham's case were just illustrative of the consequences of such a system, and that Texas was days away from executing an innocent person. When Graham's execution was stayed, the media and the public continued to focus on Graham's case for a number of reasons, including widespread interest in the issue of innocence and the emergence of new voices raising questions about the death penalty and Graham's guilt. Efforts to establish his innocence continued, but Graham was executed in 2000.

Case Example #2

Wayne Felker is another individual cited as an innocent victim of execution. Felker was a suspect in the disappearance of a woman in 1981 and was under police surveillance for two weeks prior to the body being found. The autopsy was conducted by an unqualified technician, and the results were changed to show the death occurred before the surveillance began. After Felker's conviction, his lawyers presented testimony by forensics experts that the body couldn't have been dead more than three days when found. A stack of evidence was also found that the prosecution had hidden, including DNA evidence that might have exonerated Felker or cast doubt on his guilt. There was even a signed confession of another suspect in the paperwork. Despite these and other problems, Felker was executed in 1996. In 2000, his case was reopened and Felker became the first executed person to have DNA testing used to prove innocence after execution. Although the tests were ruled inconclusive, the lack of a definitive DNA match coupled with the other testimony and the issue of the mishandling of evidence would have at least led to a new trial.

In both cases, the question of innocence is prominent. However, the outcome in case number one is very different from case number two. The difference between the two outcomes appears to be the heightened interest of the media in the emergence of the "innocence frame." The innocence frame was not enough to bring about a not guilty verdict. But, an aggressive, engaged, and involved media created a national platform for an extensive examination of both cases. This effort, created by the media in the Graham case and coupled with the collaborative partnership of an informed public demanding the exposure of truth, made an all important difference. Here again, the influence of the media proves that it is a highly formidable powerhouse for bringing light to darkness. As mentioned previously, when the media operates under the principles that govern respectable journalism, the public can rest assured that their opinions developed from information in the media have been fully informed by truth, integrity, and accountability, and that the media reports they hear are free from conflicts of interest and seek to minimize harm.

DNA AND THE INNOCENCE FRAME

With the emergence over the past ten years of new DNA technology and the innovative work of an organization called the Innocence Project, hundreds of individuals have been given a new lease on life. DNA testing has been a major factor in changing the criminal justice system. It has provided scientific proof that our system convicts and imprisons innocent people and that wrongful convictions are not isolated or rare events. Most importantly, DNA testing has opened a window into wrongful convictions so that we may study their causes and propose remedies that may minimize the chances that more innocent people are convicted. As of August 14, 2008, the Innocence Project has been instrumental in the exoneration of 218 wrongfully convicted individuals, many of whom were awaiting execution.

During the two decades preceding the mid-1990s, more than fifty people were freed from death row in the United States, including Kirk Bloodsworth, the first to be freed on the basis of DNA evidence. As a number of innocence cases emerged, media outlets devoted more time and resources to investigating the issue. For example, a groundbreaking *60 Minutes* investigative report featured the case of Walter McMillian, a black man from Alabama who had been erroneously convicted of the murder of a white female after a trial that lasted only a day and a half. This news report played a key role in McMillian's exoneration in 1993.

At this time, reporters were eager to explore why innocent people were landing on death row, and Gary Graham's case provided members of the media with an opportunity to examine this intriguing issue. As Graham's first execution date loomed, his attorneys and supporters took steps to put Graham's case before another important forum—the American people. By tapping into the emergence of 24-hour news networks and through broader use of new media, such as the Internet, to distribute news, those advocating against Graham's execution hosted press conferences, provided news reporters with access to interviews with Graham, and enlisted the help of well-known civic leaders and celebrities to focus attention on the problems associated with the case.[11] Though the efforts failed to establish Graham's innocence, they proved the power of the innocence frame to affect public opinion.

What Is the Innocence Frame and Why Is It a Stronger Base for Arguing the Death Penalty Issue?

According to a 2006 report titled "Media Framing of Capital Punishment and Its Impact on Individuals' Cognitive Responses," published in *Mass Community and Society Journal* by Frank E. Dardis and collegues at Pennsylvania State University, it is well known that the media has the ability to frame a sociopolitical issue in specific ways so as to have impact on the public's thoughts and perceptions of the issue. The report's authors analyzed coverage of capital punishment in the *New York Times* since 1960 and then conducted an experiment in which they assessed individual-level responses to differently framed news stories. They revealed (1) the dramatic emergence of a new "innocence frame" within the past ten years that accentuates imperfections in the justice system; and (2) the much greater impact of this frame on individual thoughts— especially upon those who favor the death penalty—compared to the traditional morality—based frame. The report also found that in 2000, public support for the death penalty in the United States fell to 66 percent, considerably lower than the 80 percent reported six years earlier, suggesting the impact that the innocence frame had made in just a few years.

CONCLUSION

The ability to judge impartially is a necessary attribute for individuals reporting the news or serving in the criminal justice system. Yet in recent years, the general populace has been bombarded with the influx of so-called TV news via 24-hour cable news programming and talk-radio that are no longer neutral in their presentation of news, as evidenced by the frames they present to their viewers.

Exposure to media bias affects the public's judgment. Unfortunately, today's media is ostensibly fascinated with "sensationalized" journalism. As a result, the general public has found it increasingly difficult to formulate unbiased opinions as it negotiates minefields of overt presentations of media bias. We are quickly losing our ability to be critical thinkers and make just judgments based upon facts.

Our response to sensational journalism is primarily an emotional one. One of the most notable examples of an emotional response to a justice-system case with heightened visual framing was the O. J. Simpson case. In this case, retired African American football star O. J. Simpson was accused of murdering his wife, Nicole Brown Simpson. At the time of the widely publicized trial, most African American people suspected that Mr. Simpson was guilty, but they celebrated the "not-guilty" verdict because of a value system that had been shaped by a perceived injustice toward blacks fed by years of media images. Another notable example was the case of Rodney King and the resulting lack of a just response to his beating captured on video. One must ask how the public was affected by the consistent replaying of the very public beating followed by the exoneration of the police officers who were cleared of any criminal wrongdoing. The riots that followed the verdict proved how deeply such heightened visual framing created a powerful emotional response in the public.

The media has been entrusted with the role of reporting impartial facts that are void of tainted frames, offering a slanted perspective of viewpoints that perpetuate the self-interests of certain individuals at the expense of those unable to advocate for themselves. However, the presentation of news requires a greater level of responsibility that is guided by something higher than a set of man-made standards, practices, and principles. An inner conviction of right and wrong, of what is just and fair, should always serve as the guidepost for representatives of the media.

CRITICAL THINKING QUESTIONS

1. What is the utilitarian value in use of the frame as a way to depict the crime problem and media coverage?
2. What lessons do we learn about the history of capital punishment in America relative to other countries? Is this a fair criticism? Why?
3. What is a frame? What are the advantages of using frames? Are there any potential flaws in the use of frames as a way to portray crimes committed?
4. To what standard must the media be held in the reporting of criminal offenses?
5. How do media frames shape public opinion about crimes in general and capital punishment in particular?

NOTES

1. Judge J. A. Manning, *A Chronicle of Capital Punishment*, http://www.warhol.org/education/pdfs/chronicle_of_cap_pun.pdf (accessed March 2008).
2. The American Civil Liberties Union, http://www.aclu.org/capital/facts/10602res20070409.html (accessed July 2008).
3. Kelton Rhoads, *What's in a Frame?*, http://www.workingpsychology.com/whatfram.html (accessed July 2008).
4. Diane Farsetta and Daniel Price, Center for Media and Democracy, April 6, 2006, http://www.prwatch.org/fakenews/execsummary (accessed March 2009).
5. Rhoads, *What's in a Frame?*
6. Av Westin, *Best Practices for Television and Journalists*, The Freedom Forums' Free Press/Fairness Project, http://www.freedomforum.org/templates/document.asp.documentID=17279 (accessed August 2008).
7. Bernard Goldberg, *Bias: CBS Insider Exposes How the Media Distorts the News* (New York: Harper Collins, 2003).
8. Rosalee A. Clawson and Zoe M. Oxley, "Pluralistic Roots of Public Opinion," chap. 6 in *Public Opinion: Democratic Ideals, Democratic Practice* (Washington, D.C.: CQ Press, 2008), 154–156.
9. Ibid.
10. Capital Punishment in Context, "Public Opinion and the Death Penalty" http://www.capitalpunishmentincontext.org/issues/publicopinion (accessed March 2, 2009).
11. Ibid.

CHAPTER 15

The Media and Professional Sports: The Intersect of Race, Sports, and Media in the Michael Vick Dogfighting Case*

Rose J. Bigler
Mary P. Brewster

This chapter will address the social construction of the "black criminal athlete" and will emphasize the role of the media in the construction process. A case study of the Michael Vick dogfighting case will be presented to illustrate how the press covered this story. Specifically, content analysis of the *New York Times* coverage was conducted to determine how the Michael Vick story was framed. The news coverage was investigated, in part, to discover the role that sports and race played in the coverage of the Michael Vick case in the *New York Times*.

The chapter will be divided into two main sections. The first will educate the reader about the Michael Vick case, animal abuse research and anticruelty statutes, and dogfighting as a sport. The second part of the chapter will discuss the social construction of the "black criminal athlete" and the media's contribution

* A portion of this chapter is based upon R. J. Bigler, *Animal Cruelty in the Media: An Analysis of the Michael Vick Dog Fighting Case*, an unpublished paper presented at the annual meeting of the Academy of Criminal Justice Sciences, Cincinnati, OH, March 2008.

to that construction. It will also include an overview of how the Michael Vick case relates to Richard Quinney's *Social Reality of Crime*.[1]

THE MICHAEL VICK DOGFIGHTING CASE

In April of 2007, investigators searched Atlanta Falcons quarterback Michael Vick's property in Smithfield, Virginia, and found evidence of a dogfighting ring. Over fifty-four dogs were seized that day, many with serious injuries. In July 2007, Vick and three co-defendants were indicted on federal felony and misdemeanor charges related to the dogfighting ring called the "Bad Newz Kennels."[2]

The federal grand jury indictment handed down in July 2007 alleged that these activities began in or about early 2001 and continued until their discovery by animal-control officers. Vick and his co-defendants were alleged to have "rolled" or "tested" dogs by putting the dogs through fighting sessions "to determine which animals were good fighters." They were also alleged to have executed dogs that did not perform well by methods that included hanging, drowning, and slamming dogs to the ground. In addition, they possessed sheds and kennels associated with housing fighting dogs and hosting dogfights, a "rape stand" where a female dog "who is too aggressive to submit to males for breeding is strapped down with her head in place with restraint," sticks used to pry open dogs' mouths during fights, and treadmills and "slat mills" used to condition the dogs.[3]

In August 2007, Vick and his co-defendants reached plea bargain settlements with the court thereby avoiding additional charges. On December 10, 2007, Vick was sentenced to prison for twenty-three months for running the dogfighting operation, which was consistent with the federal sentencing guidelines for this crime.

The Michael Vick case received enormous publicity in the press, mainly due to Michael Vick's celebrity status as a quarterback for the NFL Falcons. The charges were also shocking to members of the public, many of whom did not know about the crime of dogfighting. The press had an opportunity to educate the public about animal abuse and cruelty, especially the crime of dogfighting. It is important to consider how the press covered this story. Did the press include information about animal cruelty and dogfighting in the coverage of the case in order to educate the public about this crime or did they focus on sports and race? In other words, how was the story "framed"? Before answering these questions, it is helpful to understand the background of animal abuse and dogfighting.

Animal Abuse: Research and Legislation

Animal abuse and its criminalization has long been an area of study neglected by scholars.[4] Much of the scant yet important research that has been conducted thus far has tended to focus on the link between animal abuse and family violence,[5] animal abuse and family dysfunction,[6] and animal abuse and other forms of deviance.[7] Some have argued for the study of animal abuse due to its link to actual or potential violence against persons.[8] The study of animal abuse and neglect as a form of crime in itself is rare.[9] One researcher studied media coverage of animal abuse and abusers by searching the electronic and print media to find newspaper stories nationwide where cruelty of animals was evident. From those stories she worked to develop a typology of the offender based on motivation by performing content analysis of newspapers for the year 2000. She retrieved 717 cases for the year and found among other findings that dogs were the most abused type of animal.[10]

One of the reasons for the lack of research related to animal abuse in the United States is that animals are seen as property and, as such, have few legal rights.[11] Francione, a scholar who specializes in law related to animals, states that the status of animals as property has severely limited the type of legal protection that we extend to nonhumans.[12] As long as the animal owner does not act with a "malignant or vindictive purpose" by imposing pain, suffering, or death outside of the "socially accepted or exploitation," the law will not intervene.[13]

Animals, especially domesticated animals, do have a history of legal safeguards in the United States that can be traced to an ordinance in the Massachusetts Bay Colony in 1641. Today every state in the United States has anticruelty statutes. These statutes do not afford animals legal rights but serve as the primary legal protection for animals in our legal system.

As a whole, anticruelty laws specify that animals have a right to (1) protection from cruel treatment, (2) protection from abandonment, (3) protection from poisoning, and (4) the provision of food, water, and shelter.[14] State laws penalize two types of actions under their anticruelty provisions: (1) intentional acts— "acts of cruelty where the actor knowingly tries to hurt an animal by repeatedly striking an animal, burning an animal, or committing some other heinous act";[15] (2) failure to act—failure to provide food, water, necessary shelter, or in some states reasonable veterinary care may be neglect.[16] Felony provisions are for aggravated acts of cruelty where the offender commits heinous acts such as mutilation and intentional affliction of pain or death.[17]

Dogfighting

One of the most horrific types of animal abuse and cruelty is dogfighting. Dogfighting is unlawful in all fifty states and the District of Columbia, as well as in Puerto Rico and the Virgin Islands. In all states except Idaho and Wyoming, felony sanctions can be imposed on those found guilty of this crime. In some states it is also against the law to attend a dogfighting event.[18]

A dogfight takes place in a ring (a "pit") made of plywood and usually takes place in a secluded location. Dogs are pitted against one another and are made to fight for hours until one of the dogs is unable to continue. The dogs, mostly pit bulls, often sustain painful injuries such as torn flesh and broken bones. Dogs can die immediately or soon afterwards from these injuries. If a dog loses a fight, sometimes the owner will kill it out of anger by electrocution or hanging. Many dogs are found dumped after the fights or are tortured. Stolen pets, small dogs and cats, are often used in the training of these dogs to give them a "taste of blood".[19]

Dogfighting has a long history in the United States. In the colonial period, dogfighting was sanctioned and promoted. In the nineteenth century, immigrants brought dogs with them as they came to America from Europe. A man with a dog could make money (though he was unemployed) by pitting his dog against those belonging to others.[20]

By the 1860s, Henry Bergh, a citizen of New York, sought a charter for an organization that would be dedicated to the implementation of laws that prevent cruelty to animals. He appealed to the New York legislature for a statewide charter for the American Society for the Prevention of Cruelty to Animals (A.S.P.C.A). The charter was granted on April 10, 1866. Henry Bergh was unanimously elected as the A.S.P.C.A.'s first president.[21]

The most revolutionary part of the charter was its enforcement provision. The A.S.P.C.A., although a private body, was granted authority to arrest violators of the anticruelty statute in New York.[22] This legislation became the model for anticruelty laws throughout the nation.

Bergh worked hard to enforce the law that outlawed dogfighting. However, he found it difficult in a society that allowed this type of behavior. It also did not help that whole families attended the fights or that members of the police were involved as well.[23]

Dogfighting continues today and is part of the criminal subculture that can involve gang activity, illegal gambling, drug use, and drug dealing. Weapons are common at the fights, as are children.[24]

In 1976 dogfighting was outlawed in most states. Congress passed the Foley Bill, named after Congressman Thomas Foley, which amended the Federal Animal Welfare Act to prohibit animal fighting (7 U.S.C. 2156). The amendment makes it illegal to:

> (1) knowingly sponsor or exhibit an animal in a fighting venture for which the animal was moved in interstate or using foreign commerce; (2) buy, sell, transport, deliver, or receive such an animal; or to (3) use the U.S. mail, telegraph, telephone, radio, or television operating in interstate or foreign commerce to promote an animal fighting venture.[25]

In May 2007 a new federal law went into effect making interstate dogfighting activities a felony and provided for imprisonment and imposition of large fines. The Animal Fighting Prohibition Enforcement Act was signed by President George W. Bush on May 3. The law provides a penalty of up to three years' imprisonment and up to a $250,000 fine for each offense of interstate or foreign transport.

THE SOCIAL CONSTRUCTION OF THE "BLACK CRIMINAL ATHLETE": A CRITICAL ANALYSIS OF THE MICHAEL VICK CASE

A critical analysis of the Michael Vick case can help us to better understand both the behavior of the perpetrator and his companions, as well as the role of the media in presenting to the public a perception of crime, race, and sport. In his seminal work, *The Social Reality of Crime*, Richard Quinney makes clear that a critical analysis of crime can include both an attempt to explain why someone violates the law as well as a careful examination of how those with power are able to pass and enforce laws that further their interests. Additionally, Quinney emphasizes the ways in which the "reality of crime" is created and perpetuated, in part, by the media.[26]

Quinney's theory consists of six propositions related to the social reality of crime. His first proposition states that "[c]rime is a definition of human conduct that is created by authorized agents in a politically organized society."[27] The crime of dogfighting was defined as such by state and federal legislators who are "authorized agents" in U.S. society.

> Wherever men live together conflict and a struggle for power will be found. In any society, institutional means are used to officially establish and enforce sets of values for the entire population."[28]

Quinney's second proposition states that "[c]riminal definitions describe behaviors that conflict with the interests of the segments of society that have the power to shape public policy."[29] Laws prohibiting dogfighting represent the interests, norms, and values of white, middle-class Americans. This legislation represented judgment on the part of those in power regarding an activity that some members of the working class poor viewed as a form of entertainment. Some who have argued in favor of leniency for Michael Vick point out that deer hunting and horse racing are legal, yet dogfighting is not. This supports Quinney's notion that the laws reflect the interests of the powerful in society, prohibiting dogfighting while allowing other forms of harm to animals. Therefore, although the initial laws protecting animals (some dating back to the 1640s) were not meant to oppress inner-city African Americans, Quinney points out that "a criminal law may be intended for a particular interest at one time and then amended and implemented at another time for some other interest."[30]

Proposition 3 deals with the "application of criminal definitions."[31] It states that "[c]riminal definitions are applied by the segments of society that have the power to shape the enforcement and administration of criminal law."[32] Those in power in society control the application of the law. That is, the powerful determine who will be arrested, prosecuted, and imprisoned. This is interesting when we compare dogfighting to sports that are accepted by society, such as horse racing and deer hunting, and enjoyed by many, including the wealthy and powerful. One could also argue that all other things being equal, members of certain groups in society are more likely than others to be arrested for any given crime (including dogfighting). The acknowledgement of racism in the criminal justice system is nothing new.[33] Crime statistics reflect at least some bias on the part of criminal justice agents.[34]

Quinney's fourth and fifth propositions are those that interest us most in trying to understand the social construction of the "black criminal athlete." Proposition 4 states that "[b]ehavior patterns are structured in segmentally organized society in relation to criminal definitions, and within this context persons engage in actions that have relative probabilities of being defined as criminal."[35] Much of the dog men's behavior can be explained by the theories of differential opportunity, differential association, and differential association-reinforcement.

> Consequently, *persons in the segments of society whose behavior patterns are not represented in formulating and applying criminal definitions are more likely to act in ways that will be defined as criminal than those in the segments that formulate and apply criminal definitions.*[36]
>
> Man constructs his own patterns of action in participating with others. It follows, then, that the *probability that a person will develop action patterns that have a high potential of being defined as criminal depends on the relative substance of (1) structured opportunities, (2) learning experiences, (3) interpersonal associations and identifications, and (4) self-conceptions.*[37]

In attempting to understand the etiology of dogfighting, the Michael Vick case offers a unique opportunity to focus on a high profile case that received much public attention and interest. Most of society reacted negatively to the allegations against Michael Vick. Some of the swiftest response came in the Senate. Senator Robert Byrd of West Virginia shouted "Shame! Shame! Shame!" According to *The Economist*, July 28, 2007, Byrd's voice shook and his hands trembled as he said "the training of these poor creatures to turn themselves into fighting machines is simply barbaric. Barbaric! Barbaric! Barbaric!"[38]

Dog men (people who fight dogs) believe that they have been maligned in the press and society. They argue that dogfighting is just as acceptable as boxing or horseracing. A typical statement made by a dog man to justify his behavior is, "Let's face it. When you get right down to it, the sport of dogfighting is no worse than the sport of boxing."[39] Dog men also see themselves as being no different from sports coaches.[40] One such dog man stated that "[d]ogfighters are not cruel people, they are no different than boxing trainers or football coaches. The press has slandered us."[41]

Dog men see themselves as being members of a fraternity. This is a sport where loyalty and secrecy are important to those who consider themselves members of this subculture. This is especially true since dogfighting involves two forms of deviance: gambling and violation of animal protection laws.[42]

Evans and Forsyth interviewed thirty-one individuals that fight and breed pit bulls. The following interview excerpts offer insight into the perspective of those who fight dogs.

> One of the best things about this sport is the people you will meet. There are people from all walks of life involved in this game and they all have one thing in common, the dogs. Once you become known in the game, you could go anywhere in the U.S. and you will know somebody in that area who is in the game. It's like a huge fraternity. These people will accept you into their homes and offer you food and a place to stay, anytime you're traveling near their homes, just because you're a fellow dogman.[43]

> Just remember if the cops ever show up at a fight, always be prepared to leave fast. If they ever catch you, you didn't see or hear anything about dogfighting. Always be loyal to the fraternity and don't ever rat out anybody else. If they catch you they'll try to get a confession out of you. Don't give it to them.[44]

Forsyth and Evans[45] applied Sykes and Matza's neutralization theory[46] to the sport of dogfighting. According to Sykes and Matza, there are five major techniques of neutralization. First, the denial of the victim, wherein the offender maintains that whoever is harmed by an action, deserves the harm. Second, denial of responsibility, where one believes that one's acts are caused by forces beyond one's control. Third, denial of injury where one claims that no one was really harmed by the action and therefore there is no victim. Fourth, appeal to higher loyalties, wherein attachment to smaller groups takes precedence over attachment to society. Fifth, condemnation of the condemners, wherein offenders claim that those who denounce a certain behavior have themselves exhibited worse forms of behavior.

Forsyth and Evans found that dog men mainly used three neutralization techniques: denial of injury, appeal to higher loyalties, and condemnation of the condemners.[47] Denial of injury was evident in the dog men's beliefs that pit bulls are natural fighters who have been bred to fight. As Forsyth and Evans state, "it is the self-actualization of an animal who was born to fight," the dog men's loyalty to dogfighting, the long history of the sport, and their belief that they are respectable participants.[48] The condemnation of the condemners is found in the dog men's claim that people who condemn dogfighting are hypocrites who might attend sporting events such as boxing or horse racing.[49]

In other research, Evans, Gauthier, and Forsyth examined the issue of masculinity in the sport of dogfighting.[50] After interviewing thirty-one dog men and attending fourteen dogfights as well as a number of before-fight meetings, they argued that the dogs serve as symbols of their owners.[51] According to Evans, Gauthier, and Forsyth, "Any character attributed to the dogs is also attributed to the men they represent . . . If the dogs behave as heroes, then the men must be heroes also."[52]

In their interviews with dog men, Evans, Gauthier, and Forsyth found that the respondents viewed the sport of dogfighting as a way they could compete with other men for status.[53] These three scholars argued that this was especially important for working-class men since the pit offers a playing field that is equal to all men regardless of wealth.[54] As one dog man told these scholars:

> In this sport I can compete with someone who is really wealthy and whose ancestors have been in the sport for 60 to 70 years. I can beat them. If I bring a good dog to the pit, I stand just as good a chance of winning as they do. I[t] doesn't matter if they are richer than I am.[55]

If Evans, Gauthier and Forsyth are correct, then dog men have found a different avenue of opportunity to prove their masculinity and obtain status within society. One could argue that this is an illustrative example of Cloward and Ohlin's theory of differential opportunity.[56] Cloward and Ohlin posit that "individuals [are] located in two opportunity structures—one legitimate, the other illegitimate."[57] Lower-class youth may have limited access to success through legitimate means and, therefore, will consider the illegitimate opportunity structure. Just as the legitimate opportunities vary, so too do the illegitimate opportunities. Three types of deviant opportunities are described by Cloward and

Ohlin—criminal opportunities, conflict opportunities, and retreatist opportunities. Dogfighting may be considered both a criminal opportunity (e.g., an illegal means of making money) and a conflict opportunity (to the extent that those involved clearly enjoy violence and fighting). Dog men have a great deal to gain by choosing this option from among the available illegitimate opportunities. Key benefits to the dog men include money, status, and respect.

Dogfighting can also be viewed from the perspective of social learning theory. Researchers have found that animal abuse is learned behavior.[58] Sutherland proposed that criminal behavior is learned through the same processes as is noncriminal behavior.[59] Behavior is learned through interaction and communication with intimate others in one's life (e.g., peers). Interest in and knowledge of dogfighting may begin at an early age, as some dogfighting enthusiasts bring their children to events. Burgess and Akers added to differential association the idea of operant conditioning (e.g., rewards or reinforcers that increase the likelihood that an individual will learn a specific behavior).[60] Rewards abound in dogfighting and can include money, status, camaraderie, entertainment, and prestige among one's peers. Youth who are present at dogfighting events might also learn vicariously through the many rewards reaped by the dog men.

Some have argued that the learning of criminal behavior may occur within the subculture of organized sports which infuses and reinforces violent behavior outside of the sports arena. Berry and Smith summarize various scholars' arguments that "sports . . . instill antisocial values," including violence.[61] They also describe the phenomenon of "cultural spillover," the idea that the approval of violence that is legitimately used in sports may lead to "illegitimate violence by athletes outside of sports contexts."[62]

Quinney's fifth proposition pertains to the "Construction of Criminal Conceptions." "Conceptions of crime are constructed and diffused in the segments of society by various means of communication."[63]

> . . . In fact, *the construction of criminal conceptions depends on the portrayal of crime in all personal and mass communications.* By such means, criminal conceptions are constructed and diffused in the segments of society. . . . [The conceptions of the most powerful] are certain of becoming incorporated into the social reality of crime.[64]

Media coverage of crime is common. Research has indicated that it is one of the most frequently presented topics in news coverage.[65] Crime becomes a story in the press because it reflects fears and anxieties related to public safety. The public wants to know about crime in its communities and the press is eager to report newsworthy events.

Much of what the public knows about crime and the workings of the criminal justice system comes from the mass media. Research consistently indicates that the public's perception of the crime problem is not related to its reality.[66] It appears that the media is failing in its reporting of crime to correctly educate the public about crime. For example, in a content analysis of local television news coverage of juvenile crimes in Los Angeles and Orange County, Dixon and Azocar found that black and Latino juveniles were portrayed as perpetrators of crime at higher rates than were white youth.[67] The portrayal by the media of black youth as felons was disproportionately higher than their representation in official felony arrest reports.[68]

> In social psychological terms, if television news portrays more African Americans as perpetrators of crime than whites, negative stereotypes of African Americans as criminals may be perpetuated in the minds of viewers . . . The social cognitive paradigm suggests that news media images may affect viewer perceptions by reinforcing a cognitive association between a particular group (e.g., African Americans) and a particular role (e.g., criminal).[69]

This social cognition paradigm is supported by the results of a 2007 study in which research subjects were presented with a crime story embedded in a newscast. A factorial design was used in which the race of the perpetrator was not identified in some cases. The researchers found that subjects rated as high the likelihood that the perpetrator was black.[70]

The portrayal of dogfighting as a form of entertainment among inner-city African Americans, as well as among African American professional football and basketball players reinforces the public image of the African American male as violent and dangerous. The media strengthen the perception of "vicious African American dogfighting" among both the powerful and the powerless in society.

Research Methodology

In order to examine the way in which the Michael Vick case was presented to the public, the *New York Times* coverage of the case from April 25 to December 31, 2007, was analyzed. The *New York Times* was chosen with the assumption that because it is one of the most prominent and respected newspapers in the United States, its coverage would be the most educational for the reader.

The news articles were collected using Lexis-Nexis Academic. By using the search phrase "Michael Vick," 54 *New York Times* articles were found for the time period April 25 to December 31, 2007. These articles were analyzed with a content-analysis coding instrument based on the facts of the Michael Vick case.

Content analysis offers an empirical method to identify and analyze patterns in communication data. It is a "technique for making inferences by objectively and systematically identifying specified characteristics of messages. It is a way of asking a fixed set of questions about the data in such a way to provide countable results."[71] Content analysis allows the researcher to obtain an "objective and quantitative description" of the data.[72] It uses categories or a classification scheme to systematically and objectively analyze the data.[73]

The analysis was conducted to reveal the ways in which this particular media outlet (i.e., the *New York Times*) framed the Michael Vick story. Included in the analysis, based in part on the work of Spratt and associates, were the intensity or amount of coverage, and the placement of coverage within the paper, since both "are significant factors affecting framing."[74]

In addition to the intensity and placement of coverage, the content analysis included several other variables to answer a variety of questions. These questions included the following: Did the *New York Times* provide definitions and history of animal abuse/cruelty and its history to its readers? Did the newspaper's coverage inform the readers that dogfighting was a crime and a felony in forty-eight states as well as a federal offense? Did the *New York Times* state in its coverage that Michael Vick was a black man? Did the *New York Times* articles indicate whether or not Vick took responsibility for his behavior? Did the newspaper coverage present all of the facts of the case, including that the dogs were the victims and how they were victimized? Did the newspaper coverage include interviews with advocates for the dog victims or animal rights advocates? Did the *New York Times* inform its readers of the possible punishment a person could receive if found guilty of these charges? Did the *New York Times* educate its readers about the facts of this case?

The content analysis of the *New York Times* coverage of the Michael Vick dogfighting case provided some interesting results. The intensity of the coverage suggested that the story was considered to be reasonably newsworthy to the *New York Times* editors. Fifty-four articles about the case were published in the *Times* over the course of approximately eight months. Perhaps one of the most astounding and significant findings was the placement of the coverage. Of the 54 articles presented in the newspaper, all but two were presented in the sports section. The other two articles were presented in the editorial and "Week in Review" sections of the newspaper. This finding illustrates that the editors of the *New York Times* made story placement decisions to locate these articles in the sports section as opposed to a section containing more general news. Were only people who read the sports section interested in the Michael Vick dogfighting case? What about the other people who read the newspaper but do not read this section of the paper? Where would they get their information about this case if they only read the *New York Times*?

The placement of the articles also leads one to assume that the editors of the *New York Times* considered this story to be primarily a sports story since this is how they categorized the articles. Was this because the alleged perpetrator of the crimes, Michael Vick, was a quarterback for the NFL team, the Atlanta Falcons? What about the crimes committed against the dogs and society by Vick?

The placement of the articles in the sports section of the *New York Times* is also consistent with another finding from the content analysis of the articles. Never once in any of the articles did the *New York Times* define any of the terms related to animal cruelty. Specifically, the articles did not define animal cruelty or dogfighting, nor did they provide a history of dogfighting in the United States. Even if only those reading the sports section received information about the Michael Vick case, would not those people need some context in which to understand the articles? This is especially true of the *New York Times* which is considered to be one of the top newspapers in the country.

Where the *New York Times* did better in its coverage of the Michael Vick dogfighting case was in its defining of the criminal charges. Of the 54 articles analyzed, 42 (78 percent) of the articles stated that dogfighting is against the law, that it is a crime, or that an indictment was made in the case. However, only 19 (35 percent) of the articles stated that the dogfighting charges were federal charges.

Still, would not one expect that in an article covering the Michael Vick case that the *New York Times* would explain the criminal charges to its readers? These were stories about a man accused of a serious crime. Should not the coverage focus on the charges filed against him as well as the seriousness of those charges? Again, was not this information important for the reader to have a context in which to understand the articles?

One way to interpret many of these findings is to understand that the journalists writing these articles usually covered the sports beat. Perhaps the sports writers were not prepared to cover a story as complex or complicated as this one. Why did not the *New York Times* have reporters that usually covered news stories in the first couple of sections of the paper cover this story as well or at least team with the sports writers? The *New York Times'* coverage of the story and the placement of the articles in the sports section suggest that the story is one of an athlete who committed a crime rather than a criminal who happened to be an athlete. Perhaps this coverage was limited to the sports section not only because the perpetrator was a professional athlete, but because dogfighting is viewed by some as a sport, albeit an illegal one. Or perhaps because the victims were animals, not humans, the story was not viewed as important enough to warrant front-page coverage.

Another interesting finding of the content analysis is that Michael Vick's race was included in some of the articles. Specifically, Michael Vick is an African American man. Of the analyzed articles, 6 included his race as part of the coverage. Why was his race included in the articles? What did his race have to do with the story? None of the six stories explained why they included this information as part of the coverage. These six articles just stated that he was a black man.

The inclusion of race in the coverage is troubling. Would the *New York Times* have included Vick's race if he were a white man? Was race a part of the story? If it was, should not the *New York Times* explain this information for the reader? Did this piece of information prejudice Vick for some readers of the articles? Were the *New York Times* writers or editors subliminally or intentionally stereotyping Vick for the readers? The role of race in media coverage on the Michael Vick case is obvious in that some media outlets sought out comments related to the race and crime issue from such people as the interim president of the NAACP. Consider, for example, the following excerpt of a report from an NBC sports journalist:

> "[Vick] certainly was in control of his actions at all times and should be held accountable for what he did," Dennis Courtland Hayes, interim president of the national NAACP, said Thursday in an interview with MSNBC's Amy Robach.
>
> Hayes rejected the contention that dogfighting was an acceptable part of urban black culture, as celebrated in rap and hip-hop videos like "Grand Champ" by DMX or "99 Problems" by Jay-Z."[75]

The emphasis on the race issue, in conjunction with the placement of the news coverage in the sports section, further emphasizes that this is a case of a black professional athlete who is a criminal, as opposed to a criminal who happens to be a black professional athlete.

Another finding of the *New York Times* content analysis of the coverage of Michael Vick related to whether or not he took responsibility for his behavior. Of the 54 articles analyzed, only 8 (15 percent) of the articles included any information about Vick taking responsibility for his actions. In the majority (85 percent) of the articles, he was generally portrayed as a man who did not understand or take responsibility for his behavior. In fact, in many of the articles, Vick was portrayed as the victim in this case. Seven (13 percent) of the articles included interviews with advocates for Vick. Many of those advocates interviewed stated that they believed that Vick was innocent or that they did not believe that dogfighting was criminal or should be taken so seriously. Many of those advocates believed Vick was being unfairly prosecuted in the criminal courts and in the press.

The *New York Times* did present the dogs in the case as victims in some of the articles. Twenty-three articles (43 percent) included specific information that Vick's dogs were victims in the dogfighting charges. But was this coverage enough? If a man, woman or child were victimized in a crime, the *New York Times* would surely include that information as part of the story. Why were not the victims of this crime, the dogs, presented in the articles as crime victims?

When examining the victimization of the dogs, the *New York Times* was very general in the coverage of these crime victims. Fifty of the articles (93 percent) stated that the dogs were involved in dogfighting activities and 22 articles (41 percent) stated that there was abuse or cruelty with dogs as victims. However, only 17 articles (31 percent) included the fact that many of the dogs involved in the activities had died. Further, the specifics of the Michael Vick case were seldom mentioned in the coverage. Only 8 of the articles (15 percent) informed readers that many of the dogs were tortured, victims of hanging, or drowned; six of the articles (11 percent) informed the readers of the electronic dog treadmill that was used for the dogs; and 5 articles (9 percent) told of forced mating and the rape stand that were used. Only 3 of the articles (6 percent) informed the readers that many of the dogs were victims of electrocution, starvation, gunshots, or strangulation. In addition, only 2 of the articles (4 percent) informed readers that the dogs were victims of beatings, body slamming, or were caged or chained. Finally, only one of the articles informed readers that many of the dog victims had bruises or scars from the dogfighting activities.

Why were so few of the specifics of the Michael Vick dogfighting activities included as part of the coverage of this story? If the crime victims had been human, would not the specifics of the crimes have been included in the articles, even in the sports section? Why was so little value put on the well being or lives of these dogs? Is this coverage an indication of the value placed on the animals in society? What about the rights of these animals to be protected from cruelty or abuse?

The *New York Times* did include some information about animal rights as well as interviews with animal advocates. Eighteen (33 percent) of the 54 articles analyzed included animal rights in connection with the dogs as victims while 13 articles (24 percent) included animal rights advocates condemning Vick for his dogfighting activities. Seven articles (13 percent) included interviews with animal advocates about the Vick case and dogfighting. These interviews indicate an attempt by the *New York Times* to include some information about animal rights and the views of animal advocates.

Perhaps the most interesting finding was the coverage of the possible punishments for Michael Vick for the dogfighting activities. Twenty-three of the articles (43 percent) stated that Vick could receive a jail or prison sentence if found guilty of the crimes charged. Seven of the articles (13 percent) stated that Vick could be fined if found guilty. On the other hand, 29 of the articles (54 percent) stated that Vick could be suspended from the NFL for the dogfighting activities while 11 of the articles (20 percent) stated that Vick had lost endorsement deals because of the charges. The greatest emphasis related to the potential consequences for Vick's crime was related to his role as a professional athlete (e.g., suspension).

Since the articles were primarily placed in the sports section of the *New York Times*, these findings perhaps are not so astonishing. The Michael Vick case was framed as a story of a professional athlete who got into trouble. It was framed more as a sports story than as a crime story. Of course, sports writers and those who read their articles would be concerned about the suspension of a valuable quarterback from a NFL team. The inclusion so often of Vick's loss or potential loss of endorsement deals is troubling, however, when compared to so little coverage of the possible punishments Vick may receive for his crimes. This coverage indicates that the focus of the *New York Times* was on sports and not on the criminal charges of the Michael Vick dogfighting case.

Sports and Race in the Michael Vick Case

Among the most interesting findings from the content analysis of the *New York Times* was the importance of sports and race in the media coverage of the Michael Vick case. As noted in the findings, all but 2 of the 54 articles were in the sports section of the newspaper. Also in 6 (11 percent) of the 54 articles, Vick was identified as a black man and many stories used his picture, making it apparent to the reader that Vick was black. "Visual images in media coverage [have been said to] . . . shape the public's perception" of other criminal incidents.[76] Why was there so much emphasis on sports and race instead of animal abuse/cruelty and dogfighting in the *New York Times* as well as in other newspaper coverage?

The majority of crime stories appear in the first two sections of a newspaper. Also according to Chermak, crimes committed by sports celebrities appear in the sports section of the newspaper.[77] However this is not always true. Perhaps the best known exception was the O. J. Simpson case, which received front-page coverage by most newspapers during his trial. Simpson was a black man and a former football player. Why did the Vick case not receive the same type of coverage? Was it because Vick killed dogs versus Simpson, who was alleged to have killed two human beings? Despite the differences in terms of placement of coverage, both the Simpson and Vick cases received a great deal of publicity.

> African Americans in positions of social power represent an upset of the social order, a violation of social expectations. Regardless of the work or talent it has taken to achieve this status, African American athletes may be "noticed" more than white athletes for suspected criminal involvement.[78]

Berry and Smith argue that there is a "staggering" amount of news coverage on criminal athletes. They point out that the level of coverage is due to the fact that the athletes are celebrities.[79] The extent of coverage creates the impression that criminal athletes are omnipresent.

> This may be particularly true of African American sports figures since they are not only celebrities (thereby attracting attention) but are African Americans (thereby verifying racial prejudices and expectations about African Americans and crime).[80]

One of the reasons the Michael Vick case received so much coverage in the sports section of the *New York Times* is that he was a quarterback for the NFL team the Atlanta Falcons. The quarterback is the one position on the team that receives much more attention and scrutiny than the other positions.[81]

Until recently, most quarterbacks in the NFL were white among predominately black teams. Indeed to be a black quarterback was a rarity a couple of decades ago. As stated in *Ebony* magazine:

> [T]en years ago, the number of black quarterbacks in the National Football league could be counted on your left hand. Nowadays, you need the left hand, the right hand and the hands of a few friends to count the black quarterbacks on the NFL rosters.[82]

Interestingly enough, there are those who believe that it was not until the Atlanta Falcons chose Vick as the number one overall pick in the 2001 NFL draft that the doors really opened for the black quarterback.[83]

The cultural significance of the black quarterback is important. Saraceno has argued that the black quarterback helps to "begin the process of opening closed doors and yes, some closed minds."[84] How he is presented in the media is important. Since he is also a celebrity as well as a black sports figure, he can expect continuous coverage of his behavior. The media thrive on what has been called "the popular consumption of celebrity crime and violence."[85]

Sports Illustrated writers Dohrmann and Evans tried to explain Michael Vick's dogfighting behavior in an interesting way. They interviewed Andrew Young, the former mayor of Atlanta, who had a complex explanation for Vick's behavior. Young stated that Vick was "young and country" and that he primarily hung out with friends from his hometown of Newport News, Virginia.[86] According to Young, Vick was "victimized by 'ghetto loyalty.'"

> It is a heady life, being a pro athlete, but it is also a lonely life . . . And often
> the only people athletes feel comfortable with are the guys they grew up with
> on the streets . . . Many athletes are trapped in that situation . . . and it is not
> entirely their fault.[87]

The major premise behind Young's comments is that athletes—primarily black athletes from poor backgrounds—are held captive by a code that requires them to help neighborhood friends.[88] In the Vick case, those friends, who many would classify as opportunists, used Vick and eventually sold him out in the dogfighting case. His loyalty to his tight circle of friends and the code of the street led to his downfall.

Todd Boyd, a professor of race and popular culture at the University of Southern California, has studied the plight of the black athlete and states that there are four reasons to explain this plight.[89] Those four reasons fall under the umbrella of ghetto loyalty. First, black athletes are indebted to their old neighborhoods because they received a pass for participating in any criminal activity during their youth because of their athletic abilities. Second, childhood bonds are important to these athletes because they feel old friends are the only people they can trust. They consider those friends to be brothers. Third, communal pressure is heavy for these athletes. They are told often "don't forget where you come from" and "when you make it, take care of us." Lastly, many athletes fear that people might take advantage of them because of the money they possess. Because of this, they hang out with individuals they know. They feel the need to help and provide opportunities to the people they know from the old neighborhood.[90]

Quinney's ideas are summarized in his sixth, and final, proposition which states that "[T]he social reality of crime is constructed by the formulation and application of criminal definitions, the development of behavior patterns related to criminal definitions, and the construction of criminal conceptions."[91]

The social construction of various phenomena has been due in large part to the media. For example, during the start of the AIDS epidemic, the media created the "reality" that HIV was a homosexual disease and later the "reality" of HIV as a black disease.[92] The criminal conceptions created by the media result in "racialized beliefs" that can have a great impact on public reactions to crime. Dixon found, for example, that a sample of 506 Los Angeles County residents reported more punitive responses for suspects in a hypothetical criminal scenario when the race of the suspect was unidentified or when the suspect was identified as black than when the suspect was identified as a white suspect.[93] Similar results had been found in a study by Hurwitz and Peffley, in which subjects also responded more punitively toward hypothetical African American criminal suspects than toward white suspects.[94] The social construction of the race and crime link has been studied by numerous researchers.[95]

> Whites are represented in a variety of roles as perpetrators, officers, and victims on network news. However, African Americans are much more likely to be absent from network news, and when they do appear, they are more likely to be portrayed as perpetrators than as victims or officers.[96]

Criminal suspects who are African American tend to be depicted by the media in a way that "impl[ies] that they are likely to be particularly violent or threatening."[97]

Critical ontologists explore "reality" and its construction to determine whether such realities are discovered or invented.[98]

> And, if we *did* invent it, do we *admit* that we did so? Or do we—as the critical ontologist often suspects—conceal a political project behind the claim that some troubling entity has been discovered, insisting that it demands special kinds of attention . . ."[99]

Some critical ontologists would argue the following:

> [O]ur decision to *label* a set of people . . . does not indicate that we have discovered something common to all those labeled; it indicates only that we have adopted the practice of deploying the relevant label in certain ways and of coordinating our speech and action in light of the labeling practice. In so doing, . . . we have in effect *invented* a category of persons, as an element of our shared public discourse. The object [e.g., the black criminal athlete] . . . is not the cause of our labeling process, but the effect of it."[100]

It is imperative to examine "how collective memories are constructed and used," and to recognize the important role that the media, and journalism in particular, play in socially constructing these memories.[101] The impact of this construction is far-reaching and may not only create and reinforce stereotypes, but may also impact the attitudes, expectations, and behavior of the public that buys into these stereotypes.

Cultivation theory suggests that television viewers' perceptions of various stereotypes are strengthened by long-term exposure.[102] This theory is supported by research conducted by Oliver in which "greater exposure to reality-based programs specifically (but not to fictional programs) was associated with higher estimates of criminality, but this relationship was significantly stronger for estimates of black crime involvement than for white crime involvement."[103] Oliver suggests that "associative priming" theory is also supported by extant research. That is, after viewers have been exposed to crime stories, it impacts the viewers' perceptions of "subsequently-presented crime situations."[104] Media stories about violent African American criminality, for example, can create stereotypes for the viewers. The viewers will call these stereotyped images to mind with subsequent exposure to stories related to violent criminality.[105]

Oliver highlights the importance of understanding how the media helps to create stereotypes and how "existing cognitions" (and stereotypes) affect the way in which the viewer interprets stories in the media.[106] This idea of "priming" has been discussed by other authors as well. Gorham, for example, writes the following about several research studies:

> [The results] suggest that priming stereotypes of African Americans triggers cognitive processing that follows the ultimate attribution error. This process thereby enhances the ability of the news to produce not just stereotype-congruent interpretations about an individual suspect but also interpretations about the larger group that support dominant racial ideology."[107]

The Black Criminal Athlete

In 1995, O. J. Simpson, former running back and winner of the Heisman trophy, was tried for the 1994 murder/stabbing death of his white exwife, Nicole Brown Simpson, and her significant other, Ron Goldman. In 2003, professional basketball player Kobe Bryant was accused of raping a young white woman. In 2007, Michael Vick, star quarterback of the Atlanta Falcons, was charged and later pled guilty to charges related to dogfighting. The extensive coverage of these and various other African American athletes in the media results in the strengthening of "structural racism" and the popular image of blacks as criminals.[108] Widespread coverage of the infamous O. J. Simpson murder trial, Kobe Bryant's rape case, and recently the Michael Vick dogfighting case have all contributed to the social construction of the black criminal athlete, and even more so, the *dangerously violent* black criminal athlete. Berry and Smith (2000) argue that "media portrayals solidify public perceptions about minority involvement in crime."[109]

> Criminal activity seems to be attributed to African American athletes in the same way and for the same reasons that young African American men are pegged as criminals. Race is the master status defining the actor as crime-prone, regardless of other traits, skills, or accomplishments."[110]

The media create the notion "that athletes are committing crimes at alarming rates, with a hyperfocus on the alleged criminal activities of Black athletes."[111]

> When African American athletes are involved in crime, it reaffirms public opinion about media portrayals of African Americans' (on the whole) disproportional involvement in crime. That is, the *politics of representation* explains the sport-crime-race nexus, which rests upon the supposition that African American sports figures are represented as criminals, and criminal athletes are represented as African Americans.
>
> Moreover, the politics of representation lapse into the *politics of exclusion* when African Americans are represented as immoral, unappreciative, and untrustworthy, albeit sports-talented. This type of representation marginalizes African American athletes, excluding them from full participation in the social privileges that come with fame and wealth.[112]

Media journalists and editors have a responsibility to be cognizant of their role in the construction of racialized phenomena that impact the perceptions of the public, the behaviors by members of the public and marginalized groups, and the preconceptions and behaviors of criminal-justice practitioners. The extent and type of publicity in the Vick, Bryant, Simpson, and other cases presents an impression of the ubiquity of crime by "black criminal athletes." This impression contributes to the social construction of "black criminal athletes," further perpetuating the marginalization of African Americans in the United States.

CRITICAL THINKING QUESTIONS

1. Describe and discuss the social construction of the black athlete.
2. Comment on the role of the *New York Times* in media coverage of the Michael Vick story. In your opinion, what was the impact of media coverage by the *New York Times* on the perception of Michael Vick?
3. What generalizations, if any, can be made about media coverage of black athletes?
4. Is there a black criminal athlete? If yes or no, please explain.

NOTES

1. R. Quinney, *The Social Reality of Crime* (Boston, Massachusetts: Little, Brown, 1970).
2. *United States v. Michael Vick et.al.*, CriminalNo3:07CR(E.D.VoJuly11, 2007.)
3. Ibid.
4. See e.g., C. D. Bryant, and W. E. Snizek, "On the Trail of the Centaur," *Society* 30, no. 3 (1993): 32.
5. E.g., see F. R. Ascione, C. V. Weber, and T. M. Thompson, "Battered Pets and Domestic Violence: Animal Abuse Reported by Women Experiencing Intimate Violence and by Nonabused Women" *Violence against Women* 13, no. 4 (2007): 354–373; A. C. Baldry, "Animal Abuse and Exposure to Interpersonal Violence in Italian Youth," *Journal of Interpersonal Violence* 18, no. 3 (2003): 258–281; A. C. Baldry, "Animal Abuse among Preadolescents Directly and

Indirectly Victimized at School and at Home," *Criminal Behavior and Mental Health* 15, no. 2 (2005): 97–110. C. L. Curry, "Animal Cruelty by Children Exposed to Domestic Violence," *Child Abuse and Neglect*, 30, no. 4 (2006): 425–435; A. Duncan and C. Miller, "The Impact of an Abusive Family Context on Childhood Animal Cruelty and Adult Violence," *Aggression and Violent Behavior: A Review Journal* 7, no. 4 (2002): 365–383.
6. K. D. Becker, J. Stuewig, and V. M. Herrera, "A Study of Firesetting and Animal Cruelty in Children: Family Influences and Adolescent Outcome," *Journal of the American Academy of Child and Adolescent Psychiatry* 43, no. 7 (2004): 905–912; A. Duncan, J. C. Thomas, and C. Miller, "Significance of Family Risk Factors in Development of Childhood Animal Cruelty in

Adolescent Boys with Conduct Problems," *Journal of Family Violence* 20, no. 4 (2005): 235–239.

7. A. Arluke, J. Levin, L. Carter, and F. R. Ascione, "The Relationship of Animal Abuse to Violence and Other Forms of Antisocial Behavior," *Journal of Interpersonal Violence* 14, no. 9 (1999): 963–975; M. R. Dadds, C. M. Turner, and McAloon, "Developmental Links between Cruelty to Animals and Human Violence," *Australian and New Zealand Journal of Criminology* 35, no. 3 (2002): 363–382; G. S. Green, "The Other Criminalities of Animal Freeze Killers: Support for a Generality of Deviance," *Society and Animals* 10, no. 1 (2002): 5–30; See also R. Lockwood and F. R. Ascione, eds., *Cruelty to Animals and Interpersonal Violence: Readings in Research and Application* (West Lafayette, IN: Purdue University Press, 1998).

8. See e.g., P. Beirne, "For a Non-speciesist Criminology: Animal Abuse as an Object of Study," *Criminology* 37, no. 1 (1999): 117–147; M. L. Petersen and D. P. Farrington, "Cruelty to Animals and Violence to People," *Victims and Offender* 2 (2007): 21–43.

9. S. Vollum, J. Buffington-Vollum, and D. R. Longmire, "Moral Disengagement and Attitudes about Violence towards Animals," *Society and Animals* 12, no. 3 (2004): 209–235.

10. G. J. Bickerstaff, "An Exploration of Animal Abuse and Animal Abusers" (PhD diss, State University of New York, 2003), 1–187.

11. S. C. Haden and A. Scarpa, "Childhood Animal Cruelty: A Review of Research, Assessment, and Therapeutic Issues," *The Forensic Examiner* Summer (2005): 23–32.

12. G. L. Francione, *Animals, Property and the Law* (Philadelphia: Temple University Press,; 1995) G. L. Francione, *Rain without Thunder: The Ideology of the Animal Rights Movement* (Philadelphia: Temple University Press, 1996).

13. Ibid.

14. E. S. Leavitt and D. Halverson, "The Evolution of Anti-cruelty Laws in the United States," in *Animals and Their Legal Rights*, ed. Emily Stewart Leavitt and Diane Halverson (Washington, D.C.: Animal Welfare Institute, 1990); E. Leavitt and Stewart, *Animals and Their Rights: A Survey of American Laws from 1641–1990*. 4th ed. (Washington, D.C.: Animal Welfare Institute, 1990). S. Soehnel, "What Constitutes Offense of Cruelty to Animal Abuse Cases," 6 ALR. 5th 733.

15. Leavitt and Stewart.

16. Ibid.

17. D. Favre and V. Tsang, "The Development of Anti-Cruelty Laws during the 1800s," *Detroit College of Law Review* 1 (1993): 1–35. P. D. Frasch, S. K. Otto, K. M. Olsen, and P. A. Ernest, "State Anti-cruelty Statutes: An Overview," *Animal Law* 5 (1999): 69–80. P. D. Frasch, S. Waisman, B. Wagman, and S. Beckstead, *Animal Law* (Durham, N.C.: Carolina Academic Press, 2000). M. Livingston, "Desecrating the Ark: Animal Abuse and the Law's Role in Prevention," *Iowa Law Review* 87, no. 1 (2001): 1–73.

18. Humane Society of the United States, 2007, www.humanesociety.

com. Humane Society of the United States, "The Role of the Community in Reducing Violence," *First Strike Campaign Information Packet*, Washington, D.C., 2007.

19. H. Gibson, *Dog Fighting Detailed Discussion*, Animal Legal and Historical Center, Michigan State University College of Law, 2005.

20. M. Homans, *A Complete History of Fighting Dogs* (New York: Ringpress Books, 1999).

21. Favre and Tsang; Leavitt and Halverson; Livingston.

22. N. Y. Rev § 375.8; Livingston.

23. Homans.

24. Gibson.

25. M. C. Jasper, *Animal Rights Law*, 2nd ed. (Dobbs Ferry, New York: Oceana Publications, 2002), 28.

26. Quinney.

27. Ibid., 15.

28. Ibid., 11.

29. Ibid., 16.

30. Ibid., 70.

31. Ibid., 18.

32. Ibid., 18.

33. See e.g., R. M. Brewer and N. A. Heitzeg, "The Racialization of Crime and Punishment: Criminal Justice, Color-Blind Racism, and the Political Economy of the Prison Industrial Complex," *American Behavioral Scientist* 51, no. 5 (2008): 625–644; see also R. Engvall, M. A. Hallett, and S. Eschholz, *Racial Issues in Criminal Justice: The Case of African Americans* (Westport, CT: Praeger, 2003).

34. B. Berry and E. Smith, "Race, Sport, and Crime: The Misrepresentation of African Americans in Team Sports and Crime," *Sociology of Sport Journal* 17 (2000): 171–197.

35. Quinney, 20.

36. Ibid., 21.

37. Ibid., 21.

38. "Cruel and Inhumane; Dogfighting," *The Economist*, July 28, 2007.

39. J. M. Davis, "Laws Are Too Lax to Slow Dogfights, Authorities Say," *Times Picayune*, April 30, 1984, S1, 13–14; J. M. Davis, "Pit Bull Fighters," *Times Picayune*, April 22, 1982, S1, 8.

40. C. J. Forsyth and R. D. Evans, "Dogmen: The Rationalization of Deviance," *Society and Animals* 6, no. 3 (1998): 203–218.

41. Ibid., 209.

42. R. D. Evans and C. J. Forsyth, "The Social Milieu of Dogmen and Dogfights," *Deviant Behavior* 19, no. 1 (1998): 51–71.

43. Ibid., 61.

44. Ibid., 62.

45. Ibid.

46. G. M. Sykes and D. Matza, "Techniques of Neutralization: A Theory of Delinquency," *American Sociological Review* 22, no. 6 (1957): 664–670.

47. Forsyth and Evans, 206.

48. Ibid., 209.

49. Ibid., 208.

50. R. D. Evans, D. K. Gauthier, and C. J. Forsyth, "Dogfighting: Symbolic Expression and Validation of Masculinity," *Sex Roles* 39, no. 11/12 (1998)c: 825–838.

51. Ibid., 830.

52. Ibid.

53. Ibid., 834.

54. Ibid.

55. Ibid., 835.

56. Richard A. Cloward and Lloyd E. Ohlin, *Delinquency and Opportunity* (New York: The Free Press, 1960).

57. Ibid., 152.

58. See e.g., C. Hensley and S. E. Tallichet, "Learning to be Cruel? Exploring the Onset and Frequency of Animal Cruelty," *International Journal of Offender Therapy and Comparative Criminology* 49, no. 1 (2005): 37–47. S. Tallichet and C. Hensley, "Rural and Urban Differences in the Commission of Animal Cruelty," *International Journal of Offender Therapy and Comparative Criminology* 49, no. 6 (2005): 711–726.

59. Edwin H. Sutherland, *Principles of Criminology* (New York: Harper & Row, 1947).

60. Robert L. Burgess and Ronald L. Akers, "A Differential Association—Reinforcement Theory of Criminal Behavior," *Social Problems* 14 (1966): 128–147.

61. B. Berry and E. Smith.

62. Ibid., 182.

63. Quinney, 22–23.

64. Quinney, 22.

65. D. A. Graber, *Crime News and the Public* (New York: Praeger Publishers, 1980).

66. Ibid; J. F. Sheley and C. D. Ashkins, "Crime, Crime News, and Crime Views," *Public Opinion Quarterly* 45 no. 4 (1981): 492–506. S. J. Smith, "Crime in the News," *British Journal of Criminology* 24 no. 3 (1984): 289–295. S. M. Chermak, *Victims in the News: Crime and the American New Media* (Boulder, Colorado: Westview Press, 1995). L. Kennedy and V. Sacco, *Crime Victims in Context* (Los Angles, California, 1998). P. Estrada, "Juvenile Violence as a Social Problem," *British Journal of Criminology* 41 (2001): 639–655.

67. T. L. Dixon and C. L. Azocar, "The Representation of Juvenile Offenders by Race on Los Angeles Area Television News," *The Howard Journal of Communications* 17 (2006): 143–161.

68. It should be noted, however, that an earlier content analysis of national television network news found no overrepresentation of African Americans as criminals or violent criminals in the media. That is, the amount of media coverage accurately reflected African Americans representation in official arrest data. See T. L. Dixon, C. L. Azocar, and M. Casas, "The Portrayal of Race and Crime on Television News," *Journal of Broadcasting and Electronic Media* 47, no. 4 (2003): 498–523.

69. T. L. Dixon, C. L. Azocar, and M. Casas, "The Portrayal of Race and Crime on Television News," *Journal of Broadcasting and Electronic Media* 47, no. 4 (2003): 498–523.

70. T. L. Dixon, "Black Criminals and White Officers: The Effects of Racially Misrepresenting Law Breakers and Law Defenders on Television News," *Media Psychology* 10, no. 2 (2007): 270–291.

71. C. Marshall and G. B. Rossman, *Designing Qualitative Research* (Newbury, California: Sage Publishers), 98.

72. B. Berelson, *Content Analysis in Communication Research* (New York: Free Press, 1952), 18.

73. Ibid.; Marshall and Rossman; K. Krippendorf, *Content Analysis*, vol. 5 (Beverly Hills: Sage, 1980); R. P. Weber, *Basic Content Analysis*, no. 49 (Beverly Hills: Sage, 1985); R. A. Singleton, Jr., B. C. Straits, and M. M. Straits, *Approaches to Social Research* (New York: Oxford University Press, 1993).

74. M. Spratt, C. F. Bullock, and G. Baldasty, "News, Race, and the Status Quo: The Case of Emmett Louis Till," *The Howard Journal of Communications* 18 (2007): 169–192.

75. A. Johnson, "Vick Case Divides African-American leaders," NBC Sports, http://nbcsports.msnbc.com/id/20411561/site/21683474/ (accessed June 10, 2008).

76. M. Spratt, C. F. Bullock, and G. Baldasty. Interestingly, Spratt and colleagues are emphasizing the use of photos of the crime victim's (Emmett Till's) mutilated body.

77. S. M. Chermak, *Victims in the News: Crime and the American New Media* (Boulder, CO: Westview Press, 1995), 47.

78. B. Berry and E. Smith, 188.

79. Ibid.

80. Berry and Smith, 178.

81. E. Primm, S. DeBois, and R. Regoli, "An Exercise in Subtleties and the Transmission of Racism: An Analysis of *Sports Illustrated* Covers," *Journal of African American Studies* 11 (2007): 239–250.

82. B. Roquemore, "Is the NFL's Black Quarterback Boom Real?" *Ebony*, October 2001, 38.

83. S. Chapman, "Black QB's QED: The End of an NFL Myth," *National Review* 53 (2001): 11.

84. J. Saraceno, "Brisco Paved the Way for McNabb to Play," *USA Today*, February 6, 2002, 3.

85. T. Blackshaw and T. Crabbe, "Leeds on Trial: Soap Opera, Performativity and the Racialization of Sports-Related Violence," *Patterns of Prejudice* 39, no. 3 (2005): 327–342.

86. G. Dohrmann and F. Evans, "The Road to Bad News," *Sports Illustrated* 107, no. 21 (2007): 70–76.

87. Ibid., 70–71.

88. Ibid.

89. A. Baker and T. Boyd, *Out of Bounds: Sports, Media, and the Politics of Identity* (Bloomington, IN: Indiana University Press, 1997); T. Boyd, *Am I Black Enough for You? Popular Culture from the 'Hood and Beyond* (Bloomington, IN: Indiana University Press, 1997); T. Boyd, *Young, Black, Rich, and Famous: The Rise of the NBA, the Hip Hop Invasion, and the Transformation of American Culture* (New York: Doubleday/Random House, 2003).

90. Dohrmann and Evans 70–76.

91. Quinney, 23.

92. A. Persson and C. Newman, "Making Monsters: Heterosexuality, Crime and Race in Recent Western Media Coverage of HIV," *Sociology of Health and Illness* 30, no. 4 (2008): 632–646.

93. T. L. Dixon, "Crime News and Racialized Beliefs: Understanding the Relationship between News Viewing and Perceptions of African Americans and Crime," *Journal of Communication* 58 (2008), 106–125.

94. J. Hurwitz and M. Peffley, "Public Perceptions of Race and Crime: The Role of Racial Stereotypes," *American Journal of Political Science* 41 (1997): 375–401.

95. See e.g., M. Barlow, "Race and the Problem of Crime in Time and Newsweek Cover Stories, 1946 to 1995," *Social Justice* 25, no. 2 (1998): 149–183; M. Robinson, "The Construction and Reinforcement of Myths of Race and Crime," *Journal of Contemporary Criminal Justice* 16, no. 2 (2000): 133.

96. Dixon, Azocar, and Casas, 517.

97. M. B. Oliver, "African American Men as 'Criminal and Dangerous': Implications of Media Portrayals of Crime on the 'Criminalization' of African American Men," *Journal of African American Studies* 7, no. 2 (2003): 3–18.

98. S. D'Arcy, "The 'Jamaican Criminal' in Toronto, 1994: A Critical Ontology," *Canadian Journal of Communication* 32 (2007): 241–259.

99. D'Arcy, 244.

100. D'Arcy 244.

101. J. Markovitz, "Anatomy of a Spectacle: Race, Gender, and Memory in the Kobe Bryant Rape Case," *Sociology of Sport Journal* 23 (2006): 398.

102. G. Gerbner, L. Gross, M. Morgan, N. Signorielli, and J. Shanahan, "Growing Up with Television: Cultivation Processes," in *Media Effects: Advances in Theory and Research*, 2nd ed., ed. J. Bryant and D. Zilmann (Mahwah, NJ: Lawrence Erlbaum, 2002), 43–67.

103. Oliver, 9.

104. Ibid., 9.

105. See e.g., J. D. Johnson, M. S. Adams, W. Hall, and L. Ashburn, "Race, Media, and Violence: Differential Racial Effects of Exposure to Violent News Stories," *Basic and Applied Social Psychology* 19 (1997): 81–90.

106. Oliver, 17.

107. B. W. Gorham, "News Media's Relationship with Stereotyping: The Linguistic Intergroup Bias in Response to Crime News," *Journal of Communication* 56 (2006): 289–308.

108. D. J. Leonard, "The Next M.J. or the Next O.J.? Kobe Bryant, Race, and the Absurdity of Colorblind Rhetoric," *Journal of Sport and Social Issues* 28, no. 3 (2004): 284–313.

109. Berry and Smith, 173.

110. Berry and Smith, 190.

111. Leonard, 299.

112. Berry and Smith, 191.

CHAPTER 16

Legitimacy of the War in Iraq: The Role of the Media in Sorting Fact from Fox-tion

Reem Ali Abu-Lughod

On March 20, 2003, Iraq was invaded by a multinational force led by the United States and Great Britain, an event that later became known as the Iraq War, or Operation Iraqi Freedom. Justifications for going to war provided by U.S. President George W. Bush were primarily based on allegations that Iraq was developing weapons of mass destruction (WMDs) and that Iraq and Al Qaeda had been cooperating. The role of the media since the start of the Iraq war has had a great impact on the American public's perception of its legitimacy and whether or not they support or oppose it.[1]

In the United States, advancements in media technology and reporting have made it possible for every act of violence, criminality, and terrorism to become a vital part of public discourse instantly. The media in its different forms (e.g., the Internet, print media, radio, cable and satellite TV) has provided opportunities for a wider range of views to become known. It has also vastly expanded the capacity for state propaganda to saturate public opinion. One means of propaganda is through dramatization of news provided by the corporate, mainstream media. Such dramatization can result in misconceptions, especially when the media provides mostly subjective and opinionated analyses of what it reports, a phenomenon known as the media spin.[2] In all, the mainstream media has managed to reach a larger audience through myriad forms of reporting and debating the news.

The Internet is much more decentralized and since inception of the Web in the mid-1990s, it has brought together and informed people who would otherwise be unaware of pertinent worldwide events or alternative points of view.[3] Two important issues the Internet fights are the fabrication and manipulation of news. Doing so helps expose propaganda and mixed messages sent to different audiences, which contribute to serious distortions of reality. This exposure is important because depending upon the media source, the entire picture of what is really taking place is often hidden or oversimplified. For example, the conservative Fox News Channel served as a leading media advocate for the Bush Administration in support of the war, while providing an avalanche of misleading analyses and coverage. These reports falsely created the impression on the road to war that Iraq was cooperating with terrorist organizations, and that it was developing weapons of mass destruction.

One interesting aspect of the "reporting" on newsworthy events is the complex relationship between journalists and terrorists.[4] While journalists have a duty to report on a particular incident, they may be threatened for offering their own opinions and analyses of incidents, especially if they do not coincide with the terrorists' perspectives. Nevertheless, terrorists have managed to get their positions and ideologies across to viewers. Doing so has resulted in public criticism of journalists for the fine line they must walk between *reporting* news and *disseminating* terrorist propaganda. In other words, despite offering important information about media-driven foreign policy and honoring the public's right to know, the media has also contributed to making terrorist ideologies and propaganda more influential.

This globalization of news and "instant" reporting is evidenced by CNN with its around-the-clock coverage, a phenomenon known as the CNN effect.[5] Interestingly, society's concern and thirst for more information through mass media has contributed to increased fear and anxiety among the public.[6] Specifically, cable news coverage, for instance, has provided terrorists with an opportunity to impact foreign policy and international relations by making their ideologies well known. Therefore, the public's right to know is entangled in the controversial state of the media being "damned if they do and damned if they do not exercise self-restraint"[7] when covering terrorist activities. In other words, the media is held accountable for what it reports and is under scrutiny from the public.

It is a known fact that different media sources and venues (cable news, the Internet, live journalistic coverage) may hinder the public's right to see the "whole truth" of a particular event through a distortion of the events. Such media bias includes factual, or analytical, omissions and selectivity. Factual bias is making false claims or omitting true facts to support a moral stance or political position, and selective bias is purposely *choosing* facts that support a political, moral, or ideological stance while ignoring others.[8] The problem of media bias is further complicated because the public frequently takes for granted the legitimacy of media reports.[9]

This chapter focuses primarily on how different media venues have portrayed the war in Iraq. It begins by discussing definitional issues related to terrorism, followed by an examination of how crimes are portrayed by the media and the obstacles faced when reporting news. This chapter also discusses how "terrorism" has become an issue of public discourse, with a primary focus on the Iraq war, followed by the public's attitude about the war in the United States and abroad.

IN SEARCH OF CONSENSUS ON DEFINING TERRORISM

Many questions arise when examining "acts of terror" and fear of crime in society. Can all *criminal* acts that result in massive losses be defined as "terrorist acts?" What differentiates terrorism from nonterrorism? Does a militant group have to be identified as a *terrorist* group? In an effort to answer these questions and to differentiate between terrorism, criminality, and violence, many different definitions of terrorism have been developed. Terrorism, for example, has been explained as an emotional state,[10] as the systematic use of violence,[11] or as any negative compulsions.[12] Governmental agencies provide even more definitions. The FBI, for example, defines terrorism as "the unlawful use of force or violence against persons or property to intimidate or coerce a government, in furtherance of political or social objectives."[13] In contrast, the U.S. Department of Defense defines terrorism as "the unlawful use of, or threatened use, of force or violence against individuals or property to coerce and intimidate governments or societies, often to achieve political, religious, or ideological objectives."[14] Another analytical approach is to classify terrorism as a tactic, even as a strategy, not a goal.[15] According to Simonsen and Spindlove, terrorism is "a means to an end—nothing more and nothing less . . . "[16] In other words, those involved in acts of terrorism are more concerned with winning the attention of world leaders and the media than with articulating a particular vision. Thus, there remains ambiguity in efforts to define terrorism.

In this chapter, an integration of the official government definitions of terrorism is used: It is argued that acts of terrorism are unlawful violent actions that contribute to moral panics; psychological, political, and physical harm; and an increase in fear levels among citizens.[17] Thus, terrorism harms, even devastates a nation or community through violent acts and increased levels of fear and insecurity, all resulting from extremists acting on their ideologies in pursuit of goals through terror tactics.[18]

CRIME AND THE MEDIA

According to Griset and Mahan, three main issues arise when the media provides coverage about terrorism: interference, cooperation, and commercialism.[19] Interference refers to journalists providing their own analyses of certain incidents that may be contrary to the terrorists' goals. In general, interference challenges social actors' decisions on which information should be aired live, aired after the fact, or never aired to the public.[20]

In contrast to interference, cooperation is a more controversial concept in news reporting, especially when journalists support terrorist goals, if not interests.[21] In short, the media may be easily viewed as a *cause* of terrorism in its reporting strategies, and self-censorship or state-censorship may ensue.[22]

The third issue at stake with respect to news reports includes commercialism. With commercialism, there is no doubt that the mainstream media has evolved into a highly monopolized set of giant, profit-seeking, corporate conglomerates dependent upon advertising to generate revenue. When "selling" or commercializing news, the media is more focused on "nonstate" forms of terrorism and what it perceives as a threat to the "national interest."[23] Very rarely is the United States or its allies mentioned when state terrorism is reported. It is only when "foreign," especially revolutionary movements interfere with U.S. capitalism that the episodes are labeled as "terrorism."[24]

Taken together, a conflicting, news-reporting tension remains between a group of people who strive for fair and accurate discourse on reported events and journalists' (and corporate managers') sensitivity to the interests involved in the reported events.[25] What remains in question, however, is the complex relationship between the mainstream media and alleged acts of terror.

ARROGANCE OF THE WEST TOWARD A GREAT CIVILIZATION

Terrorism targeting the West has gained much public discourse in the United States and has resulted in an extraordinarily self-serving and arrogant approach to Iraq, all highly amplified and manufactured through the media. This misguided view is partly blamed on the media's lack of exposure to Iraq and its people, resulting in a mistaken belief among many Americans that all or most Iraqi people are oppressed and uneducated, and lack democratic values.

Since the U.S. invasion, the economic conditions of Iraq have worsened. Equally important, the conflict has negatively impacted U.S. national security and the U.S. government's ability to advance its foreign policies. The American public seems to have become desensitized to the horrible damages inflicted upon millions of innocent children, displaced refugees, and other civilians. These negative effects of the war have been masked largely by what the media portrays as a tough "fight for freedom and democracy."

Until recently, images of Iraq and the Iraqi people have been portrayed by the media as violent and corrupt, or innocent and freedom-loving extremists who are also thirsty for democracy, depending on the occasion. What has remained largely invisible from media coverage is the richness of the Iraqi civilization, the diversity of its people, and the devastating experiences of the innocent as a result of U.S. policies and actions. In reality, the damages incurred in Iraq seem to represent all that is wrong with the notion of "nation-building" by a world power on a failed state. In his writings, the late

Edward Said argued that a world power's conquering criminality is reflected in the hijacking of words like *democracy* and *freedom*.[26] Despite the lack of a universally accepted definition of the term *democracy*, most accept that its main principles of sovereignty of the people and self-determination involve all members of a particular society having equal access to instate power and representation, and enjoying universally recognized liberties and freedoms. Therefore, democratic values exist embedded in a culture's functioning; a way of life the West seems to ignore unless it is its own export. From this perspective, it becomes obvious that the great civilization of Iraq, its culture and language, values and morals have been violated in an attempt to introduce U.S. style "stability" and "democracy." Ironically, in the U.S. view, bringing democracy to Iraq required war and other behaviors that are antidemocratic in nature.[27]

PUBLIC OPINION POLLS ON THE WAR IN IRAQ

> While we cannot assert that these misperceptions created the support for going to war with Iraq, it does appear likely that support for the war would be substantially lower if fewer members of the public had these misperceptions.[28]
> —Steven Kull

One of the most observed behaviors among the American public stems from viewpoints largely propagated not just by its government but by compliant media venues. The early supposed proven intelligence that Iraq was supporting Al Qaeda and creating weapons of mass destruction have been disproven and discredited. It is interesting, nevertheless, that the Bush Administration's changing motive to go to war with Iraq was consistently supported by Americans who watched or heard conservative news media, such as Fox News, or talk-radio personalities like Rush Limbaugh.[29]

According to the Program on International Policy Attitudes (PIPA) at the University of Maryland, people's perceptions about the war varied depending on their source of news. Those who primarily gathered their information from mainstream media such as NPR, CNN, and NBC had fewer misconceptions about the war in Iraq than those who depended on Fox News, known for its conservative news coverage. Fox News became one of the most popular cable networks in the United States advocating for the invasion of Iraq. What news channels like Fox have created is an audience that is largely dependent on their subjectivity to interpret all reporting incidents, which has contributed to a homogenous narrow-mindedness among TV viewers and a disconnect between public awareness and the "truth." Interestingly, the "Fox" effect—known as "Fox-tion," a euphemism for fiction—has not only impacted the American public's views, but has also created a divide between the two major political parties in the United States.

Beyond cable and network news, the Internet has added a new, alternative venue for acquiring war news, but without the mainstream media's mass reach.[30] News channels outside the mainstream reflect different views than domestic U.S. media but are hardly pursued by the U.S. public.[31] Despite such alternative news coverage of the war, including blogs and e-mail transmissions, it remains difficult for these alternative views to compete with the most dominant corporate news channels.[32] Nonetheless, the Internet has provided more people with instant information about world events, if they are willing to seek it.

An International Perspective

A 2006 report by the Pew Global Attitudes Project found that most people in the Netherlands, Germany, Jordan, France, Lebanon, China, Spain, Indonesia, Turkey, Pakistan, and Morocco believed the world was safer before the U.S. invasion of Iraq.[33] As for the Iraqi population, a World Public Opinion (WPO) poll conducted on September 27, 2006, examined their perception of U.S. troops and security-related issues in the country.[34] Seven out of ten Iraqis demanded complete U.S. withdrawal from Iraq within one year. Regarding security, the poll showed that the majority of Iraqis believed that the U.S. presence only provoked insecurities and internal conflict in Iraq, a result different from what the U.S. had promised to accomplish. The Bush Administration used the media to promote the notion that the Americans would stabilize and democratize the Middle East region and seize weapons of mass destruction from Saddam Hussein.

Eager to cover the war, the mainstream U.S. media did not seriously question the Bush Administration's intent or actions in the lead up to the war or in the early years of the war, nor did the media question the government when it was clear that the public had been misled. In other words, while the Bush Administration is certainly guilty of misleading the public, the mainstream U.S. media (it can be argued) abandoned its responsibility for independent investigative reporting and just went along with the official narrative. Despite U.S. propaganda, much of the world saw the injustice of the war. A BBC World Service poll conducted in January 2007 of more than 26,000 people in 25 countries found that 73 percent of the global population disapproved of how the U.S. has handled the war in Iraq. By September 2007, two thirds of the world's population believed that the U.S. should withdraw its troops from Iraq.[35]

CONCLUSION

Objectivity in U.S. media reports remains a major challenge, particularly when Americans rely on a favorite network's analyses and interpretations of incidents, what is referred to as "media spin." While the media is expected to report fairly on events both locally and internationally, the media is often faced with a "news triage" where it prioritizes what it regards as a priority. In the case of the war in Iraq, the media regards the event as a main concern to the American public because it has impacted the nation's troops, oil and gas prices, economy, foreign policy, and many other geopolitical and domestic social issues.

Understanding the significance of media coverage is vital to understanding the potential impact of certain selected events taking place around the world. In this chapter, emphasis on the media was used to highlight mediawide omission of important information about the war in Iraq, and how Internet sources and other alternative media are struggling to inform the American people.

CRITICAL THINKING QUESTIONS

1. How has the modern media impacted the perception of the American public in regards to their support or opposition to the war in Iraq?
2. How do the three issues of media coverage—interference, cooperation, and commercialism—contribute to the subjectivity of information and the complex relationship between journalists and so-called terrorists?
3. Despite the lack of consensus in defining terrorism, provide your own interpretation and analysis of the term and explain whether "one man's terrorist is another's freedom fighter" is a justification of committing terrorist-related activities.
4. Statistically, support for the war in Iraq has declined since the invasion in 2003. Has this decline been a result of the American public's lack of interest in the war, a change in the U.S. government, a downturn in the economy, or the American public's awareness of the misconceptions of going to war in the first place? Also, how has the media played a role, if at all, in the decline of support to the war in Iraq?

NOTES

1. L. Rainie, S. Fox, and D. Fallows, "The Internet and the Iraq War: How Online Americans Have Used the Internet to Learn War News, Understand Events, and Promote Their Views, PEW Internet & American Life Project, 2003.

2. Gus Martin, *Understanding Terrorism: Challenges, Perspectives, and Issues* (Belmont, CA: Sage, 2006), 391.

3. Beverly Kees, "Net Can Renew Democracy for Disenfranchised," *Freedom Forum*, August 12, 1998, www.freedomforum.org/templates/document (accessed June 7, 2007).

4. Sue Mahan and Pamala Griset, *Terrorism in Perspective*, 2nd ed. (Belmont, CA: Sage, 2008).

5. Piers Robinson, "The CNN Effect Revisited," *Critical Studies*

in Media Communication 22, no. 4 (2005): 344–349.

6. Allison Anderson, "Communication, Conflict and Risk in the 21st Century: Critical Issues for Sociology," *Sociological Research Online* 8, no. 4 (2003).

7. Brigitte Nacos, *Terrorism and the Media* (New York: Columbia University Press, 1994).

8. Erich Goode, *Drugs in American Society*, 6th ed. (New York: McGraw-Hill, 2005).

9. Steven Chermak, "Marketing Fear: Representing Terrorism after September 11," *Journal for Crime, Conflict and the Media* 1, no. 1 (2003): 5–22.

10. Eugene V. Walter, *Terror and Resistance: A Study of Political Violence* (New York: Oxford University Press, (1969), 5.

11. Jacob Benjamin and S. Hardman, "Terrorism" in *Encyclopedia of the Social Sciences*, eds. Edwin Robert Anderson Seligman and Alvin S. Johnson New York: Macmillan, (1934), 14, 575–76.

12. Moore Barrington Jr., *Terror and Progress—U.S.S.R.: Some Sources of Change and Stability in the Soviet Dictatorship* (Cambridge, MA: Harvard University Press, 1954), 11.

13. Terrorist Research and Analytical Center, National Security Division, Federal Bureau of Investigation, *Terrorism in the United States 1995* (Washington, D.C.: U.S. Department of Justice, 1996), p. ii.

14. U.S. Departments of the Army and the Air Force, "Military Operations in Low Intensity Conflict," *Field Manual 100-20/Air Force Pamphlet 3-20* (Washington, D.C.: Departments of the Army and the Air Force, 1990), 3–1.

15. Nathan I. Yungher, *Terrorism: The Bottom Line* (Upper Saddle River, NJ: Pearson/Prentice Hall, 2008).

16. Clifford Simonsen and Jeremy Spindlove, *Terrorism Today: The Past, The Players, The Future*, 2nd ed. (Upper Saddle River, NJ: Prentice Hall, 2004).

17. David C. Rapoport, "The Politics of Atrocity in *Terrorism: Interdisciplinary Perspectives*, eds. Yonah Alexander and Seymore M Finger (New York: John Jay Press), 47.

18. Martin, 42.

19. Griset, Pamela and Sue Mahan, *Terrorism in Perspective* (Thousand Oaks, CA: Sage Publications, 2003), 131.

20. Alicia Shephard, "Safety First," *American Journalism Review* 22, no. 1 (2000): 22–28.

21. Edward S. Herman and Gerry O'Sullivan, *The Terrorism Industry: The Experts and Institutions That Shape Our View of Terror* (New York: Pantheon, 1989).

22. Paul Wilkinson, "The Media and Terrorism: A Reassessment," *Terrorism and Political Violence* 9, no. 2 (1997): 51–64.

23. Mahan and Griset, 134.

24. Edward S. Herman and Gerry O'Sullivan, *The Terrorism Industry: The Experts and Institutions That Shape Our View of Terror* (New York: Pantheon, 1989).

25. Gabriel Weimann and Conrad Winn, *The Theater of Terror: Mass Media and International Terrorism* (New York: Longman, 1994).

26. Edward Said, Writings published in News Center retrieved from Common Dreams, http://www.commondreams.org/views03/0420-04.htm.

27. Edward Said, "The Appalling Consequences Are Now Clear: What Is Happening in the United States?" *The Symptom Online Journal*, (2003).
28. Steven Kull, Clay Ramsay, and Evan Lewis, "Misperceptions, the Media and the Iraq War," *Political Science Quarterly* 118, no. 4 (2003–04).
29. Ibid.
30. Junho Choi, James H. Watt, and Michael Lynch "Perceptions of News Credibility about the War in Iraq: Why War Opponents Perceived the Internet as the Most Credible Medium, *Journal of Computer-Mediated Communication* (2006): 209–229.
31. N. Hamdy and R. Mobarak, "Iraq War Ushers in Web-Based Era," in *Global Media Go to War: The Role of News and Entertainment Media During the 2003 Iraq War* (Spokane: Marquette Books, 2004), 245–254.
32. Choi.
33. *Pew Global Attitudes Project*, Pew Research Center.
34. PIPA, "The Iraqi Public on the US Presence and the Future of Iraq," conducted by the Program on International Policy Attitudes (PIPA), 2006, www.worldpublicopinion.org.
35. BBC, "World View of US Role Goes from Bad to Worse," BBC World Service Poll, 2007.

PART IV

Conclusion

CHAPTER 17

A Look Back and What Does It Mean

Robert L. Bing III

It is abundantly clear to me that while much has changed, many things remain the same. The media is the focal point of so much information, but a recent cartoon in the *New York Post*—showing cops killing a chimpanzee in New York City—raises questions about whether or not progress has been made. The media is omnipotent and shapes our views about the world. It informs us about crime and crime rates. The media has an obligation to provide balanced news coverage, but it does not always do so and it consequently bears responsibility for the development of stereotypes. The chapters in this book unmask the stereotypical portrayals of blacks and other ethnic minorities.

The chapter on racial profiling and the chapter on rape, race, and media coverage both discuss the media's tendency toward mostly negative coverage of blacks. The chapter on the portrayal of women of color and the portrayal of blacks as victims and offenders shows progress toward fair news coverage but much still needs to be done, especially in reports about blacks accused of violent crimes against white victims. In coverage of missing people, there is little (if any coverage) about missing black men and women. In contrast, the media has a special fascination with missing white females. This coverage points toward the relative importance or interest in females who are in nonwhite categories. With respect to crime rates and crime data, it is interesting to point out that media use of "aggregate" data adds to the confusion by concealing potentially important relationships. In addition, the media's use of the Uniform Crime Report (UCR) carries with it the potential for distortion. UCR data are data reported by the police that may be biased against poor people and visible minorities, creating opportunities for all sorts of misrepresentations. In another situation pertaining to the use of UCR data by the media, many readers do not know about the hierarchy rule, which results in the underrepresentation of crimes committed by all offenders, regardless of color. According to this rule, if an offender commits a burglary, rape, and homicide, only the highest of these offenses are reported.

The point to be made here is that if the media relies upon UCR data in its reporting of crime, the potential for misrepresentation does exist.

In all, there remain many challenges for the media in the years ahead. These challenges extend from traditional print media to other media forms. Today, we have the Internet and 24-hour news channels, including Fox and Nancy Grace, and each source has its own spin on the crime story. Nancy Grace's television shows almost always pertain to something that is extraordinary—and not necessarily representative. For many weeks, as an example, her CNN Headline News program provided unprecedented coverage about a missing white female in Aruba. Similarly, MSNBC's weekend coverage about prisons has the potential to glorify crime and criminals behind bars.

With respect to race, the chapters in this book provide strong evidence to support the call for the media to accept greater responsibility and offer more context and balance in the reporting of crimes. If it does not do so, stereotypes will continue to fester, viewers (both black and white) will have unfounded fears, and public policy will be based upon a truncated version of reality, one that is biased against poor people and visible minorities.

Contributors

David R. Montague, Ph.D., is an assistant professor of criminal justice at the University of Arkansas at Little Rock. He is the coordinator for the UALR Master of Science Program in Criminal Justice, focusing on public policy for criminal justice professionals. Montague serves on the UALR Chancellor's Race Committee, which completes dialogue on race via many departments. Montague has published and presented several works pertaining to race and crime.

Steven Chermak is a professor in the School of Criminal Justice at Michigan State University. His research interests include identifying effective strategies for reducing crime/violence, policing, domestic terrorism, and media coverage of crime and justice. His current research projects include an examination of the criminal activities of far-right extremists, and a National Institute of Justice–sponsored project to examine the intelligence practices of state, local, and tribal law enforcement agencies.

Jesenia M. Pizarro is an assistant professor in the School of Criminal Justice at Michigan State University. She earned her Ph.D. from the School of Criminal Justice at Rutgers University. Her research focuses on the social ecology of violence, homicide, and the social reaction to homicide. Her recent work has appeared in the *Prison Journal, Criminal Justice Policy Review, Journal of Criminal Justice,* and *Homicide Studies*.

Jeffrey Gruenewald is an assistant professor at Florida International University. His research interests include the relationship between race, crime, and media; bias crimes; domestic terrorism and extremism; homicide; and restorative justice. He has coauthored articles appearing in peer-reviewed journals such as *Justice Quarterly, Policing,* and *Journal of Criminal Justice and Popular Culture,* and has authored and coauthored book chapters related to the topic of domestic terrorism. His current research focuses on the nature of far-right-wing extremist homicide incidents and participants, and how they compare to other bias-motivated and nonideological homicides.

Robyn Rosenthal is a doctoral student in the Justice, Law, and Crime Policy program at George Mason University. Her research interests include American criminalization of mental illness and drug abuse, public opinion and crime policy, structural violence, and disproportionate representation within the offender population.

Nickie D. Phillips is an assistant professor in the Sociology and Criminal Justice Department at St. Francis College in New York. She received her Ph.D. from City University of New York Graduate Center and holds an M.A. in forensic psychology from John Jay College of Criminal Justice. Her research interests include hate crimes, cultural criminology, and media representations of crime and justice.

Natasha A. Frost is an assistant professor in the College of Criminal Justice at Northeastern University. She holds a Ph.D. in criminal justice from the City University of New York's Graduate School and University Center. Natasha's primary research and teaching interests are in the areas of punishment and social control. Specifically, she is interested in punitiveness (both individual and state level), the role of the media in the development of support for punitive criminal-justice policies, and the effects of incarceration and prisoner reentry on individuals, families, and communities.

Charles J. Corley, a native of South Carolina, received his B.A. in sociology/ social work from the Hampton Institute in 1981. In 1984 he received his masters degree in sociology/criminology from Bowling Green State University and in 1986 received his Ph.D. in sociology/family relations, with a minor in demography. Dr. Corley is an associate professor of criminal justice at Michigan State University. His research writings/publications and training workshops focus on juvenile justice processing, adult corrections, program evaluation, organizational leadership training, familial processes, substance abuse, the black family, and minority-majority race relations.

Charisse Coston holds a Ph.D. in criminal justice from Rutgers University. She is an associate professor of criminal justice at the University of North Carolina at Charlotte. She teaches courses in the subtopic areas of victimology, sexual assault, serial murder, criminal justice management and policy, the portrayal of crime in music, correctional field experiences, and research methods at the graduate and undergraduate levels. She is also a teaching affiliate in the Honors College, International Studies, Africana Studies, and Women's Studies. Her research activities and publications focus on the criminal victimization experiences among and between especially high-risk targets of criminal victimization both nationally and internationally.

Mary Brewster, Ph.D., is a professor of criminal justice and director of the Master of Science Program at West Chester University where she teaches courses on research and statistics, theoretical criminology, victimology, and corrections. She has published articles, book chapters, and an edited book on a variety of topics related to domestic violence and stalking, drug courts, juvenile justice, and corrections.

Rose Bigler, Ph.D., is a professor of criminal justice at Curry College, where she teaches courses in corrections, theoretical criminology, victimology, juvenile justice, and media and crime. Her research interests and publishing have been in these areas and in the area of children's rights and politics and crime.

Jason Naumann, a native of north Texas, has studied political science with a concentration on criminal justice and has been actively involved in the Innocence Project of Texas. His research interests include the rehabilitation and exoneration of the wrongfully convicted.

Erica Thomas is a graduate of the University of Texas at Arlington, where she received her M.A. in criminology and criminal justice. She earned a B.S. in advertising/public relations from Texas Christian University. Her research interests included the portrayal of people of color in the media as victims and criminals, the victimization of women and children, prisoner reentry in communities, and community policing.

Reem Ali Abu-Lughod is an assistant professor of criminal justice at California State University, Bakersfield. She joined the faculty at CSUB in 2006, following completion of her Ph.D. in Urban and Public Administration from the University of Texas at Arlington. Her research interests primarily focus on global terrorism, race and ethnic relations, gender-based domestic violence among Palestinian refugee women, issues of forced migration and social displacement. She has also been a consultant to government and private agencies in the United States, providing training and awareness on issues related to cultural and religious barriers with an emphasis on the Middle East.

Stephanie A. Jirard is an associate professor of criminal justice at Shippenburg University. She holds a J.D. from Boston College. Professor Jirard is a former U.S. Navy JAG Corps officer, trial attorney for the U.S. Department of Justice, assistant U.S. attorney, assistant federal public defender, and Missouri State public defender in the Capital Litigation Unit. Her 2008 textbook, *Criminal Law, Criminal Procedure and the Constitution*, was published by Prentice Hall.

Robert L. Bing III is an associate professor of criminology and criminal justice at the University of Texas at Arlington. He received the Ph.D. in Criminology from Florida State University and completed his undergraduate coursework at the College of the Holy Cross. His research interests include race and crime, issues in higher education, and courts and corrections. He is the author of over twenty-eight articles and many technical reports.

Linn Washington Jr. is an award-winning writer who teaches in the journalism department at Temple University in Philadelphia. Washington writes a weekly column entitled "Race Matters" for the *Philadelphia Tribune*, the nation's oldest African American–owned newspaper. Washington's reporting and research concentrate on issues of inequities and racism in America's criminal justice system and its news media. An associate professor at Temple University, Washington is the director of the print news sequence in the department of journalism and codirector of the department's Multi-Media Urban Reporting Lab (MURL). Washington is a graduate of the Journalism Fellowship Program at the Yale Law

School. His professional career includes serving as special assistant to the chief justice of the supreme court of Pennsylvania. Washington is the author of *Black Judges on Justice* the first book presenting in-depth interviews with black jurists. Washington holds a B.S. in communications from Temple University and a masters degree from the Yale School of Law.

Elaine Sutton Mbionwu is a certified correctional health professional and re-entry expert/consultant, with expertise in the field of reintegration. In 2008, she graduated from the Morehouse School of Medicine's National Primary Care Center Executive Faculty Development Program. In 2008, Ms. Sutton Mbionwu completed a federally funded project with the Council of State Government, which resulted in the release of a handbook titled *The Re-Entry Partnership Guide for Faith/Community-Based Organizations.*

Frankie Y. Bailey is an associate professor at the School of Criminal Justice, University at Albany (SUNY). Her areas of research are crime and mass media/popular culture, and crime history. Her most recent books are *African American Mystery Writers: A Historical and Thematic Study* (McFarland, 2008), and with Alice P. Green, *Wicked Albany: Lawlessness & Liquor in the Prohibition Era* (The History Press, 2009). Bailey is also the author of the "Lizzie Stuart" mystery series.

Renee Bradshaw received her B.A. in psychology in 2004 and her M.A. in criminology and criminal justice in 2008, both from the University of Texas at Arlington. Her research interests include terrorism, gender issues, domestic violence, and the media. She is currently working on her doctorate in public administration.